CE

THEOLOGY AND MODERN LIFE

Harris Franklin Rall

THEOLOGY AND
MODERN LIFE

Essays in Honor of
HARRIS FRANKLIN RALL

Edited by
PAUL ARTHUR SCHILPP

Essay Index Reprint Series

BOOKS FOR LIBRARIES PRESS
FREEPORT, NEW YORK

First Published 1940
Reprinted 1970

STANDARD BOOK NUMBER:
8369-1727-8

LIBRARY OF CONGRESS CATALOG CARD NUMBER:
70-117852

PRINTED IN THE UNITED STATES OF AMERICA

FOREWORD

HARRIS FRANKLIN RALL this year celebrates two anniversaries of service to humanity. Forty years ago, at the very turn of the century, he first officially joined that noble band of men known as Methodist ministers. Fifteen years later, in 1915, he joined the faculty of one of Methodism's leading theological seminaries, taking the chair of systematic theology at Garrett Biblical Institute. To this seminary he has now given a full quarter-century of distinguished service and of unflinching devotion. In both of these capacities his record is unique by reason of the profundity and breadth of his scholarship, the maturity and kindliness of his sterling personality, and the Christ-likeness of his character which has marked him everywhere and among all men as " a good minister of Jesus Christ."

It is only natural, therefore, that some of Dr. Rall's former students as well as a group of America's greatest living theologians should desire, on the occasion of this double anniversary, to pay their tribute to this great Christian teacher. There is not one of us who has contributed to this volume who does not realize that, in the most significant sense of the word, it is impossible for us to honor Harris Franklin Rall with anything we might do. The living testimonial to his honor is indelibly inscribed upon the lives of the many hundreds, yes thousands, of men upon whom he has shed the light of a deep and abiding faith, the insight of an ever searching and tireless mind, the benediction of a sweet reasonableness, and the tremendous power of a personality mag-

nificently held together by one dominating purpose and
commitment: to give himself unsparingly to the cause of
humanity and the cause of the church in order that through
such self-giving others might be enabled to " grow in stature
and in wisdom, and in favor with God and men."

It is, then, in humility of spirit that these gifts are brought.
They are laid upon the festive altar of those two anniversaries
in the hope that they may not be altogether unworthy of him
in whose honor they were written and for whose sake they
have here been collected into a single volume. Each contributor, I venture to say, would be particularly delighted
if the reader of these essays should find himself intrigued by
the bibliography of Professor Rall's writings at the end of
the volume to dig more deeply than he may previously have
done into the published works of this great twentieth century theologian. Such a result would be far more significant
than if the reader were to remain satisfied merely with what
he may find between the covers of the present book.

Two further words of explanation may be in order here.
First, the reader needs to keep in mind that Dr. Rall himself
cannot, of course, be held responsible for any of the ideas
expressed in these pages. Although each of the contributors
has undoubtedly been influenced by Dr. Rall's thought, every
one has tried to write his contribution out of the mature
thought and judgment of his own growing and developing
mind. Dr. Rall himself would not want it otherwise. It is
quite conceivable, therefore, that points of view may here
be represented with which Professor Rall might not find
himself in complete or even in partial agreement.

The other fact needs to be stated just as frankly. The
editor has made no attempt whatever to harmonize the ideas

of the various contributions, any more than it has occurred
to him to limit contributions to those who would be in complete theological agreement with Dr. Rall. In fact, when
all is said and done there is formally only one thread which
holds these essays together: each was written in honor of
Harris Franklin Rall. Despite the title of the volume, it
cannot even be said that all the essays are theological in character. When the editor invited the various contributors to
this volume, each writer was informed concerning the general nature of the book, and the choice of subject as well as
manner of treatment was left to him. Each contributor is
therefore entirely responsible for the subject as well as for the
content of his chapter. So far as the order of the essays in the
volume is concerned, it may be noted that — after the biographical essay, which, of course, belonged in the first place
— the essays begin with the more nearly historical contributions, proceed through the theological discussions to those in
the area of the philosophy of religion, and culminate in those
essays which make the more direct, practical application of
contemporary religious thought to the life of modern society
and more particularly to that of the church.

The editor is happy to be able to round out these intro-
ductory remarks by an acknowledgment of his indebtedness
to those without whose magnanimity this volume might
never have become a reality. This joint tribute to a great
teacher, theologian, Christian thinker, and friend has been
made possible largely through the generosity of other friends.
All who have thought herein to pay their sincere respects
to Dr. Rall feel themselves especially obligated to Mrs. Henry
Pfeiffer and to Mr. and Mrs. Gustavus A. Pfeiffer of New
York City, who have been more than generous in their un-

stinted and wholehearted support of this enterprise and to whom, therefore, much of the credit for this volume and for what it has made possible must go.

P. A. S.

Department of Philosophy
Northwestern University
Evanston, Illinois
New Year's Day, 1940

CONTENTS

THEOLOGY AND MODERN LIFE

HARRIS FRANKLIN RALL

IRL GOLDWIN WHITCHURCH
Garrett Biblical Institute

T WO STRONG interests entered in to shape my thinking about religion." So writes Harris Franklin Rall
in the chapter on "Theology, Empirical and Christian," which he contributed to the symposium on *Contemporary American Theology* which appeared, under the editor-
ship of Professor Vergilius Ferm, seven years ago. "First
there was the concern with religion as a personal matter."
One catches at once the characteristic Methodist note in that
affirmation. It speaks out without qualification, and without
apology. "My interest in theology sprang first from the
meaning that religion had for me in my own life. That had
its mystical side; religion meant God, and in my boyhood
home and in my own life God was something very real. And
it had its practical side: it was through religion that I sought
the deepest satisfactions of life. I conceived the goal of life
through religion, and in the fellowship with God I sought
the help for living my life. This personal religious interest
and the experiences that have gone with it have furnished my
point of departure for theological thinking to this day. My
theology has not been a philosophical system which left in-
cidental room for religious needs. Its concepts have gained
alike warmth and substance from this ongoing life in which
God has meant fellowship and help, and in which he has
given life its supreme meaning and worth."

"My second interest in religion"—and here the modern scholar takes up this *apologia*—"lay in my search for a rational world-view and philosophy of life. The impulse to philosophize was not independent of religion, a matter of curiosity or of separate intellectual concern. Religion itself meant to me seeing life whole, knowing that the object of trust was real and was the ultimate reality, and finding some meaning and purpose for the world order and human life. The rational had for me a religious meaning. I agreed with Plato: 'The unexamined life is not worthy of a man.' Religion was the summons to think as well as to live — or rather, to think was itself an essential part of life at its highest. Faith in God meant for me faith in a world that had unity and order and meaning. I found a genuine religious note in Browning's word:

> This world's no blot for us nor blank;
> It means intensely and it means good.
> To find that meaning is our meat and drink.

"To these two interests, which may be called the mystical and the rational, I must add a third, the social interest, and I realize in retrospect how much my thinking has been affected by this." Here begins to speak the philosopher who has never known what it means to take refuge in an ivory tower. "That interest began with my college days. In the nineties I came into contact with that rise of social interest among certain religious leaders which Rauschenbusch has sketched in his *Christianizing the Social Order*. I read Washington Gladden, Josiah Strong, the early writings of George D. Herron, and later on Rauschenbusch and the rest. I was present at one of the first conferences held at Grinnell College by a group that called itself 'the men of the Kingdom,' and read their weekly journal, *The Kingdom.*

"The Methodist Federation for Social Service, which I joined in its first year, brought me the stimulus of fellowship with Francis J. McConnell, Harry F. Ward and others. Ten years of pastorate in New Haven and Baltimore gave abundant opportunity to express this social interest in the pulpit and in practical relations. That opportunity was largely increased during five years as president of the Iliff School of Theology in Denver, with a summons to apply religious ideals to civic and state affairs.

"From the first this social concern furnished me material for my religious thinking. This was for me religion, though I did not cast overboard my concern with religion in other forms. Nor could I go with those whose newly found social interest, even while they remained within the church, led to an easy neglect of basic problems of thought or a general contempt for theology. It may be, as some have told us, that the concern with theology as with ritual and architecture means for some men simply a flight from the challenge of social problems. But it is equally possible that men may flee from intellectual difficulties to the eager discussion of social problems or a devotion to social service. The remedy for an inadequate theology is not the disavowal of all theology." *

It would be difficult, if not impossible, to put more succinctly the process by which Dr. Rall has come to exert so profound an influence on the students who have filled his classroom for three decades, as well as on the thinking of the

---

* *Contemporary American Theology,* Second Series. Edited by Vergilius Ferm (New York: Round Table Press, 1933). Further quotations in this essay stemming from Dr. Rall's own pen are taken either from this same essay or from his *A Working Faith.*

Methodist Church and of American Protestantism as a whole. Here are the three characteristic notes of a teaching career whose influence has reached far beyond the ivy-bound walls of the schools of theology in which it has been pursued. Reflection upon the relevance of these three stressed elements to the confusions and despairs of contemporary life will show why it has seemed fitting that this triple anniversary in Dr. Rall's career — forty years in the Christian ministry, thirty years in theological education, twenty-five years as professor of systematic theology at Garrett — should be marked by this volume. But only those who have experienced direct contact with the mind and spirit of the man in whose honor this book is presented can fully realize its inadequacy as a token of the debt under which the church stands.

I

Harris Franklin Rall is a son of German pietism, transplanted to the Nebraska and Iowa prairies, and reared under the disciplinary privations of a pioneer circuit rider's parsonage. Sometime in the fifteenth century an Italian ancestor, bearing the name Rallo, following northward the German count whose attendant he was, had settled in Württemberg. There the name became Germanized as Rall, and the family as well. One who knows the quickness of mind and gaiety of spirit (I can think of no better descriptive term) which mark this modern theologian will find it as easy to trace the influence of his Italian ancestors as of the generations of Germans who have left their stamp in the rigorous ordering of his thought.

Dr. Rall's father, Otto Rall, left Württemberg for America as a lad of fifteen, finally settling in Pittsburgh during the decade which preceded the opening of the Civil War. There he met Anna Steiner, who had come with her widowed mother from the Swiss canton of Graubünden on the upper reaches of the Hinter-Rhein, and had settled in that same Pennsylvania city on the invitation of her father's cousin, the noted church historian, Philip Schaff. Otto Rall and Anna Steiner were married in 1860. For ten years, following a clear conversion experience, the young immigrant, who had been nurtured in the devout atmosphere of Swabian pietism, felt the urge toward the Christian ministry. Family obligations stood in the way, but the time finally came when he took the decisive step of seeking ordination, and entered the ministry of the Evangelical Association, now the Evangelical Church. What manner of man he was is revealed by a vow of consecration which he wrote during the first year of his ministry, but which was not found until after his death:

On this day, the 14th of December, 1870, I enter into covenant with my faithful Father. May the grace of my faithful Redeemer help me.

In the name of my God I commit and devote myself to him as his sole possession: my spirit, soul, body, talents, time, influence, possessions, my feelings, desires, my failings also and my corruptions, everything that now is known to me and that the Spirit of God and his Word shall reveal to me, my love for my wife and my love for my family. May the dear Savior thus receive me, cleanse, sanctify, consecrate me, and use me for the glory of his name. I for my part will accept my Christ as my all, and leave it to him to give me the full assurance of my sanctification. May he use me for the glory of his name and the spread of his cause.

OTTO RALL

It was into a home warmed by this spirit of consecration that Harris Franklin Rall was born at Council Bluffs, Iowa. At seventeen he entered the University of Iowa, where he

experienced what he has called his " first intellectual awakening" under Professor G. T. W. Patrick. Late in his un-
dergraduate course he decided to enter the ministry. Gradu-
ating from the Yale Divinity School in 1897, he spent two
years on the Hooker Fellowship in postgraduate study in
Germany. There he studied theology and philosophy at
Berlin and Halle under Harnack, Kaftan, Pfleiderer, Paul-
sen, Kaehler, Loofs and Reischle, and took his doctor's degree *magna cum laude* with a dissertation on Leibniz written
for Alois Riehl, then at Halle and later for many years head
of the department of philosophy at the University of Berlin.

Returning to this country, Dr. Rall spent a year of further
study and lecturing at Yale, after which he entered the
Methodist ministry. His first appointment was at East Berlin, Connecticut, from which he was transferred after five
months to Trinity Church, New Haven. Four years later
he became minister of the historic First Methodist Church of
Baltimore. After six and a half years in that pastorate he was
elected president of the Iliff School of Theology at Denver.
His primary interest, however, lay in teaching. Accordingly,
when the opportunity offered in 1915 to exchange his administrative duties at Iliff for the chair of systematic theology
at Garrett Biblical Institute, he accepted. He has been at
Garrett ever since.

II

It has been as a teacher, therefore, that Dr. Rall has made
his principal contribution to the developing life of the contemporary church. Something will be said presently as to
the content of his teaching, but for the moment I wish to
speak of its method and quality. Four vivid impressions are

carried away by those who share the privilege of participating in this teacher's classes. First, there is a sense of his unremitting personal interest in the student. Be the other demands on his time what they may, he has never been too busy to turn aside to give help in meeting the personal problems of his students. Wisdom for the perplexed, sympathy for the wounded, counsel for the inexperienced, rebuke for the indolent and careless, patient instruction for the slow of mind — all these have been poured out without measure through the years until it may be doubted whether a single student has left these classes without feeling that he has found there an understanding and faithful friend.

Equally characteristic has been Dr. Rall's insistence on clear thinking. Theological discussion too often falls prey to the temptation to wander off into a misty land of abstractions where nothing stands out in sharp definition. But there is never any fog floating about in this teacher's classroom. It was not without significance that the first thing he did after being installed in his present chair was to change its name to that of *systematic theology*. "Theology for me," he has said, "must be empirical, it must be a theology of faith, and it must be Christian." That first requirement has meant that his theological ideas must not only grow out of experience, but that they must be presented in a clear-cut, orderly fashion. And woe be to that student who has tried to substitute wordy formulas for the logical conclusions which are possible only when ideas are reduced to lucid meaning!

But even this does not satisfy Dr. Rall's conception of the full responsibility of the theologian. In his view, the theologian must not only know the meaning of his own formulas, but he must be able to make that meaning clear to the mind without academic background. The Christian minister must not only have a reason for the faith that is in him; he must be able to express that reason in such terms as to be " understanded of the people." Theology must be able to walk the crowded ways of life, and make its interpretations plain and compelling to the bewildered and too often despairing common folk who wonder whether meaning can be found in their existence. No student with the Rall hallmark on him ever tried to propagate religion by speaking in an unknown tongue.

And finally, it would be impossible to list these characteristics of Dr. Rall's teaching without mentioning what — again for want of a better term — I will call its liveliness. Perhaps " aliveness " would be more exact, if the dictionary offered any authorization for the word. What I have in mind all who have endured boredom and fought off sleep in theological classrooms of another sort will at once understand. If, as I have said, there is no fog floating around where Dr. Rall is teaching, there is still less dust, and never the smell of mustiness. Here is a theologian who is not afraid to let his students *enjoy* the time spent in his classes, even though they are wrestling with ultimate issues. When I drop in at his home I notice that the current issue of the *New Yorker* is as likely to be lying beside his reading-chair as the *Journal of Religion*. I am sure that he would insist (and rightly) that the one can cast quite as much light on the problems of contemporary theology as the other.

This, then, is the sort of teaching which has brought distinction to the theological department at Garrett for the past quarter-century. It was a career deliberately chosen, and has been undeviatingly pursued. The administrative bypath had no attraction, even though its public honors might have proved greater. The temptation to secure ecclesiastical distinction by engaging in the manipulations of church governing bodies — the sort of thing that Methodist ministers usually embrace in the comprehensive and faintly scornful term, "conference politics" — made no appeal. Because of the eminence of his learning and the admiration of his former students, there has never been a time in the last two decades when Dr. Rall would have had to do more than express a readiness to accept denominational honors to have had them heaped upon him. His ambition has not been of that sort. He has wanted to be but one thing — a Christian teacher. "This one thing I do." He has done it. He is still doing it.

In assessing Dr. Rall's contribution to Garrett one is at the same time paying high tribute to the school which, in its turn, has made its contribution to the man. It was Garrett's tradition of complete academic freedom which provided the opportunity for an untrammeled search for truth. This enabled Dr. Rall to expand the usual conception of theology to include the independent study of systematic ethics and of the philosophy of religion. This same liberal spirit made possible the thoroughgoing study of theological education and revision of its curriculum which Garrett undertook in 1921. The work was done by a committee of which Dr. Rall was chairman. But his colleagues not merely aided in the work and welcomed the results, but they are to this day maintaining this same policy of constant self-criticism to the end of a training for the Christian ministry which shall meet the needs of the contemporary situation. In his colleagues Dr. Rall has always found the sympathetic and like-minded spirits who have helped to make the newer Garrett possible. A

bond of deep appreciation and intimate fellowship has tied
him to the three presidents under whom he has served,
Charles Macaulay Stuart, Frederick Carl Eiselen, and the
present incumbent, Horace Greeley Smith, who has been
leading Garrett through these difficult days to a new and
larger life. I know Dr. Rall would not have us speak of his
work for Garrett without voicing his oft-expressed appreciation of what the school has meant to him: the privilege
of teaching in an institution marked equally by freedom of
thought and loyalty to the Christian faith and way, and the
deeply prized fellowship with his associates.

III

Yet even this does not suggest the full measure of Dr. Rall's
influence as a teacher. In some respects it is not unfair to
say that his most important teaching has been done beyond
the boundaries of the theological seminary. Early in his
career he made his mark on student conferences, and some of
his first books, such as his *Life of Jesus, Teachings of Jesus,*
and more particularly his *New Testament History,* helped
to set a new standard for lay instruction in those fields. The
latter book is probably still the most widely used text in
American college courses on the New Testament. After the
period in which these texts appeared there followed *A Working Faith, The Meaning of God, A Faith for Today,* and a
series of widely circulated pamphlets which were designed to
bring within the grasp of the general reading public an interpretation of modern theological thought.

But none of these ventures in authorship has equaled in
importance the work of Dr. Rall in behalf of candidates for
the ministry who have not been trained in theological schools.

This work he has carried on especially for such men in the Methodist Church, but it has set an example which has had a large influence on other denominations. For a hundred years, beginning with 1816, the Methodist Church had been satisfied to do no more to equip its theologically untrained clergy than to provide them with a list of books, which they were expected to read and on which they were required to submit to examination during a four-year period. Once in four years a committee of the church's Board of Bishops revised this list of books. Some curious recommendations resulted from the system, and many even more curious examinations.

In 1914 the presidents of Methodist theological seminaries were asked by the committee of bishops to recommend books for the new list about to be announced. Instead, Dr. Rall, then president of Iliff, proposed that they should present to the bishops a detailed and balanced educational plan for the guidance of these untrained ministers which should take the place of the combined book list and examination. No reply being received from the bishops to this proposal, it was brought before the Methodist General Conference in 1916, and adopted. This plan envisaged features now familiar to the church: a permanent Commission on Courses of Study, the publication of especially prepared texts, a series of handbooks giving directions and help to the student, a plan for correspondence study, a system of summer schools of theology with required attendance, graduate courses for ministers who had completed their formal studies, an annual coaching school for those in charge of this educational program in the various annual conferences, and a complete reorientation of this whole venture in adult education by the church which found illustration by changing the name of the administrative agency from the " Board of Examiners " to the " Board of Ministerial Training." The effect which this single development has had in raising the level of the ministry can hardly be overestimated.

During the last few years the "supply pastors " of Methodism also have been brought under the same general plan. This group of relatively untrained men, commonly working in the most difficult fields and with the smallest educational opportunities, in years past have been left largely to their own resources, save for the occasional and often superficial supervision of overburdened district superintendents. Yet there were frequently as many as a quarter of the charges in what was then the Methodist Episcopal Church listed in the records of the denomination with the phrase, "to be supplied." At Dr. Rall's urgency the necessary legislation has now been enacted to extend the system of balanced, supervised and progressive theological training to all members of this clerical group. For this service alone the congregations in five thousand churches, dependent for their religious nurture on these hitherto unschooled pastors, should rise up in the judgment to call this theologian blessed.

IV

Harris Franklin Rall is a churchman of the highest order. His churchmanship not only has a philosophy; it assumes specific and concrete forms. One cannot otherwise understand the devotion with which he has served the cause of securing a better trained ministry. Always that training was ultimately for the sake of the kingdom on earth, but more immediately for the church which mediates the divine ideal,

The church has not been for him a bloodless abstraction.
The church is first a divine ideal for human life, which creates a fellowship of persons who sincerely desire the realization of that ideal in themselves and in the world. In a sense,
the church stands for a living embodiment of God's Holy
Spirit. Not that the embodiment is as complete as a Christian desires. Indeed, the misuse of the powers of the church
by ambitious earthlings is the common sorrow of Christians.
Why? Because the fellowship represented by the churches
is the very hand by which God would lift humanity to a
higher plane.

Dr. Rall has served the church in many capacities. During
these years of teaching there have been few periods when he
was not likewise carrying on his ministry from a pulpit. In
the revision of the Methodist ritual in 1916 he bore a large
part as secretary of the commission charged with the task.
He was a delegate to the World Conference on Faith and
Order, which met in 1937 at Edinburgh, and was a member
of the American commission which presented to that body
the reports on "The Church's Unity in Life and Worship."
He is now serving as a member of the American Theological
Committee of the Faith and Order movement.

Yet it is equally important to point out that he is no churchman in any constricted sense. The spirit of exclusiveness
finds no home in his thinking or practice. Viewed through
his eyes, all men are potentially churchmen. Churches are
here to serve in every possible manner every conceivable need
of men in every land, whether they be men of little faith or
of none at all. Here is the point at which Dr. Rall's relation
to the Methodist Federation for Social Service is most significant. From the year of the organization of that pioneering

body, he has been among its most active members. When it was less than a year old, in 1908, he was elected as its treasurer and made a member of its executive committee. Later he became vice-president, a position which he still holds.

The relation of this social awareness to his theology, Dr. Rall has himself put into words which deserve to be pondered. "Our modern social movement," he has written, "may be looked at in two ways. We may look at it from without in terms of changing political and economic organization. But we may look at it also from within in terms of the new social ideals and insights. The latter is what is significant for us in relation to theology. It is perhaps best expressed by the term democracy, which is increasingly being used to indicate a social faith rather than merely a form of political organization and would seem preferable to the ambiguous term humanism.

"Basic for this new social faith are certain convictions: the supreme worth of human personality, personal freedom alike as a good and as a way of achievement, faith in human nature and in the forces of truth and justice and good will as compared with physical compulsion, justice as the concern of all in securing the fullest opportunity for each, human solidarity, and the obligation of cooperation in service. This higher social faith, or social conscience, is at once an expression of the influence of religion and, conversely, a development of human insight which religious thinking must take into account.

"Religion, like this new democracy, is concerned with the values of life and the way in which they may be achieved. Its basic conviction is that in some way goodness and power are one. It sees in the values of life the clue to the nature of the final reality. These social insights into human values then should be of significance alike for the doctrine of God and of salvation. As regards the idea of God, this is the line that was followed by the Hebrew prophets and Jesus. With them, as with our present-day social thought, the ethical and personal were determinative. . . .

" Our second great concern in religion is with the way in which the good is to be realized, and here again our social insights are determinative for theology. Our concept of God and our idea of these goods both point away from the positions of traditional theology. We cannot longer hold to the sacramentarian magic which came in with Eastern theology. That went with a God that was conceived in terms of eternal and incorruptible essence that must somehow be communicated to man and so transform in quasi-metaphysical fashion the finite and corruptible human nature.

" Nor can we think of salvation in terms of sovereign power, as Augustine and Calvin set it forth, with its arbitrary decrees and irresistible grace. That which is ethical and personal can be realized only by processes that are congruous in their nature; what is more than that is magic, for the essence of magic is the effort to secure given ends by means that are unrelated in kind.

" It is quite a mistake, however, to assume that this view rules out all idea of transcendence, that it leaves us with a God who is no more than the sum of man's aspirations and efforts, and a salvation that sees in man himself the only savior. This same social viewpoint, thought through, involves a real transcendence. If the personal and ethical are a casual by-product of an impersonal order, then they can have no such ultimate value and authority as our social faith assumes. If they have supreme value and authority, then they must point to the nature of ultimate reality. That means a God who, as personal and purposive and good, transcends this changing time-space world. The tragedy of non-theistic humanism is that its cosmic faith, or lack of it, denies a basis for those values which its social faith affirms and so commits it to a fundamental dualism.

"The problem then for the new theism which seeks to do justice to these social insights is to work out such a conception of God, and of the relation of God and man in the process of human redemption, as shall do justice to all that we have learned from history and psychology and ethics and man's social experiences. Barthianism certainly has not found the way. We can appreciate its reaction against those modern tendencies which have put man at the center of religion instead of God, but we cannot accept its denial of significance to the historical and the human. Non-theistic humanism gives up the problem by canceling the other side. Our clue must be in our conception of God as rational and personal and ethical. If religion be a relation that is ethically conditioned, then it can be maintained only by a response that is rational, ethical, active, and free.

"On the other hand, the old externalism and absolutism have gone from this conception of God, and we reach the idea of a conditioned or limited though not necessarily a finite God. Assuming the idea of God as purposive and creative Good Will, our social insight makes plain that the ends in view condition the processes by which they are achieved. If we trust our social-ethical insights, if we use them to interpret our world, then that world must be one in which there is a measure of freedom as well as of order.

"But must we not go farther than this? Life is all of one piece; you cannot separate human nature from other animate nature, nor even draw a line to divide astrophysical evolution from the later biological evolution. Should we not expect even on the lowest level that element of contingency which modern physics has suggested to us, and on each succeeding level an increasing measure of freedom as a condition of development? Have we not here one of those ultimates which we have to accept 'with natural piety'?"

V

It would be impossible for me to conclude this sketch without some comment on the impression which Dr. Rall's theology has made upon me, one of his students. The whole question of theological method has been raised in recent years with a new earnestness. Since the Renaissance, theology has had the protective shelter of authoritarianism gradually torn away. Religious ideas have been forced to walk with other respectable ideas in a world of mutually interpreted facts, where justification depends upon adequate evidence. A cursory examination of Dr. Rall's books will reveal that he is thoroughly alive to this situation.

Since the seventeenth century five major attempts to formulate an empirical theology have been made. In the first, religion was completely victimized by an abstract rationalism in the name of a scientific religion. The results we know in early deism. The second venture started at the opposite pole of experience — with the psychological make-up of man. Romanticism is its name and Schleiermacher is its major prophet. Its contribution lies in two directions. It embodies partly an emancipation from the natural logic of deism, but more especially the insight that religion lays hold on the entire personality and inspires unqualified surrender to God. A third attempt tries to combine the strength of the first two. Voluntarism in religion seeks to relate a passionate devotion to the divine within one's entire world, a world of nature as well as of persons. But here the nerve of the religious life is cut, because a deep vein of agnosticism lies at the center of this thought. A fourth attempt seeks to repair precisely this damage, and so becomes essentially a theory of religious certainty by means of intuitional insight. A fifth attempt stems from Kant and extends across the years through the development of an adequate theory of value judgments.

As a theologian Dr. Rall has developed and retained a fine sensitivity to this changing religious situation. In company with other modern thinkers he has wrestled with the problem of a theology that is rationally grounded. The first question which naturally arises in this connection is that of authority and method of approach. Historically, there has persisted a religious tradition within which certain untouchable assumptions serve as the point of departure. That was one of Dr. Rall's comments on the Edinburgh Conference, to which he was a delegate. Some theologians were ready to raise pertinent questions only after they had been assured that their sacred presuppositions were not to be examined. Such a procedure skirts the edge of dishonesty. Within that atmosphere of authoritarianism a living theology is irrelevant. A religious view which shrinks from the light of examination betrays its own fears and excites suspicion. In theology, as in all honest investigation, authority rests on a rationally grounded faith.

Evidence, and evidence alone, can ground a valid religious faith. It is understood, of course, that evidence means evidence that is relevant to the religious situation. No *ipsissima verba* of some spokesman for church or creed or council must be allowed to push proper evidence aside. Neither can theological evidence be found in flirtation with our commonly accepted notion of "proof." Too frequently we speak as though evidence means proof, and proof means mathematical or physical evidence. Its authority now attaches to the phrase, "scientific proof." Ministers often want to be as sure about God or immortality as they are that two times two makes four. Others look for physical evidence to support articles of faith. No doubt mathematical proof is adequate in its own field and physical evidence is relevant to physical situations. But we must avoid trying to apply them inappropriately, as well as from falling into the trap of assuming that no other kinds of evidence are available or adequate for other aspects of experience. A rationally grounded theology has freed itself from the shackles of speculative authoritarianism and explores all the relevant evidence. To that end Dr. Rall writes " for men who want a faith by which to live, who wish to hold it intelligently, who want to face honestly all the facts bearing upon the matter, and then with equal honesty ask what such a faith means for life."

The sciences, as Dr. Rall views them, have not only revolutionized our mode of living by reason of their practical application, but they have given us a new world of nature and of knowledge. By the impact of the sciences, both as an attitude and a technique, philosophical and religious thinking has been profoundly influenced. During more recent years, especially, the psychological and social sciences have come into places of prestige. For religion, an uncritical use of them has resulted in theories about the illusory character of religious experience and in nontheistic interpretations of religion. Dr. Rall's reaction is to point out how the scientific temper serves religion by helping to remove dogmatism, and by keeping our knowledge up to date. On the other hand, the sciences must not be illegitimately extended into a naturalistic philosophical outlook.

Scientific methodology has directed the sciences primarily toward physical nature, but only a question-begging procedure assumes that such a nature is the *only* real. Scientific knowledge is undoubtedly valid within its appropriate realm, but " there are other ways of knowing than that of science." Moreover, "science can create power; it cannot tell us whether to use our machines to till the soil and produce goods, or to employ them to blow up ten million of our fellows in a World War." Naturally, in a scientific era like ours the question of empirical method is perpetually alive. Among other things it brings up a whole nest of implicative relationships with scientific thought and with pseudo-scientific philosophical speculation, known as naturalism. Some liberal theologians may toy with a naturalistic theism or a theistic naturalism. It is a safe prophecy that Dr. Rall will remain a liberal theologian, but that no tincture of such a naturalism will infect his theology. He understands the utter incompatibility of these two logics.

One of the great themes in Dr. Rall's thought is that religion comes to us as personal help. That explains his deep appreciation for the best in romanticism, for what mysticism at its higher reaches has sought to make clear. In salvation God lays hold on our inner personal nature, and this operation of his Spirit can be illuminated by psychological studies. These studies are especially valuable in guiding methods of approach to personalities. But psychology is a science, not a philosophy. When one follows the nerve currents of religious experience they lead to God, to ultimate reality; religion has an incurably philosophical bent, and its questions cannot be evaded either in the name of scientific verification or of the presuppositions of a positivistic naturalism. Hence voluntarism in religious thought serves superbly only within the bounds set when the limits of knowledge gained through the sciences are recognized and the active, adventuresome, and practical character of faith is emphasized.

Just as certainly does a voluntarism betray its devotees if its agnostic tendencies are permitted to cut the nerve of the objectivity-seeking spirit of religion. In the end religion finds its source of help in a transcendent personal God, not in an impersonal immanent process. Religion includes the four main relations which constitute the sphere of man's life: nature, self, man's fellows, and God. "Religion includes all and emphasizes the last, but the relation with God is not just a fourth added to the other three. . . . The supreme relation, God, the last dimension of life, the Eternal, transforms all the rest as it takes them up into itself."

Theological doctrines about the world and God cannot rely upon high-sounding verbiage or unction of spirit. Religion needs to know. There is no point to mere affirmation. Psychological certainty is not enough. The reality of God must come within the area of illuminated experience. Knowledge and reality are correlative terms. Therefore the question, How can I know God? The answer calls for important distinctions. Knowledge is of various kinds and is

a matter of degree of understanding. A one-way revelationism is not open to this theologian. Facing the complex processes of knowledge, Dr. Rall's answer leans heavily upon
insight, spiritual awareness, intuitional understanding, or
whatever designation you prefer. Only one must keep these
things clearly in mind: The whole man is implicated in this
spiritual awareness; he lives under the constant necessity of
growth; the knowledge of God is morally conditioned.

The idea that religious insight is a function of personal
character leads one near the center of Dr. Rall's theology.
His students invariably carry with them the one overpower-
ing idea: Christianity is a Christ-centered religion. Perhaps
the best commentary on that theme is a word from Paul's
letter to the Corinthians which is a favorite with Dr. Rall:
" The light of the knowledge of the glory of God in the face
of Jesus Christ." This great theme serves a double purpose.
First, it discloses the influence of the value-judgment approach to religion made famous by Albrecht Ritschl. Second, as Ritschl points out, this approach opens the way to
focus attention upon the moral personality of Jesus. In him
we come face to face with a God of perfect righteousness
through whom we enter into the life abundant. Here is a
way that is open to every man. " Face honestly your convictions as to what is just and good; be absolutely loyal in
action to every ideal, to every least measure of faith that you
hold; go just as far as you can. If you do that, you will know
God, for this is his voice, here is his presence; and as you
move on, the way will open before you."

It thus appears that Dr. Rall is a theologian of a new order,
mainly because through the years he has retained his love
for the temper of philosophy and his contacts with the living

currents of philosophical thought. Too often theology has meant the explication and defense of doctrines commonly held by a church, a creed, or a leader. To Dr. Rall such an outlook is blind in both eyes. To be sure, historic faiths develop out of great experiences and so constitute part of the indispensable materials of comprehensive religious thinking. But the crucial point comes in the use made of these doctrines. They must be taken for what they are, *claims* to the truth about religious experience. They must never be taken for what they are not, final editions of truth that need only defense. They belong properly among the raw materials of the critical theologian. He must examine them and make the truth in them stand out bold and clear. Their historic character constitutes a presumptive claim to a degree of validity. But their real value lies precisely in their validity, and in that alone.

Religious ideas that are true have everything to gain and nothing to lose under the light of examination. Only after such examination can they perform a second great service for the spiritual life. The religious man inhabits a world. His religious ideas must be at home in the whole welter of ideas which fill his world. Religion cannot retire into some sequestered corner of experience. Experience is not made on that pattern. Only religious ideas that have stood the test of careful scrutiny can face the world unafraid. How often we hear men say that religious faith needs certainty. Yes, but certainty may be of two kinds. One rests solely upon emotional conditioning; the other arrives with marshaled evidence. The first ignores the conditions of stability and of value. More than certainty, religious faith needs to lay hold on an object that is worth being certain about.

At this point Dr. Rall has laid broad and deep the foundations of a theology that has two main concerns. One is with
the character of the object of faith, and the other with a dependable or valid knowledge about that object. That is why
it can be said that his thinking is traditional in the best sense
of being alive to the great truths of the Christian faith, and
living in its alertness to an ever enlarging truth about human
life in God's world. His theology thus performs a double
task. First, it must sift the claims of religious faith in order
to find a true faith. Second, it must seek to co-ordinate its
truth with the best available knowledge about human experience in its full sweep and at its highest reach. That is what
I have in mind when I say that Dr. Rall's theology is philosophical in the best sense of the word.

VI

The fruits of a Christian spirit are many. For the sake of
clarity their names might be called. In one modern Christian gentleman, at least, some stand out. In a world where
so many not altogether consistent demands are made upon
us, and where we are called upon to play so many parts, it is
an inspiration to see that a man can maintain a unified self-
hood. Perhaps that is one reason why we esteem so highly
a certain transparency of character. The problem is not new.
The ancients remarked upon play-acting, and thought it a
mark of honor when the inner and outer man were consistent parts of one whole. Socrates once offered a prayer to
beloved Pan to grant him such harmony of spirit. The New
Testament warns against doubleness of spirit and commends
sincerity. A healthy soul is wholly sincere; that is, sun-clear,
transparent to the most penetrating light. In this thorough-

going sense Dr. Rall is sincere. He is what he appears to be, and you know in advance where to look for him.

A sincerity which works itself out into a transparent spirit commands more attention for the whole than for a part. But notable parts are here to be found. Modesty, courage, and humility go together as reflecting a sense of the expansive richness of life. Patience, too, is required of all of us. A double portion has seemed to be asked from Dr. Rall at times. I have seen him in situations where patience under misrepresentation was exacted. That patience was unflinchingly given, and without a word of complaint. In fact, it sprang in part from a deep-grained kindliness of spirit that was so sure of the good will of all men that it appeared he did not know that he was being subjected to misrepresentation or attack. Through the years he has exhibited a wholesome good humor which relieves him from carrying the world, Atlas-like, on his shoulders. God made the world with a fairly solid and benevolent framework. His sons are born to live in it, unafraid, in faith and joy.

Dr. Rall continues a most stimulating teacher at Garrett. His writing goes on to enrich the Christian cause to which he has dedicated his life. He lives in a world made kindly by the good will of friends, because he is worthy of their every trust. There is a legend that Plato used to thank the gods that he was born in the time of Socrates. In a similar spirit of gratitude, I am certain that I am but one of a host who will continue to be thankful that we have lived in the company of Harris Franklin Rall.

OUR IMMORTALITY

SAMUEL S. COHON
Hebrew Union College

The idea of immortality cannot be argued by itself; it is contingent upon one's world view, one's faith. And neither this particular belief nor the larger faith can be successfully grounded merely upon a philosophy of nature. Neither the theory of panpsychism nor a consideration of process and matter will suffice, even if we call the process personality-producing or endow the matter with a good supply of unrealized potentialities. Our thought must be empirical but our empiricism must be more inclusive, and the experience of the spiritual, of values, must have a primary place in our consideration.

HARRIS FRANKLIN RALL
Christian Century,
July 4, 1934

THE UNIVERSALITY of the belief in the survival of the soul after death and its persistence through the changing millenniums, amid differing conditions of knowledge as of ignorance, testify to its vital significance for human life. Savage and savant alike have found in it bread for their heart's hunger, a staff of support for their weary feet, and a star of hope to guide them through the dark. Sometimes through glimmers of light and more often through unquestioning faith, the generations of men of varying races, tongues, cultures, and creeds have tenaciously held on to this belief, despite the doubts, questionings and denials of large numbers. Like Cicero, so most men have preferred being wrong with those who affirm immortality to being right with those who deny it.

This belief derives from the subsoil of human nature, from the realm of sentiment, feeling, and desire, and from the will to live, more than from conscious reflection. We fail to understand its true inwardness and tenacity unless we bear in mind the reasons of the heart of which reason takes no account. Psychological grounds, to a greater degree than most thinkers recognize, color their philosophies. What recommends itself to them as a logical deduction may grow out of a yearning or a hope. Strictly examined many a so-called proof appears at best but an intimation.

The belief in immortality climaxes *man's rebellion against finitude*. He is painfully aware of the fact that like the rest of nature he is a creature of time and a victim of its ravages. His life-span, while longer than that of many other beings of the organic world, is not as long as that of others. However, unlike them he refuses to let the number of his days be the true measure of his existence. He discovers within himself qualities that enable him to escape destruction. He builds civilizations, invents arts, and creates literatures, sciences, ethical systems, and religions whereby he bridges the chasm of mortality. Even after his worn body is become food for maggots, his life-stream courses in his offspring and his creations touch for good or ill the race of men. He projects " his insights across the bars of space and time " and makes his best moments live after him. In his will to live he storms the citadels of death.

With his spiritual and intellectual advance man turned this product of his unsatisfied hunger for life into an object of faith and of reason. On the highroad in quest after assurance of immortality, the theistic religions and numerous philosophies meet. Psalmists, sages and mystics from East and West advance together. Plato, Aristotle and Plotinus lead their hosts of disciples from synagogue, church, and mosque. In the procession we discern Philo Judaeus, Maimonides, Mendelssohn, and Bergson by the side of St. Augustine, St. Thomas, Eckhart, Leibniz, and Emerson, along with Al-Ghazali, Avicenna and Averroes and their followers from all parts of the world. Some walk with firmer step than others. A number of distinguished figures in the world of religion and of philosophy are absent. But the company of choice spirits in the procession moves steadily on to triumph over death.

I.   FOUR FORMS OF THE BELIEF IN IMMORTALITY

The negation of mortality assumed several forms. The first is physical continuance. It figured in the religious life of ancient Israel. At death a person was " gathered to his fathers." He also continued in his children. His life coursed in them. Their prosperity and well-being were his, and so were their defeats and misfortunes. The Psalmist holds out the hope to the God-fearing man: " His seed shall be mighty upon the earth; the generation of the upright shall be blessed. . . . The righteous shall be held in everlasting remembrance." [1] The dead continue within the family and the people and are bound up with the endeavors of the living. Their merits and their vices affect their descendants. Preserved within the memory of the beloved, of the family and the community, they may be said to live in the history of their people and to help bind the generations into a united holy congregation. [2] Hermann Cohen finds here a logical connection between the continuance of the individual and the messianic reign, which represents the victory of the good.[3] The sum of all persons composing the nation may be regarded — to use modern terminology — as a " collective individual," whose duration extends indefinitely. While the assurance that their individual beings will be preserved in the larger life of their people has afforded ground for hope to vast numbers, it can hardly be taken for the real hope of religion. Families and even nations have run their course and have been lost without a trace in the maelstrom of history. The records of the past seem like inscriptions on the graves of once powerful nations that have been swept away by wars, pestilence and famine. Furthermore, within the " collective individual " individuality vanishes and memories are quickly forgotten. Whatever true significance the idea possesses derives from the fact that it makes for the preservation of values — a consideration to which we shall turn later. For personal continuance religion has been forced to look elsewhere.

The second form taken by the desire for immortality is the notion of transmigration, which may be viewed as a form of continuance. The deceased comes to life in a new body. Under the sharp dualism of body and soul, the transmigration is transferred from the physical to the spiritual. The soul of the departed reincarnates itself in an offspring, kinsman or stranger. The idea of a cycle of rebirths appeals to men at various stages of thought as a semi-scientific account of heredity. In reality it harks back to primitive thought. The idea of the soul's passage into members of another species, whether animals or birds, plants or stones, probably derives from totemistic belief. With the growth of conscience it was put into the service of morality and thus invested with some worth. The successive removals of the soul into other bodies are conditioned by its deeds and misdeeds in previous states. This idea satisfies rudimentary ideas of retribution, as well as the longing for expiation of past sin and for self-purification from evil.

This belief, while foreign to biblical and talmudic thought, found its way into Judaism in post-talmudic times. But despite the commanding role which it played in the cabala, it never attained the position of an accepted principle of Jewish faith. Generally its hold on the West has never been as strong as on the East. In India it is the doctrine of future life par excellence. There, too, it displays its chief weaknesses. In addition to its fantastic character, it has proved to be a joyless conception of life. The dull and weary round of change has bred a spirit of fatalism and of pessimism. Little that the individual may do can free him from the mechanical chain of law which holds him prisoner. The soul is too inexorably bound by its past to enjoy any real freedom of development in the present. Man ceases to be an original source of self-determination. He is what he is because of what he was in former states. Such a belief makes for moral paralysis and discourages social progress. The Hindu caste system has been bolstered by it.

Despite the high authority of Plato and despite the spell which this doctrine has cast upon some thinkers in the West, its hold on the modern mind is feeble. From being a deeply cherished conviction it has passed into folklore and legend and serves as an occasional embellishment of poetic imagination.

The third form of immortality, too, is physical and is best

exemplified by the Egyptian process of mummification of the dead body, a practice intended to preserve it for a future awakening. In Israel this idea took on a national character before it became personal. Ezekiel's vision of the resurrection clearly refers to the restoration of the nation.[4] Daniel, on the other hand, definitely holds out the hope of individual resurrection:

And many of them that sleep in the dust of the earth shall awake; some to everlasting life, and some to reproaches and everlasting abhorrence. And they that are wise shall shine as the brightness of the firmament; and they that turn the many to righteousness as the stars forever and ever.[5]

Appearing in response to the deep craving for righteousness, this belief has been inseparably bound up with man's moral strivings. Its connection with the messianic hope stressed still further the ethical nature of the idea of final judgment. The bliss of the hereafter, while stored up for all, is in reality to be shared only by the righteous.

The fourth concept of immortality is spiritual and comes to light in various forms of animistic belief on the one hand, and of philosophical ideas of the soul's immortality on the other. It came to full expression in Plato and attained a commanding place in the advanced theistic religions. It underlies the beliefs in transmigration as in resurrection and retains also an independent character.

Of the four ideas, only that of the resurrection of the body attained to the rank of a cardinal dogma in Judaism, Christianity, and Islam. Serious consideration was given to the condition of the body in the resurrection. Would it arise with all its earthly defects or in a perfect state? Would it

be old and worn or renewed in unfading youth?[6] The hope
was strong that while the raised body would be the same
as during its days on earth, it would yet be new, rebuilt and
refashioned. The mortal and corruptible frame would be
exchanged for an immortal and incorruptible one. It might
even be invested with celestial and angelic qualities.[7]

The orthodoxies of Judaism, Christianity, and Islam still
cherish this faith. The Maimonidean Creed, which voices
the conviction of historical Judaism, reads: "I believe with
perfect faith that there will be a resurrection of the dead at
the time when it shall please the Creator, blessed be His
name, and exalted be His remembrance forever and ever."
In line with the purer teachings of Maimonides himself and
of Mendelssohn, Reform Judaism has eliminated references
to a future resurrection of the body from its liturgy, and emphasizes instead the immortality of the soul.[8] Men appear
less disturbed by the dissolution of the body and are not concerned about its renovation in the future. For many of us
such anxieties belong to a childish state of mind.

Though we glory in the strength and agility of the body
and find in it the perfection of an Apollo and the beauty of
a Venus, we refuse to identify the human being with the
physical frame. We feel that what gives man pre-eminence
over all other living beings is his reflective reason, his ethical
and spiritual idealism, and his creative will. Coupled with
freedom these gifts of heart and mind give man a godlike
power. Constituting the chief elements of his distinctive
humanity, they are of the essence of his self and give him
whatever worth he possesses in life and in death. The hope
of immortality is, therefore, associated with the inward self
rather than with the corporeal being. For us only the im-

mortality of the spirit has sanctifying power and moral value. The consciousness that there is something at the core of one's being which is imperishable invests life with transcendent seriousness and worth. Physically ephemeral, a child of dust and brother to the worm, man is yet linked with the stars and related to the Infinite. The life of the humblest man may be of some moment to the life of the All. His hopes, his dreams, his strivings — puny though they appear to himself — may prove to be of value to the world even beyond his earthly days. The belief in immortality thus appears not only as a high valuation of personality but also as a dynamic of victorious living.

Religion rejects the notion of human insignificance and transience. In its view the naturalistic admission of Ecclesiastes that " the pre-eminence of man over beast is naught, for all is vanity," fails to do justice to the true nature of man and to satisfy his moral and religious sense. Human life would lose all worth if the spirit of man were nothing more than a passing breath. Both moral trust and the sense of mystery attaching to life embolden him to posit something more permanent in his makeup. In the words of the modern paraphrase of an ancient Jewish prayer: " Our life would be altogether vanity were it not for the soul, which, fashioned in Thine own image, gives us assurance of our higher destiny and imparts to our fleeting days an abiding value." [9]

II. NATURALNESS OF THE BELIEF

Our immortality thus recommends itself to us as (1) natural, (2) reasonable, and (3) helpful. It may be claimed that, besides the will to live, no psychological factor has contributed more to the belief in immortality than the *inability of consciousness to negate itself.* This mental limitation expressed itself in the early notions of the unnaturalness of mortality and of survival after death. Dream experience among primitives strengthened the belief that the dead continue to exist as phantoms if not in a physical state. Analogical reasoning among more advanced peoples tended to corroborate the belief that man is redeemed from the grave. The life-stream flows on ceaselessly. Like the Nile it winds itself uninterruptedly from its hidden sources to the open sea, though here and there it loses itself in the desert sands and courses underneath. Death only makes a change in the stream but does not terminate its course. It is not the end but only a new beginning.

The naturalness of the conviction of continuance beyond the grave has suggested itself as a strong proof of its reality. The sense of eternity is implanted within our hearts.[10] The inability of consciousness to negate itself and to conceive of nonexistence probably forms the basis of the universal assent of man that death is not the end, and may be at the root of the belief that the notion of immortality is innate.[11]

An old master taught that " when a righteous man departs he is lost only to his generation. It is like unto a pearl that was lost by its owner. Wherever it is it remains a pearl. Its loss is only the owner's." [12] The dead depart from us but not from Him who is the source of our being.

The saintly Rabbi Nahman of Brazlav spent his last days in Uman in a house facing the cemetery. Frequently he took his stand by the window and meditated on the hereafter: " What difference is there for him between life and death? Only first he lived here, and soon he will set up his dwelling yonder, in the grave, and live there." Death is but moving from one room into the other.[13] We encounter the same feeling in the speculations of more critical thinkers. Death is but an illusion.

III. REASONABLENESS OF THE BELIEF

As a reasonable doctrine, the belief in immortality is grounded in the nature of the soul, on the one hand, and in the nature of God and the universe, on the other. From the standpoint of empiricism we may still maintain with Rabbi Abraham ibn Ezra: "The conclusion of the matter is that man does not understand the nature of the soul, whether it be a substance or an accident, whether or not it perishes after its separation from the body, and why it is attached to the body." [14] What the eye of reason fails to see, the eye of faith may behold. But the vision of the two must be brought into focus if they are to function normally. Hence the persistent endeavors to find empirical and speculative grounds for the belief in the reality and eternity of the soul.

Not all the attempts in this direction have proved satisfying. The efforts of the rationalists who banish the soul altogether, or regard it biologically as germ plasm, vital principle, or thinking substance, or define it in physical and quantitative terms, if correct, may render a service to science but are of little or no value to religion, for they fail to endow life with sanctity and to link man with God. The Platonic method of defining the soul a priori as not subject to decomposition because it is a simple substance, incorruptible because it is invisible, and deathless by virtue of its essence, appears arbitrary and leads to a purely verbal reality, but it contains a valuable element often overlooked by those who would pursue the empirical method. It claims for the soul a transcendent quality over and above the physical and psychical life. A vagueness naturally attaches to the concept which cannot be cleared up by microscopic analysis in the laboratory. The soul or self can have meaning for religion not by itself but only as related to the Divine, as a monad reflecting the immanent activity of the World Soul, the Divine in man, a bearer of moral and spiritual values. However, while polytheistic religions may conceive of the soul as a minor deity, monotheistic faith discreetly distinguishes between the soul and God. The two are not identical. He " who stretched forth the heavens and laid the foundations of the earth, formed the spirit of man within him." [15] The soul is a divine creation and is separate and distinct from God. " A candle of the Lord is the soul of man," [16] a spark from the Undying Fire at the heart of all being. Its light is derived from Him but it has its own being. It is an ultimate principle of being, a substantive in its own right and not a mere adjective defining someone else.[17]

From the standpoint of religion the soul is the divine element in the human self or personality, the noumenal as distinct from its phenomenal or empirical elements. It is beyond consciousness and beyond mind though it manifests itself in and through them. It is the principle of individuality, viewed from the aspect of divinity. Viewing it as a monad, we must nevertheless regard it as capable of sustaining relations with and affecting other monads. Appearing at birth as a potency within the organism (as was held in somewhat different form by the advocates of creationism), the soul develops with the growth of the person into ever fuller powers, or withers and decays. The Aristotelians spoke of the actualization of the soul through reason. They may have taken too narrow a range in limiting the higher life to knowledge. We should think of the soul as unfolding not only through intellectual pursuits but also through love that does not falter, through unwavering justice, through self-discipline and self-sacrifice, through moral courage and struggle on the battlefields of truth and duty, through lofty vision, high aspiration, and steadfast devotion; in short, through a life with God. Realizing its potentialities, it becomes a permanent part of the divine life. Dependent upon the physical organism for its coming into existence and for its growth, it may be separable from the organism and capable of surviving it.

The reality of the religious conception of the soul is contingent upon the general world view. It is untenable if we regard the universe as meaningless, purposeless, and dead, a mere mechanism operated by fortuitous happenings. Such a materialistic view of the world leaves no room for the phenomena of consciousness and mind as well. All attempts to explain spirit by derivation from inert matter appear singularly unconvincing. It is far more satisfactory to look at the universe as an ordered whole, of real meaning and purpose — though the exact nature of these escapes human knowledge — and essentially alive. We can think of the soul as real only when we believe with the Psalmist that "with Thee is the fountain of life; in Thy light we see light." [18] This conviction alone offers ground for the belief that the human spirit is real and that the earthly life is but a stage in its development. It is instructive that the religion of Israel advanced not from the soul to God but from God to the soul.

The doctrine of ethical monotheism carries a double conviction: first, that one God unites, governs and sustains the vast all; and second, that his workings are ethical — i.e., that they are ordered according to law, making for the ultimate well-being of all things both for themselves and in their totality. In other words, the whole of nature — including man as part of nature — came into being and is preserved through the holy, just and good World Will and World Mind, the Fountain of life. All forms of being and of consciousness have their roots in the living God. Man, in whom the life-process has reached the highest level, reflects most closely the "image of God." So capable of nobility of spirit, so infinite in faculty, man cannot be merely the quintessence of dust. By virtue of his reason, his creative power, and his moral sense, he shares with God in the work of creation. Being one with Him in life, man cannot be cast off in death. God delivers the soul from destruction.

This doctrine of religion is basic also to idealistic philosophy. L. P. Jacks finds the essence of its teaching in the proposition that "life and immortality, not death and mechanism, are the keywords of the real universe;" and that, insofar as we are its true children, "life and immortality are the keywords of our reality also." While idealists differ on many issues, they all tend to agree that the universe is, as Goethe called it, "the living garment of God." They all dissent from the view that life and consciousness are chance occurrences in a dead universe. If they were mere accidents, we might expect them to end as they began, and all conscious lives to be "refunded into the universal empire of death." But with conscious life as the essence and reality of the universe, we may have ground for anticipating something better.[19]

The belief in an immortal soul constitutes part of the religious birthright of man. As far as we are able to ascertain, the animal world is neither concerned with spiritual values nor troubled with questions of death and deathlessness. Man alone seeks to endow his transiency with permanence and to link his fleeting moments with eternity. In his naive realism he, too, sometimes inclines to abandon this thought. On the one hand, he cannot bring himself to recognize the naturalness of mortality, and on the other he questions the reality of immortality. To his cloudy vision all things seem to come and go, with nothing abiding. Destruction appears to be the final arbiter of all that exists. An end seems to await all things under the sun. He sees the senses falling into eternal slumber and the body stiffening into the sleep that knows no waking. As he is reconciled to the decay of the flesh, so he sometimes appears content with the annihilation of the spirit.

Among the chief exponents of this alternative to immortality in the ancient world were Epicurus and Lucretius. Their disciples continued the great denial during the Middle Ages and still do so today in the name of materialistic philosophy. We encounter it in religious experience as well. It was held in the early religion of Israel as against the cults of the dead, and is voiced by advanced monotheists in several Psalms, in Job and in Ecclesiastes. The Sadducees may have adhered to it in opposition to the novel teachings of the Hasidim and the Pharisees regarding the future life. However, this point of view could not maintain itself in the face of the human craving for continuance and of the advancing logic of ethical monotheism. Neither could it hold its ground in the light of idealistic philosophy. It can be enter-

tained only if spirit can be shown to be a by-product of matter and if the universe can be demonstrated to be dead. A
living universe, the ultimate ground of which is God, rules
out the thought of annihilation.[20]

Another alternative, not to immortality but rather to the
preservation of personal identity after death, claims our attention. The Stoics held that at death we are " absorbed in
the unfathomed depths of universal being." As Marcus
Aurelius expresses it, the spirit, surviving for a time, is finally " absorbed in the generative principle of the universe."
Some interpreters construe Ecclesiastes 12:7 in this sense.
Thus Rabbi Abraham ibn Ezra taught that the soul loses its
individuality at death and is reabsorbed by the *anima uni-
versalis*. This is essentially the idea of pantheism. Spinoza
affirms in one of his propositions that " the human mind
cannot be absolutely destroyed with the body, but there is
some part of it that remains eternally." [21] In the previous
proposition he maintains that in God there is necessarily the
idea which expresses the essence of the human mind under
the species of eternity. This can pertain only to the essence
of the mind, for the actual mind endures only as long as the
body endures. While the soul is immortal that which represents its individuality or separate personality vanishes with
the death of the body. The soul itself " sinks back into the
vast undercurrent of boundless life," which is the vital force
of the pantheistic universe. Schopenhauer, too, held that
individuality is not " the thing in itself, but only the phenomenon presented in the form of time; and therefore with
a beginning and an end." The real being is free from the
limitations of time and individuality. It is present in every
individual, and no individual can exist apart from it. Death

terminates that which is distinctive in man and leaves only the universal.[22]

While this conception, representing an escape from egocentricity, fascinates many minds, it suffers from the general difficulties of pantheistic thought, which obliterates the distinction between God and the universe. The part is identified with the whole, and personality is deprived not only of immortality but also of self-realization, of responsibility, and of freedom, and is logically reduced to illusion.

Ethical monotheism supplies that which pantheism misses. Claiming that we live in a world " the final ground of which is a supreme moral and spiritual Being," it finds personal immortality a reasonable belief. Josiah Royce well expressed the logic of ethical monotheism: " Just because, then, God is one, all our lives have various and unique places in the harmony of the divine life. And just because God attains and wins this uniqueness, all our lives win in our union with him, the individuality which is essential to their true meaning." [23] God is, indeed, " the God of the spirits of all flesh." [24] From this viewpoint we may think of the destiny of the soul not as absorption in God but rather as communion with God. Retaining its integrity, it rediscovers itself in him. Though it be manifestly an overbelief, we may contemplate the possibility that God needs our spirits to be truly himself even as they need him to partake of the fount of being. As he sends us into life to do his will, so he may have tasks for us beyond the span of our earthly career. Thus the rabbis taught that " the righteous rest not either in this nor in the future world, but advance from strength to strength until ' every one of them appeareth before God in Zion.' " [25]

Monotheistic faith thus leads to the belief in personal immortality. The ethical nature of monotheism strengthens the belief with an ethical argument. The theological and the ethical arguments often appear together. So Plato suggests, in the *Timaeus,* that our souls, at least in their higher part, are the work of God; and that he cannot will to destroy his own creation. A just God cannot deal unjustly with his children. The argument reduces itself to trust in God. In the words of the Psalmist, " In Thy hands I commit my spirit." The ground for this confidence is that " Thou wilt not suffer Thy godly one to see the pit." [26]

The moral argument, as Galloway reminds us, is not based on proof in the scientific or philosophic sense. Instead of being deduced from empirical data, it is a demand of moral conscience. "It is a claim that man, as an ethical being, makes on the universe in which he lives and acts. In other words, it is a postulate put forward to harmonize the facts of experience, and to make them consistent with the demands of the moral consciousness." It stems not merely from the heart's desire for the maintenance of the bonds of love and friendship beyond the grave and from the refusal to think lightly of oneself and the universe, but also from the demand of practical reason for the moral organization of experience.[27]

This argument has assumed various forms in both the religious and the philosophic traditions. In its simplest and most prevalent form it is bound up with the belief in other-worldly retribution. The sinner who flouted justice on earth will reap the harvest of evil in the beyond. There can be no escape for him. In the same way the righteous person who pursued the paths of justice will enjoy the fruit of his doings in the hereafter. The topsy-turvydom of the world cannot upset the ultimate balance of things. This craving is still present in people who may not be particularly sensitive to religion. If there is no hell, they say, there ought to be one for rogues and sinners. As God's justice cannot be merely punitive but must be essentially corrective, the religious mind recoils from the thought of endless punishment in the hereafter. After a period of purgation, the soul is redeemed and restored to God's grace.

The belief in otherworldly retribution, growing out of the moral sense, rested in great part on fear. In the experience of the three monotheistic religions, as of some polytheistic creeds and even of the atheistic religion of Buddhism, this idea operated as a deterrent to evil and as an incentive to right living. In vast parts of the world it still serves a useful end. In the Western world, however, among both Jews and Christians it has lost its force. Men endure so much misery in this world that they are not frightened by the thought of more of the same kind after death. If men still shun evil and pursue the good it is because of the consequence in the here rather than in the beyond. To the degree to which they act on reflection they are guided by the thought of the moral law of cause and effect, of evil producing more evil and of good leading to more good. However, the principle of immanent justice in social and individual life does not seem to work adequately. It is not the most callous and crudest but the most sensitive and refined who feel most keenly the pain and the misery of the world. The truest servants of God are most often the men of sorrows, bearing upon themselves the stripes and chastisements of their generation. Even if it be recognized that vicarious suffering forms part of the spiritual education of the race, the question forces itself upon the moral conscience: " Shall not the Judge of the whole earth do justly? " [28] Does justice not prevail in the organization of the universe? Considerations of this nature persist in giving urgency to the expectation of the ultimate rectification of the inequities of human affairs in another world, despite the skeptical turn of the modern mind.

A subtler expression of the ethical argument is found in Mendelssohn's *Phaedo,* patterned after Plato's dialogue but voicing eighteenth century ideas. The argument is based on the teleological world view. Creation, it may be claimed, came into existence for the sake of rational beings, who shall advance step by step, increase in perfection, and thereby attain happiness. That this advance should pause midway and be thrown back into the abyss with all the fruit of its endeavors wasted cannot be the choice of God and part of his plan for the world. As rational beings men strive after ceaseless growth and progress toward godlike perfection. This is their highest goal. It cannot be that man should be created with infinite capabilities without being able ever to satisfy them. A kind God cannot be conceived as having implanted in man the thought of immortality only to mock him in the end. Providence has not endowed man with longing for eternal bliss in vain. Unattained in this life, the progress toward moral and spiritual fulfillment will be attained in the hereafter.[29]

A similar form is given this argument by Kant, but without the theistic ground. It is based on the fragmentary and radically incomplete nature of man's spiritual life and on the discrepancy between his vision of the ideal and his ability to realize it. It appears inconceivable that man would dream of perfection as his highest goal if it were wholly un-attainable. As this highest good cannot be achieved during one lifetime, we are led to suppose "the endless *duration* of the *existence* and personality of the same being. . . . The *summum bonum,* then, practically, is only possible on the supposition of the immortality of the soul; consequently this immortality, being inseparably connected with the moral law, is a postulate of pure practical reason." [30]

To deny this claim amounts to asserting that moral chaos obtains at the heart of reality. And the moral law which bids us transcend our physical being and live as "aspirants of eternity" appears as a satanic delusion. Thus the postulate of the soul's continuance and fulfillment beyond earthly life helps to save us and our convictions about God from moral bankruptcy.

As to the bliss or misery awaiting the spirit in the here-after, about which dogmatic faith had much to say, reserve seems the part of wisdom. There is point to the claim that hell is but the nightmare produced by our sense of condemnation of the evils which harass our earthly life. Similarly heaven with its realms of unending bliss, radiant splendor, and infinite goodness is merely the idealization of our approbation of virtue. The fairly general lack of curiosity regarding both of them is one of the marked features of contemporary religion. Unlike our forebears we do not press for previews of the fires of hell or of the glories of heaven; neither do we worry concerning the changes that come over the soul at the shock of death and in consequence of its adjustment to its new environment and its new tasks. The efforts on the part of psychical research to lift the veil of the unknown fail to stir the believing world. Men of

deepest spirituality are most content to leave the mystery to
God. They share the Psalmist's faith: " My flesh and my
heart faileth: but God is the strength of my heart and my
portion forever." [31]   At the hour of sunset, they confide their
spirits to him, assured that having experienced his presence
in life they will not be abandoned in death. In rabbinic
metaphor, they will find " shelter under the wings of the
Shekina [Divine Presence]." The pursuit of truth, goodness, and holiness — i.e., living with God — that is heaven;
surrender to sin, wickedness and falsehood, which is es-
trangement from him, is hell, whether in this life or beyond.

IV.   HELPFULNESS OF THE BELIEF

Is the belief in immortality helpful? Lotze argued that
whatever has come into being will continue eternally as
long as it retains unchangeable value for the organic unity
of the world.[32] Whether or not the soul has abiding value
for the organic unity of the world we have no way of ascer-
taining. But we know that it is of transcendent value to
personal and social well-being. There are, indeed, some
temperaments which find comfort in the thought of total
extinction or of loss of individuality through absorption in
the Absolute. The longing for nirvana on the part of
Buddhists indicates that such a prospect may even be welcome from the standpoint of religion. They look for the
extinction of all desire and interest, including that of survival, and for deliverance from the dreary wheel of change,
the dull and gloomy round of continuous reincarnations.
Among Jews and Christians, too, there are many weary fight-
ers of life's stern combats who long for dreamless rest.

The late C. G. Montefiore voiced the sentiments of many

religious spirits for whom faith in immortality is "a necessary corollary" of the belief in a righteous God: "If a divine
voice should say: 'There is no immortality for you, but God
is righteous all the same,' I sometimes feel as if I should be
satisfied and at rest." Again, the revelation

would not, I think, make any marked difference to my manner
of life. It would still seem best, and most in accordance with the
divine will, to live worthily today, though we are utterly extin-
guished tomorrow. One would be less ready to die, sorrier to lose
what was to be one's only chance of consciousness, of knowledge,
of love. But . . . I should feel that mankind had received a blow
from which it could hardly hope to recover. Jowett said: "The
denial of the belief takes the heart out of human life: it lowers
men to the level of the material." [33]

Destroy the confidence in the abiding worth of human
personality and in the continuity of the ethical and spiritual
life — whether in a transcendental or social realm — and
you remove thereby the strongest prop of human endeavor.

The fallacies of otherworldliness are sufficiently evident.
Men have deferred living and fighting for justice and abandoned "this world as a rotting hulk." It is no less fallacious
to imagine that by abandoning all thoughts of survival life
will grow richer and the efforts for justice intenser. There
is the wisdom of experience behind Paul Elmer More's argument: "If we perish like beasts, shall we not live like
beasts?" [34]

In a speech from the tribune in 1794, Robespierre addressed a question that has lost none of its force for us:

Will the idea of annihilation inspire man with purer and more
elevated sentiments than that of his immortality? Will it inspire

him with greater respect for mankind or for himself? more devotion for his country, more boldness against tyranny? . . . The
idea of the Supreme Being, and the immortality of the soul is a
continual appeal to justice.[35]

The skeptical philosopher Renan predicted:

The day in which the belief in an afterlife shall vanish from the
earth will witness a terrific moral and spiritual decadence. Some
of us, perhaps, might do without it, provided only that others held
it fast. But there is no lever capable of raising an entire people if
once they have lost their faith in the immortality of the soul.[36]

Emerson warned us against the moral paralysis which creeps
over us with the abandonment of this belief. Pessimism
rears its head, human affections grow feeble, and moral
values become ephemeral. Its loss casts a dark shadow upon
our present life.[37] The decline of this belief under the pressure of materialistic and racial or biologic philosophies accounts, in great part, for the frightful disregard of the sanctity and worth of the individual in Russia, Germany, and
Italy.

V. PRESERVATION OF VALUES

Worse than man's physical extinction is the extinction of
his values. Man's true life is not within the tracks of his
body but within his ideal purposes, as creator of the values
which form the basis of our civilization. Humble or great,
his work is of worth to the whole. It may be the work of
the brickmaker, bricklayer, architect, or designer — but it
is of moment to the entire social structure. What are our
cities but the product of human lives? Every inch of the
streets upon which we walk or travel, each subterranean

pipe which supplies us with water, each wire which links us with the rest of the world, each house or public building we inhabit, each theater, library, school, or temple we attend, each newspaper, magazine, book, play, or picture, each movement, ideal, or vision — represents the distilled essence of human lives, of labor, love, thought, sacrifice. Each life in turn is the product of other lives. It is the fruitage of the love not only of a father and mother, but of countless other forebears. It is, indeed, the heir of all generations.

L. P. Jacks objects to the idea expressed in George Eliot's "The Choir Invisible" that we are dissolved into a stream of moral tendency and live on after death "in minds made better by our presence." Using one person as a means to the ends of another, Jacks thinks, violates the fundamental principle of the moral order, in which — as Kant taught — persons, individual persons, are treated as *ends in themselves* and not as means or instruments to other ends.[38] The Kantian ideal is essential to the preservation of human rights. No personality may be reduced to a mere tool or machine. It is quite other for a person to give himself willingly for the well-being of others, as the mother gladly gives herself for her child, as the lover sacrifices himself for the sake of the beloved, as the patriot surrenders himself for his country, or as the man of science offers his life that knowledge may be increased. The cosmic order would be unintelligible if the law of sacrifice were ignored. According to the Talmud, Alexander the Great asked the sages of the South: "What shall man do to live?" "Let him die unto himself," they replied. "What then shall he do in order to die?" asked the conqueror. "Let him live for himself," the sages answered.[39] Considered by itself each soul is a monad, an end in itself; from the social side it is also a means to other ends, to other souls.

The interest shifts from mere physical continuance and from the survival of the vital or rational principle to the preservation of the soul as the divine in man, the bearer of ethical and spiritual values. The significance of the shift may be made clear by an illustration. In the divine book of life each person may be said to constitute a single word. In combination words form sentences and paragraphs and convey meaning. Human beings, too, derive their significance, not from themselves alone, but from their relations to others. In cooperation or in conflict with others they play out their roles in life's drama. The greater the person—i.e., the greater the meaning of his being and its significance to humanity—the greater is its relationship to others, imparting purpose and value to them. At death the elements that form the person fall apart, but their meaning in the scheme of humanity remains. To carry the figure a little further, we may assume that even as the movable type which composes the word, when broken up or taken apart by the printer, is not necessarily destroyed, so the elements that make up personality continue even after they have been separated by death.

These elements are not merely physical, but also spiritual. Consequently the words of Ecclesiastes, " And the dust returneth to the earth as it was," [40] present only part of the epilogue of the human drama. There is more to be added. We have already dealt with the idea expressed in the second half of the same verse, " And the spirit returneth unto God who gave it." What of the values through which the spirit grows and matures? Our previous observations on this point

should have sufficed were it not for the overclaim of some
that values retain their intimate union with the soul and continue with it in its life with God. The grounds for such a
claim seem to lack validity. We have no warrant for thinking of values as substantive in their own right. They are but
the effects and objects of the spirit, relations, and attitudes
of persons to themselves and to others. While coming to
fruition in the lives of individuals, they are social in character. As the honey produced by the bee ceases to be its own,
so values achieved are no longer private but become a social
possession. We can speak of their conservation not in a
transcendental realm but in the lives of men, in the circle of
the family, community, country, and humanity. In short,
personal values have meaning to the extent to which they
function in the lives of individuals and contribute to the good
of society.

The fear that the dissociation of values from persons at
death deprives man of pre-eminence over the beast is without
foundation; for his pre-eminence consists in being a pro-
ducer of values. Thereby he forges his soul and becomes a
co-worker with God. To conserve his efforts for the good
of his fellow men is his chief concern as an ethical being. To
characterize this concern, as is often done, as the mere craving for the perpetuation of personal influence does scant
justice to it. Though something of this desire is present in
most men, this craving is of much deeper nature. It is the
urge to express oneself as a creative being. Whether it
operates in us blindly or consciously, it forms the very essence
of our lives.

" Social immortality," far from conflicting with the personal, enriches its significance. Only the spirit that has con-

tributed to the larger life of mankind may be deserving of
unbroken communion with God. This idea also justifies the
hope of personal continuance, with which we dealt in the
first part of our discussion. To the claim that our lives flow
on in the life-stream of the race, this idea adds the assurance
that moral, spiritual, and intellectual endeavors abide as part
of the heritage of civilization. Immortality, whether personal or social, is ultimately predicated upon the belief that
the Creative Spirit ever hovers over the deep, working out its
designs and ends and endowing the universe, of which we
are part, with endurance and with meaning. The spirit, as
the bearer of values, derives from God and strives after him.
Its life is a continuous growth. Progress forms part of its
nature. Thus it is linked with the universal striving after the
victory of the good, which is the natural climax and goal
of ethical monotheism.

From the standpoint of values, immortality appears not
only as an intrinsic attribute of the soul but also as an acqui-
sition and an achievement. Instead of merely projecting its
vision beyond the misty portals of the grave, this belief makes
for a " transfigured personal life in a transfigured social
order." Its " otherworldliness " tempers this world. The
sharp line between " this world " and " the world to come "
fades away. One grows out of the other. They are inter-
bound by striving, suffering, and achievement. It also
checks the tendency to circumscribe our moral and spiritual
efforts by the bounds of temporal and mundane society,
whether of class, nation, race, or church. Important as these
are, they are only fractions of the whole. The full goal of
human life must be the universal and the eternal. Man
must so live in society as to invest his life with eternity and
partake of the divine life.

Immortality concerns itself with the realization of life's highest ends, with the sanctification of the self, and with its complete surrender and dedication unto the All-just, the All-good and the All-holy. Identified with eternal causes, the spirit of man partakes of their deathlessness. Having experienced the Infinite, man need not fear relapsing into finitude. Faith, hope, justice, love, rout fear and despair and sweep away all negations. The possibilities of a mysterious universe, governed by the righteous God of life, reveal inexhaustible realms of wonder to the aspiring spirit.

NOTES

[1] Ps. 112:1–6.

[2] See Deut. 29:13–14. Cf. Taanit 5b: "Our father Jacob did not die. . . . Even as his seed is alive so he lives."

[3] *Religion der Vernunft* (Leipzig: Gustav Fock, 1919), Chap. XV.

[4] Ezek. 37:1–14.

[5] Dan. 12:2–3. See also Isa. 26:19, 25:8.

[6] See Sanh. 91 ff.; 1 Cor. 15:35 ff.

[7] A strikingly original version of this belief is found in the epitaph which Benjamin Franklin composed for himself at the ripe age of twenty-two: "The body of Benjamin Franklin, Printer (like the cover of an old book, its contents torn out and stripped of its lettering and gilding) lies here, food for worms; but the work shall not be lost, for it will (as he believed) appear once more in a new and more elegant edition, revised and corrected by the Author."

[8] For the manner in which the Anglican Church has given up the belief in the resurrection of the flesh, see Kirsopp Lake, *Immortality and the Modern Mind* (Cambridge, Mass.: Harvard University Press, 1922), pp. 38–44. See also K. Kohler, *Jewish Theology* (New York: The Macmillan Co., 1928), p. 297.

[9] *Union Prayer Book* (Cincinnati: Central Conference of American Rabbis, 1924), I, 66. See Israel Abrahams, *Annotated Edition of the Authorized Daily Prayer Book* (London: Eyre & Spottiswood, Ltd., 1914), p. xxi.

[10] Eccles. 3:11. For a modern appraisal of this proof see A. E. Taylor, *The Faith of a Moralist* (New York: The Macmillan Co., 1937), I, 268 ff.

[11] Cf. Wordsworth's "We Are Seven." For an especially forceful illustration of this state of mind, see James Oppenheim's poem "Death," in Caroline Hill's *The World's Great Religious Poetry* (New York: The Macmillan Co., 1923), pp. 685–86.

[12] Meg. 15a.

[13] Kahana, *Sefer Hahasidut,* p. 338.

[14] Commentary to Exod. 23:20.

[15] Zech. 12:1.

[16] Prov. 20:26.

[17] "The soul in man," Emerson says, "is not an organ, but animates and exercises all the organs; it is not a function, like the power of memory, of calculation, of comparison, but uses these as hands and feet; it is not a faculty, but a light; it is not the intellect or the will, but the master of the intellect and the will; it is the vast background of our being, in which they lie, an immensity not possessed and that cannot be possessed. From within or behind, a light shines through us upon things, and makes us aware that we are nothing, but the light is all." Man is but the organ of the soul. "When it breathes through his intellect, it is genius; when it breathes through his will, it is virtue; when it flows through his affection, it is love. And the blindness of the intellect begins, when it would be something of itself. The weakness of the will begins when the individual would be something of himself. All reform aims in some particular, to let the great soul have its way through us; in other words, to engage us to obey." — *The Over-Soul.*

[18] Ps. 36:10.

[19] L. P. Jacks, *A Living Universe* (New York: Doubleday, Doran & Co., 1924), pp. 103-4.

[20] The soul being nonphysical, its reality or nonreality can be argued from material analogies only provisionally. A suggestion may be derived from the doctrine of conservation of matter and energy. Is it unreasonable to allow that the law of conservation has its analogue in the realm of the spirit? Some men of science seem to think it is not. For example, Dr. Heber D. Curtis, while admitting "a gap between the world of matter and that of the spirit," asks: "With energy, matter, space and time continuing, with nothing lost, are we ourselves the only manifestation that comes to an end, that ceases, is annihilated at three score and ten?" (Cited in *Religious Education,* XXIII, 291.) At the same time we must note the difficulty which inheres in the analogy. Wilhelm Ostwald calls attention to the hopelessness of identifying any bit of energy. "By coming into contact with another quantity of like energy it is at once lost as completely as a drop is lost in the ocean. It retains its existence only in that it adds its share to the common quantity of energy, and no means is known by which this token of its existence can be destroyed." — *Individuality and Immortality* (New York: Houghton Mifflin Co., 1906), pp. 41-42.

[21] *Ethics,* V, prop. XXIII.

[22] *Immortality — A Dialogue.*

[23] *Conception of Immortality* (New York: Houghton Mifflin Co., 1900), p. 75.

[24] Num. 15:22.

[25] Berachot 64a, after Ps. 84:8. See Matthew Arnold's tribute to his father in "Rugby Chapel;" John Laird, *The Idea of the Soul* (New York: Doubleday, Doran & Co., 1924), p. 177.

[26] Pss. 31:5; 16:10.

[27] George Galloway, *The Idea of Immortality* (New York: Charles Scribner's Sons, 1917), pp. 151–52.

[28] Gen. 18:25.

[29] Moses Mendelssohn, *Gesammelte Werke* (ed. 1843), II, 175–76.

[30] *Critique of Practical Reason* (trans. by Abbot), pp. 218–19.

[31] Ps. 73:26.

[32] Cited by Garvie, article "Immortality," *Encyclopedia Britannica* (11th ed.), XIV, 337.

[33] "The Desire for Immortality," *Jewish Quarterly Review*, Old Series, XIV, 105–7.

[34] *On Being Human* (Princeton, N. J.: Princeton University Press, 1936).

[35] Cited by E. E. Holmes, *Immortality*, p. 42.

[36] Cited by Garvie, *loc. cit.*

[37] *Natural Religion*, Postscript. See also Hocking, "The Meaning of Life," *Journal of Religion*, XVI (1936), 275.

[38] L. P. Jacks, *op. cit.*, pp. 106–8.

[39] Tamid 32a.

[40] Eccles. 12:7.

THE SIGNIFICANCE OF CRITICAL STUDY
OF THE GOSPELS FOR
RELIGIOUS THOUGHT TODAY

FREDERICK CLIFTON GRANT
Union Theological Seminary

I

WHAT DIFFERENCE, if any, does the critical study of the Gospels make for religious thought at the present day? There are some who reply, "None at all. Religious thought goes on and will go on its way regardless of the theories of literary and historical critics. Religious thought is no mere set of inferences from a body of assured historical data, but is centered in a direct and independent apprehension of truth. Theology is not dependent upon history. And as for preaching and religious education, they have for a long time operated in complete freedom from critical researches, and no doubt will continue to do so. The center of religious thought, devotion and education, the source of their present inspiration, is to be found in worship, in the deep emotional response of the soul to the Christian tradition as a whole; and this has no need to wait for the critics to give some word of assurance that Christian faith is justified, and that one may properly go forward in confidence and trust."

We must recognize the large amount of truth in this argument. Indeed, we may even thank God for it: Christianity is a still living, still vital religious faith, and moves by an

56

inner momentum regardless of the changing views of men, however important in their own sphere. True, the argument — or rather its conclusion — is sometimes stated in curious ways. For example, I know an Orientalist who is prepared to apply literary and historical criticism to every field outside the Gospels, to the Old Testament and equally to early Christian literature (outside the New Testament) with the same freedom he exercises in the study of the history, literature, and religion of ancient Babylon or Egypt, early Islam, or the Christian sects of the East; but when he comes to the New Testament, he insists, " I prefer to take the Gospels just as they are." But such an extreme view is surely untenable for the majority of students. A distinction must be drawn between the devotional use of the Scriptures, including the Gospels, and their use in the critical reconstruction of the course of the beginnings of the Christian movement in history. The former may be valid, in its own sphere: in fact, almost any kind of writing may be treated devotionally — witness the interpretation of the Song of Songs. As Emerson says somewhere, men can gain spiritual nourishment from even the most unpromising of sacred literature — " as Balboa's men, crossing the Isthmus, boiled and ate their boot tops; " and how much the more, then, such inspired, and inspiring, literature as the Gospels! I once knew a godly pastor who enriched his own devotional life and that of his people with meditations on the obscure word " Selah," found in the Psalter — which he interpreted to mean *"Nota bene"* — " Note carefully! Think of it! " We must recognize in fairness that such devotional study may be genuinely enriching, even though it uses the greater meanings of Scripture to cover or support the less, as the brilliance of a chandelier hides the weaker bulbs in a blaze of light. They say there was a story in circulation at the University of Berlin thirty years ago, as follows: Some adverse and captious critic had said of the great Professor Harnack that " a scrubwoman knew the Bible as well as he." When Harnack heard it he remarked, " *Ja; vielleicht noch besser* " — " Yes, and probably much better! " It is not, of course, the devotional use of the Gospels with which we are now concerned, but with their use for historical and doctrinal purposes. Though naturally we must recognize that if historical and literary criticism should by either chance or necessity some day reach the conclusion that the Gospels are purely mythical and contain no element of truth of this tangible kind whatsoever, and if the conclusion could be proved, then probably the day would be done for their devotional as well as for their doctrinal or historical use. But even so, we may remember that some persons, for example the late Barrett Wendell, would prefer a purely mythical, symbolical sacred literature, wholly detached from history, of permanent religious meaning simply because new meanings can be read into it from time to time and age after age. Wendell gave this as his reason for preferring the Fourth Gospel above the other three; no doubt there are others who hold this or a similar view. One meets Hindus who maintain that the Bhagavad Gita is superior to the New Testament for the reason that it does not pretend to relate history, but only a simple myth, shot full of later speculation, philosophy, and the fruits of exalted insight into spiritual truth.

There are also those who, in the name of Christian doctrine, would dispense with the historic truth of the New Testament. The " Word of God " which it contains, or rather which it presupposes, is superior to the contingencies of time and place, even in a sacred and inspired record. They cite Lessing's principle, viz., that eternal truth is not dependent upon proofs derived from the relativities of history; and they refuse to admit that the New Testament (i.e., specifically, the Gospels) can provide the basis for Christian doctrine. This view is a long remove from our traditional attitude toward the New Testament, especially toward the historical books it contains; and it is difficult to make out just what place the Gospels are to continue to occupy in such a scheme of ideas. The fact — the historical fact! — is that the Gospels never were the *basis* of Christian doctrine. The old " high " Anglican view has to some degree characterized all Christian thought from the beginning: "The church to teach, the Bible to prove." That is to say, the Christian faith, the Christian gospel, is something distinct from, even if reflected in, the four canonical writings known as " Gospels." There was a gospel before there were any Gospels, as there was a faith before there were any creeds. But this is not quite the view we are describing. The tendency now, in certain areas, is to ignore the Gospels themselves, as well as Gospel criticism, and to base Christianity upon the total phenomenon of the New Testament, as the culmination of the Old; or rather upon the majestic historical phenomenon of which the New Testament is the partial record and various reflection. To some extent, this view may be the result of discouragement, or even of despair, over the results of a century and more of higher criticism. *If* the results to date of all this effort are so negative and so unsatisfying; *if,* as Schweitzer maintains, Jesus is only a stranger and an enigma to our generation, and now more a stranger than ever before in these nineteen long centuries; *if* the New Testament, and chiefly the Gospels, are recognized to belong to an ancient

and now long forgotten era, and to another and wholly different world of social, economic, and religious attitudes and
relationships, namely, those of the old Semitic Near East,
superficially Hellenized by the first century but still anything but modern — *then* the question arises, What can provide the basis for Christian faith and practice? Since the
foundations have begun to subside, like those beneath one
of the medieval cathedrals, what will support Christianity
while new footings are being provided, new piers and pedi-
ments which will go down to the solid bedrock far beneath
this shifting soil of time? It cannot hang in thin air, like the
houses of Laputa; and on the older view, according to which
the foundations were solely and exclusively historical, the
structure must inevitably collapse. Some of the skepticism
of history now popular in certain circles and some of the
dogmatism now rampant in religious thought are surely
closely related, not merely as contemporary intellectual phenomena but in the order of cause and effect. Criticism may
be inevitable: but what is to survive the full application of
the critical method and process? Should we not, before it
is too late, retrace our steps, and go back to a simpler, perhaps a more naive, certainly a more religious attitude toward
the Gospels? That is, supposing we are unable to accept the
modern theological device of divorcing faith from history,
or of locating the basis of our faith, not in detailed facts or
events but only in the general or total impression of revelation which the New Testament records or reflects.

II

But such a proposal is thoroughly impractical. We cannot, if we would, go back to the naive and uncritical attitude

of our forefathers. Historical and literary criticism is now applied in every field of our knowledge of the human past. This was not so in our great-grandfathers' days — not only the Bible but other books as well enjoyed a veneration which set them above criticism. For example, Shakespeare was idolized; " literary criticism " was chiefly engaged in pointing out his excellences. Certain heroes were idolized: Washington, for example, in many circles. Certain theories of government were beyond criticism — democracy in some circles, monarchy in others. But in these modern days, when free and unfettered criticism is the rule in every department of human interest, it would be tragic folly even to attempt to withdraw the Bible or certain of its books (say the Gospels) from the acid test and scrutiny of criticism. Nothing would more quickly or conclusively prove, to the satisfaction of many persons, that the Gospels could not be expected to survive the test, and so were being withdrawn in order to forestall a discovery of their worthlessness. Criticism is inevitable. And so, instead of lamenting the fact, we ought to see that criticism is fairly applied, and that its positive results are as fully and accurately recorded as the negative, and that the religious evaluation of these results is given as much consideration as are the historical or the literary. These are three aspects of " the significance of critical study of the Gospels for religious thought " with which I wish to deal in this paper.

1. In the first place, we must see that criticism is fairly applied. Every subject of criticism has its own peculiarities. In this respect works of literature and art share with all living phenomena, as opposed to inanimate things. You may

run every specimen of rock or metal through the same laboratory process, without distinction — for you have a standard, a goal before you, an element you are determined to detect and extract. But when you study a living species in its native habitat, whether flower of the field or beast or bird, a hundred factors at once condition its behavior, its response to environment, its method of meeting and mastering the fate that threatens it. Even more important are the marks of individuality or of peculiarity when we study a human person or group, and attempt to evaluate his or their behavior. And a book, or a collection of books, a literature, shares this human quality — no two are alike; " types " are rarely found in a pure state but almost always in complicated crossings; and nature — or history, or God — never quite repeats. So it will not do to set up some a priori theory of what a religion ought to be, or how it ought to take its origin, on the basis of some generic pattern which we think can be made out by a " comparative " study of religion, or by grouping sects under various academic categories. Your nimble Tartar, as Emerson said, always leaps over the Chinese wall of intellectual classifications — whether Hegelian or more recent. I do not deny that similarities exist, and are often illuminating — as the late Eduard Meyer illustrated ancient Judaism and early Christianity from the history of the Latter-day Saints. But our eyes should be just as keen to see uniqueness and distinction, newness and fresh emergence, as they are to recognize likeness and to detect signs of an underlying pattern.

One of the distinctive features of early Christianity, shared with Buddhism, for example, but not with Islam — with which in some other respects it has far more in common — is the fact that not one word of the sacred literature was written by its Founder.

The oldest accounts of the Buddha which we possess grew out of the conversations which his monastic disciples held, even during his lifetime, in the neighborhood north and south of the middle Ganges. There, in the cool of the evening, groups of them gathered in the fragrant groves and engaged in edifying dialogue, exchanging in exalted mood their recollections of what they had themselves seen and heard or received from the " teacher," as he had let some incident from his own life slip into the current of his discourse.[1]

On the other hand, for Islam we have the Koran, gathered and arranged soon after Mohammed's death by his successor Abu Bekr, garnered from the retentive and accurate memories of his fellow warriors, edited in a standard text by order of the Caliph Othman, with its surahs arranged in order of length — all this within thirty years of the hegira, and most of the Koran dictated directly to his followers by its author! With the later noncanonical traditions the case is different — no modern writer on Islam would think of placing these on a par with the canonical utterances of the Koran. When we turn back to Christianity, we are confronted with a situation that is both similar and yet distinctive and peculiar. Little in the Gospels can have been dictated by rote, like the Koran; the variations between passages are enough to prove this — e.g., the Lord's Prayer, or the Beatitudes. Moreover, the sayings have been translated out of another language, and the original nuance and implication are now lost in more than one of the Lord's utterances. On the other hand, the Gospels were not the product — like the sayings of the Buddha — of quiet monastic communities where every word of the Master was treasured and reverently repeated: the Gospels, as Martin Dibelius rightly insists, grew out of preaching, their materials were used over and again in public proclamation of the message and in private teaching — but with a difference; for the preachers of the gospel took it for granted that the end of the age had arrived, and there was little need to preserve the precise diction of the Master for a posterity which would never exist.

Another factor involved in the fair application of criticism is the length of time covered by the literature. The Old Testament covers a period of a thousand years, more or less, from its earliest fragments of folk poesy to its latest finished books, and reflects the most varied types of social organization, from nomadism to a settled agricultural economy, through monarchy to exile and dissolution of the state, then on to the later priestly theocracy, with a brief revival of monarchy under the Maccabees, and the final extinction of political independence in the Roman period. The religious outlook and ideas of men were conditioned all along the way by the external circumstances of their common life. But the New Testament arose within a comparatively brief period — probably not more than a century at most, if we except the Second Epistle of Peter, which dates from approximately 150 A.D. Part of this literature, including the early Gospel traditions, comes from Palestine; the larger part comes from the Greco-Roman world outside — chiefly from the cities about the Aegean, from Rome, and perhaps from Alexandria. The New Testament comes from an area of highly developed and still advancing civilization; but it comes from people who had little at stake in organized society, who were convinced that " the fashion of this world " was " passing away" and was soon to disappear, and who accordingly had but slight concern with civic responsibilities — in fact, for the majority of the early Christians such responsibilities probably did not even exist. Their only concern was obedience to "the powers that be," for the sake of a temporary truce which was to last until the end of this present evil age. The divine reign was soon to succeed and supplant that of the Caesars. This attitude clearly prevailed with the majority of those who handed down the Gospel tradition. No wonder then if certain elements in Jesus' teaching were underscored, and others neglected, with the result that Jesus is represented as much more of an apocalyptist than he really was. We know there was another side to his teaching, since many of his sayings simply cannot be stretched upon the Procrustean bed of apocalyptic.

Now there is variety enough in the New Testament. Different types of mind and of faith contributed to its making. Contrast for example the authors of the Epistle of James and of the Gospel of John, Paul and the author of the Gospel of Matthew, Luke and the author of the Epistle to the Hebrews! [2] A similar variety is to be seen within the Gospels, and in their sources; the recognition of this variety is one of the most important contributions of New Testament research to modern religious thinking. For the Gospels certainly must be interpreted in the light of their own purposes and interests, and so likewise must their underlying sources be interpreted. The interests of Q and of Mark are different — Mark is greatly interested in methods of exorcism, Q only in the results, or in the implications for the kingdom of God. Matthew, for example, is interested in church organization and the later Christian mission; his source M, whether document or cycle of oral tradition, identifies Jesus' teaching with the Law of Moses — as its full and final exposition and application. Mark and Q have a high " Son of man " Christology; L appears to have no Christology at all, or certainly a very inchoate one — Jesus is a prophet, a healer, a *Hasid*.

But there is unity as well as variety — not the unity of the Koran, derived from a single author, or of the oldest Buddhist traditions, handed down in a united monastic group, but the unity of a faith with a common center and a common purpose. The faith was directed to the " kingdom " or reign of God, already present in power, about to be realized in complete actuality; the common center was Jesus, now the exalted Lord of his community and at the same time the heavenly Messiah seated at God's right hand; the common purpose was to prepare and make ready for his return, for the last judgment and the great $\kappa\alpha\tau\alpha\sigma\tau\rho\circ\phi\acute{\eta}$ in affairs, human and superhuman, which was soon to take place. This unity in variety is most important. Professor Dodd is even prepared to rest the case for historical validity upon the agreements of Mark and Q, and he lists a number of these data which cannot be viewed otherwise than as primitive and fundamental to the whole historical development of early Christianity.[3]

Nevertheless, from the contrast with the Old Testament which we have mentioned and with other religious literatures which might have been cited, there are certain very important inferences to be drawn. For one thing, the Old Testament is the surviving sacred literature of a nation; the New Testament is the literature of a movement, of a church. Much, probably most, of the New Testament presupposes the

Old — either in the oral Aramaic Targum of the Palestinian synagogues (or possibly in the Hebrew, which no doubt many Jews understood, then as now), or in the Greek translation, the Septuagint of the world outside and to the west. This presupposition of the Old Testament is enormously important for early Christian ethics as well as for early Christian doctrine. Jesus did not set forth a new code of ethics; instead, he presupposed the Mosaic Law, reinterpreted and deepened its meaning and application, repudiating much of the current Pharisaic exposition and modification of its terms. But if you set Jesus' "ethics" apart from its historical context and background in Judaism, and then view it as an independent system, you get an impossible and preposterous code — which men may profess to admire but will make little effort to apply.[4]

Another inference from the contrast between Old and New Testament applies to what is called form criticism. Undoubtedly there are " laws of form," principles at work in the transmission of oral literature, more or less determinative of the external formulation of tradition, and observable everywhere. But just what these laws are, and how they are to be defined — we are not so sure of this. Meanwhile, research is steadily proceeding in this field.[5] But even when the laws have been made out — and probably many of them will be exemplified by the Old Testament quite as fully as by any other sacred literature — it will still need to be remembered that the traditions in the Gospels had only a comparatively few years of oral transmission, not the centuries upon centuries say of the legend of Moses in the Old Testament. The Samuel cycle, the David cycle — these are closer comparisons; but even here a sharp difference is to be seen. For

these are popular stories, folk tales, legends of national heroes. The Gospel traditions, on the contrary, are the traditions of a religious movement, of a cult. Moreover, it
is hard to see how their form can be wholly predeter-
mined: here surely, if anywhere, " law " is simply " gen-
eralization from experience." What of the poet, what of
the prophet, what of the innovator with some fresh word,
some new vision? Is he to be ruled out of order? Can
no man in the primitive church have " uttered a word from
the Lord " as valid and authentic as the sayings found in
Q — or, let us say, as *other* sayings found in Q? Or can
he not have reformulated, reinterpreted such a saying — or
sayings? Must the laws of folk tradition, the primitive,
anonymous, legend-making faculty of the teller of tales in
ancient Israel and elsewhere, set the pace and standard for
the transmission of tradition in the early Christian communities? — Surely there is something new and different
here!

That is to say, the creation of *new* sayings and parables
must be accounted for, not merely the transmission of an
inherited body of tradition. We can see the process at work
in certain passages where the authors or compilers of the
Gospels, or of their sources, are doing their best with the materials at hand. For example, Mark 8:17-21, where the editor is weaving together the two parallel series, 6:34 — 7:37
and 8:1-26; or Matthew 17:27, which is almost certainly
legendary; or Matthew 5:17-20, which diametrically contra-
dicts Mark 7:1-23, but which may well have read, originally
(i.e., in its oral form), " Think not that *he came* to destroy
the law or the prophets . . . ; " or Matthew 10:5 f., 23 —
contrast Mark 13:10, and even Matthew 28:19! But there are

surely other passages where early Christian *prophets* with
their " word from the Lord " have contributed to the stream
of tradition — words which no one in the primitive community, least of all the prophets themselves, questioned as
authentic. Paul had such messages; the Apocalypse of John
contains some; the Gospel of John is full of them. The in-
troductory form may have been the simple one still surviving
in the Oxyrhynchus papyri (the so-called *Logia Iêsou*):
" Jesus saith; " compare Revelation 2:1, 8, etc., " These things
saith he. . . ." But more important than the form is the
content, which springs out of immediate religious experience
rather than out of historical recollection. As Professor Fors-
ter has put it, " In John, the sayings are *more* important if
not spoken by Jesus but derived from the experience of the
primitive church: as for example, ' Napoleon is the greatest
of generals ' is a more important testimony on the lips of his
marshals than as an assertion of Napoleon himself." Here
lies the fundamental problem of Christian origins — a problem which cannot even be approached without taking seriously the basic presupposition of all primitive Christianity,
viz., the reality of the spiritual world, of the inspiring Spirit,
of the exalted, heavenly Lord who " is the Spirit."

There is a further peculiarity to be noted. If the Gospels
stand in close relation to the Old Testament — and I for one
still think the Old Testament is far more important for the
understanding of the New than, let us say, the apocalyptic
literature, Enoch, iv Ezra, ii Baruch, and the rest — they are
no less closely related to what follows, the " surviving early
Christian literature," apostolic fathers, apologists, the earliest
liturgies and hymns, the earliest church orders, the epi-
graphic and other archaeological remains of early Christian-

ity, even the apocryphal Gospels ("the Sunday afternoon literature of the early church," as Adam Findlay called them). The inclusion of these other early Christian writings helps to widen our base, our parallax, and gives us a sense of the historical setting and continuity of the Gospels, and of their place in the life of the church, which is indispensable if they are to be properly evaluated. If criticism is to be fair, the Gospels must be seen in their proper setting, as " church books," not as individual literary creations wholly detached from the movement which created them and which they were designed to serve. New Testament history is really chapter one in the history of the Christian church. New Testament theology is really chapter one in the history of Christian doctrine.

2. Not only must criticism be fairly applied, but its positive results ought to be as fully and accurately recorded as the negative. Unfortunately, some of our contemporaries are more impressed with the negative results than with the positive, and speak or write as if criticism had undermined — or were endeavoring to undermine — the Christian faith. But the losses occasioned by criticism have been compensated by gains. What has taken place is a shift in focus, with the result that certain features in the Gospel tradition stand out more clearly than before, others are recognized as still obscure. Nothing turns out to be valueless and fit only to be discarded. Not even the " wildest " variant reading in the New Testament text is wholly without significance, a point upon which Professor Riddle insists when he calls textual criticism "a historical discipline." [6] This principle is signally true of the criticism of the Gospel tradition. For ex-

ample, suppose the Great Rejoicing (Matt. 11:25-30) is an early liturgical hymn, as Professor Rist [6a] and others would have it, rather than an authentic utterance of Jesus. Suppose that in order to get at its real historical meaning the third person ought to be substituted for the first (as Canon Streeter suggested [7] with reference to the discourses in the Fourth Gospel):

All things have been delivered unto him by his Father.
Come unto him, all ye that labor . . .
Take his yoke upon you, and learn of him;
For he is meek and lowly in heart,
And ye shall find rest unto your souls.
   For his yoke is easy,
   And his burden is light.

Has the passage lost anything of its real religious significance? I think not — though certainly no one would prefer the prosaic third person to the dramatic, liturgical first person of the saying as it stands in the Gospels! But then how came it to be written in the first person? Perhaps in the same way that the appeal of Divine Wisdom [8] is dramatized in other passages, in both Old Testament and New. You must allow for poets, even in the Gospel literature! And if someone replies, " Yes, but why not recognize Jesus himself as the poet, in this instance as in others? " — I agree that it is possible; [9] but I am only insisting, at this moment, that the religious value of the passage is not lost, and that even such " extreme " criticism as this has a positive value as well as a negative.

Or take the total resulting situation in regard to the life of Christ. It is a commonplace of present-day criticism that no one will ever again be able to write a full and detailed

" Life of Jesus." Only the briefest sketch, no longer perhaps than Professor Bultmann's *Jesus and the Word,* can
now be written — a short article indeed for some " Universal
Cyclopedia of Biography," say, and replete with many a hy-
pothesis, many an " if " and " perhaps." But is this so new
a thing? Believe it or not, Alfred Edersheim recognized the
situation when he wrote his huge *Life and Times of Jesus the
Messiah* — as we have it upon the authority of the late Percy
Gardner: " The materials for a life of Jesus, in any objective
sense, do not exist." [10] Some of us have tried writing the life
of Jesus, using only the positive data of the Gospel traditions.
The result is a meager outline, hardly to be compared with
what we should like to have, viz., a standard modern two-
volume life! But the positive result is that we are now
forced to recognize, as never before, that the materials for
the life of our Lord are precisely the kind we might expect in
the particular historical situation in which he lived. There
were no biographies of Jewish saints and leaders of the first
century. Wilhelm Bacher, in his *Agada der Tannaiten,*
gathers all the material on the life of Hillel into ten pages —
and those largely filled with critical footnotes! Jochanan
ben Zakkai has twenty; Akiba with all his sayings, authentic
and apocryphal, and all the incidents of his life, together with
Bacher's critical discussion, fills only eighty pages! The Gospels are not biographies, and were never meant to be. They
contain biographical material, but that is not the same thing.
And the positive side of this recognition is that the Gospels
are documents of religion, of a faith and worship, of a new
" way " of life " in accordance with the sayings of the Lord,"
not documents of secular history — or even of " history " at
all, primarily, even on its religious side. The Fourth Gos-

pel is of course outstanding in this respect; but all four have
a share in this quality or character. And so what applies to
John applies also to the others, in various degrees. We are all
aware that it will not do to cite the Fourth Gospel, either the
narrative or the discourses, as accurate stenographic tran-
scripts of what once took place or was uttered in Palestine by
Jesus of Nazareth. This does not lessen the value of that
Gospel: rather, it relieves the strain of trying to combine John
with the Synoptics, and it enables us to recognize the value
of John's interpretation of the life of Jesus in terms of the
needs of the whole world, intellectual, moral, religious. But
the same caution must be extended to certain elements in the
Synoptics. We must recognize the growth of legend, wherever the evidence clearly points to such growth. We must
recognize the presence of interpretation, even in some of the
sayings and parables. And we must do more than allow for
certain "tendencies," ecclesiastical or other, that have been
operative in the tradition; these "tendencies" are part and
parcel of the tradition itself — for it is "church" tradition
the Gospels contain, from start to finish — nothing purely
secular, nothing *in vacuo,* nothing purely individual. And
this recognition certainly has a positive value: it enables us
not only to recognize what the New Testament essentially
is, viz., a book of religion, not of bare history divorced from
religion (as if that were conceivable!); a book which gathers
up the sacred archives of a cult, if you will, and which can be
understood not only best, but understood at all, only in the
light of that growing, expanding, developing cult. And by
the same token this new recognition of the real nature of the
Gospels throws a flood of light upon the nature of our religion.

3. This brings us to our third point: the religious evaluation of the results of criticism must be given as much
consideration as is given to the historical or the literary
evaluation. Why do we, why does anyone, study the New
Testament? I hope I do not underrate its value as literature;
but it is not as literature that the New Testament has influenced Western civilization. Nor is its value as history insignificant; yet the history it contains, as history, can be
crowded easily into a page or two of the history of antiquity
— as Breasted does in his *Ancient Times.*[11] It is really as the
sacred literature of our religion, a fragmentary, selected literature, the sole survival of the first age of Christianity, that
we study the New Testament. But this does not mean that
historical and literary criticism are unimportant. Quite the
contrary; for Christianity is a historical religion, i.e., it takes
history seriously, and views the knowledge of God as something specifically revealed at a particular time, not as a system of metaphysics, or of ethics, or of spiritual discipline,
which has been thought out by masters of the spiritual, moral,
or intellectual life without any relation to history, and without
reference to social conditionings or problems or tasks. From
one aspect, Christianity is " an ethic, pure and simple; "[12]
but the ethics are not separable from the religion,[13] and so,
from another aspect, it may be said that Christianity is a religion, pure and simple, one more of the many codes and
cults of mankind, the highest and purest, no doubt, but still
a cult with an appropriate code. And yet how little a way
this takes us in an understanding of Christianity! How little
it prepares us for the flaming ardor of Paul, Augustine,
Francis! How slight an introduction it affords to such a
book as *The Imitation of Christ,* or the *Theologia Ger-*

manica, or William Law's *Serious Call to a Devout and Holy Life!* How little it suggests the heroic abandon of Henry Martyn, or the crystal-clear thinking of Aquinas, or the self-less devotion of Studdert Kennedy, or the social enthusiasm of many another Christian of today!

I would close as I began: there is something new and unique here, " the power of God unto salvation; " the fresh forces of the age to come, released in the midst of a humdrum and pedestrian age, and still at work remaking society and individuals in an age almost as humdrum and pedestrian as the first century, and with equally exciting interludes — war, discovery, epidemics, novel ideas, and a steadily growing concentration of political power at the top. What the Gospels have to contribute is not obscured, but is really uncovered, by the new critical approach to their contents. For we see them now as the records — not the sources but the deposit — of a transforming moral and spiritual movement which was then entering upon its course of change and revolution in the accustomed ways of men. That the energies of the gospel have not gone farther in transforming the world than the present state of society shows, is something that need not discourage us. Nineteen centuries are only a very brief interval in the story of a race at least three hundred thousand years old, with habits of thought and behavior deeply ingrained by long custom and really inherited, in large measure, from an ancestry reaching back for perhaps three times as long — a thousand millenniums! In view of the recency of its arrival, it is surely safe to say that " we are the early church," and to view the small progress already made as a real encouragement of hope. Hence instead of abandoning " the present evil world " to the pessimists, as some of our contemporaries would do — even some theologians! — we claim the future, not only in the sense of the eternal kingdom which lies at the heart of the Christian gospel, but also in the sense of the world here and now. God's reign is advancing, even in this world, despite temporary setbacks and discouragements, and it is bound to triumph in the end. In brief, both worlds are ours!

There are those who say, All that criticism has done is to whittle away the great positive affirmations of the New Testament, and it has left us religiously impoverished. For example, the virgin birth of Jesus is questioned or denied; his miracles are explained away as examples of faith-healing; his teaching regarding the end of the world is ascribed to contemporary Jewish apocalyptic; the resurrection is viewed as a series of appearances — apparitions! — to the baffled and discouraged disciples; and so on. But, on the other hand, it may be recalled that there were many Christians in the first century who had never heard of the virgin birth — including some who were saints and martyrs. As for the miracles, they surely were understood as mighty works of God in response to human faith — and were so understood by no one more explicitly than by Jesus himself, who refused to ask God for "signs." As for the eschatological teaching — e.g., in Mark 13 and the parallels in Matthew and Luke — what is there to distinguish it from similar predictions in all the apocalyptic writings, in Enoch, IV Ezra, II Baruch, and the rest? And the resurrection, the real hinge and pivot about which all of primitive Christianity swings, the absolutely indispensable datum for the rise of early Christianity — the resurrection was not only described from the very outset in the technical language of vision (" he appeared to . . ."), but Paul unhesitatingly lists his own experience of the risen Christ along with the appearances to Peter and the others (1 Cor. 15:5-8). Far from minimizing the supernatural, modern criticism confronts us with it in its most refined and compelling shape — the supernatural which is, as von Hügel defined it, only our attempt to label and describe the life in grace. What these early Christians were talking and writing about was not a series of events in past history, or even in quite recent history; instead, they were relating not so much *facts* as *acts,* that is to say *acts of God.* The whole process of redemption, the whole great movement and outpouring of the Spirit which they had experienced and were still experiencing when they wrote, took its origin from God. In the strictest sense it was a supernatural movement, superhuman, divine in its initiation and continuance. In brief, they were men on fire with faith, and they described everything from the one point of view of religion: no science, no philosophy, no literary ambition or taste had anything to contribute. Naturally they described the acts of God in terms of their own inherited religious outlook; and we, with ours, must face this and attempt to understand. If in the meantime modern science and philosophy have arisen and altered " the face of the earth " to some extent, that does make a difference — in our understanding, but not in the act or the acts of God who was then engaged in a " mighty work " at the very crossroads of human history. This way lies the true interpretation of the New Testament: it is the record, human and fragmentary and imperfect, but sufficient, of the saving act of God in Christ. Criticism is indispensable for the understanding of the record, and should be granted its full freedom, as is the right of every legitimate science. But indispensable as it is, criticism is not enough. Only *faith* can understand and grasp what it is these simple, earnest, primitive Christians are writing about, and living and dying for!

NOTES

[1] Edmund Hardy, *Buddha* (Leipzig, 1903), p. 9.

[2] See the article, " Divergence and Growth in the New Testament," in *Christendom*, Autumn 1939. — One of the clearest statements of this variety in the New Testament is the chapter in Vol. XI of the *Cambridge Ancient History* devoted to the rise of Christianity (chap. vii). It was one of the latest writings of the late Canon Streeter, provost of the Queen's College, Oxford, and has all his literary brilliance and keen historical insight combined with accurate, painstaking attention to details. I mention it because too few New Testament students are acquainted with the *Cambridge Ancient History* or have discovered this chapter — as compact a sketch of primitive Christianity as could possibly be written in forty pages.

[3] C. H. Dodd, *History and the Gospel* (London: James Nisbet & Co., Ltd., 1938), especially chap. iii, " Historical Criticism of the Gospels."

[4] See the article, " The Church's Present Task," in *Religion in Life,* July 1939 (especially pp. 346 ff.).

[5] For example, two volumes of the three planned by the Hardwicks on *The Growth of Literature* (London: Cambridge University Press) have appeared, and the third is promised for an early date. The work deals with the *oral* literatures of Europe and Asia.

[6] See *Anglican Theological Review*, XVIII, 220 ff.

[6a] *Journal of Religion*, XV, 63 ff.

[7] *Cambridge Ancient History*, XI, 285 note.

[8] E.g., Luke 11:49.

[9] In fact it is *probable*. See C. F. Burney, *The Poetry of Our Lord* (Oxford: Oxford University Press, 1925).

[10] *A Historic View of the New Testament* (London: A. & C. Black, 1901), p. 74.

[11] Pp. 661 ff. (Boston: Ginn & Co., 1916).

[12] E. F. Scott, *The Ethical Teaching of Jesus* (New York: The Macmillan Co., 1925), p. xii.

[13] *Ibid.*, p. v.

THE CHRISTIAN DOCTRINE OF MAN

ALBERT CORNELIUS KNUDSON

Boston University School of Theology

MUCH HAS been said in recent years about the Christian doctrine of God. There has been an insistent demand that theology be made more theocentric than it has been during the past century. This demand, as voiced by Barth and his associates, has not been without its value. It has served as a corrective of a one-sided humanism and has done much to reawaken interest in some of the more fundamental problems of theology. But, on the other hand, it has itself been carried to a one-sided extreme. Its motto, "Glory to God Alone," has been emphasized in such a way as to obscure essential elements in the Christian doctrine of man and to make it important that this doctrine also receive renewed attention.

The fundamental elements in the Christian view of man are clearly indicated by two figures of speech employed in Scripture: the image of God and divine sonship. Man was made in the image of God, and is a son of God. The exact import of each of these biblical figures has been the subject of not a little discussion and difference of opinion. But the differences have not been especially significant. On the general meaning of the figures there has been and is widespread agreement. They mean that man is akin to God, that he is a spiritual and free being, that his personality is sacred and of permanent worth. In a word, they affirm the essential spirituality of man and the infinite value of the human spirit.

These two affirmations are practically one. Spirituality and eternal worth imply each other, and in the union of the two we have the essential element or elements in the Christian view of man. This high estimate of human nature and destiny was expressed by Jesus in various ways. He taught the superiority of man to the animal world; [1] he put human values above all institutions, no matter how ancient and holy they might be; [2] he set the worth of the individual soul above that of the whole world; [3] and he affirmed the resurrection of the dead. [4]

Over against this Christian anthropology there are three competing views that give a certain urgency to the Christian message with respect to man. There is the pantheistic view with its underlying assumption that man in his personal life has no enduring value. His life is maya, illusion. Second, there is the naturalistic view with its underlying belief that man in his essential nature is an animal, though an animal of superior intelligence. Finally, there is the dualistic view with its underlying conviction that man in his essential nature is a sinner. He has no native capacity for God and can of himself do no good thing. A brief consideration of each of these views may serve to set off somewhat more clearly the Christian doctrine and its significance.

I. THE PANTHEISTIC VIEW

We begin with the pantheistic view, the view represented by the great religions of the East, especially by Buddhism. Here we have a sharp antithesis to the Christian emphasis on the sacredness of personality and its eternal worth. For

Buddhism, at least in its historic form, personal life is not good. It is an evil from which we should seek to be delivered. Redemption for the Buddhist means redemption *from* life rather than the redemption *of* life. This obviously runs directly counter to Christian teaching. Christ came that we might have life and have it more abundantly. Christianity most emphatically affirms life.

This fundamental contrast between the Buddhistic and Christian conceptions of human life has a manifest significance for Christian missions in the Orient. It provides a motive and, I should say, an adequate motive for them. " The canker at the heart of heathenism," said T. R. Glover, is " the absence of any certainty that life has a permanent value." And in Buddhistic circles not only is there this uncertainty. There is something deeper still. There is virtual despair of life in its personal form. The future has nothing in store, even for the enlightened and emancipated spirit, to which he may look forward with hope. If there be a future for him at all, it is only as a shadow, a mere wraith, of personal life.

Christianity has, then, a message of hope for the Buddhistic world. And this message applies not only to the life to come. It applies equally to the life that now is. Buddhism has placed the stamp of disapproval upon desire. It aims at the ultimate extinction of desire and in so doing it has cast a blight over life in its present personal form. It has detached the sanctions of religion from the common goods of life and attached them to ascetic practices. It has made the religious life to a large extent a life of negations. It has not stressed adequately the distinction between good and evil desires, and it has not placed upon the desire for moral and social reform the sanction and blessing of religion as it ought. The result has been that the life that now is has been impoverished. What the Buddhistic world imperatively needs is a revaluation of life in its personal form, a new realization of its sanctity and its permanent worth. And this Christianity alone can give it. The Christian doctrine of man has the utmost significance for the Buddhistic and the whole non-Christian world.

It is asserted by Professor Pratt and others that Buddhism because of its impersonal metaphysics and its spirit of tolerance has less to fear from modern science than has Christianity. But in making this statement Professor Pratt overlooks the fact that modern science grew directly out of a personalistic or Christian metaphysic; and he also overlooks the still more significant fact that modern science is built most emphatically on the Christian affirmation of life as distinguished from the Buddhistic negation of it. This may, of course, also be said of our whole Western civilization. It is based on a fundamental optimism with reference to human life. And in this respect the spread of our scientific civilization is one of the most potent factors in the spread of Christianity. No doubt in certain other respects its influence is evil and a hindrance to Christian missions. But insofar as it is optimistic and affirms the value of life in its personal form, it tends to undermine the asceticism and pessimism of the East and thus to prepare the way for the Christian faith. Modern science, like nature, is too strong for the ascetic, and in the religious conflict between the East and the West it is almost certain eventually to exert an important, if not decisive, influence in favor of the optimistic personalism of Christianity.

II. THE NATURALISTIC VIEW

Western civilization, however, is not wholly Christian. It is imbued with a deep-seated naturalism. In it we have a denial, not of life itself, but of spirituality as the essence of human nature and as the true type of human life. Life is affirmed — there is no sympathy with Buddhistic quietism and pessimism — but it is life on its lower or secular level.

This secular or naturalistic view of life has in modern times been invested with an almost religious significance, and that in three different forms. With many it has become a religion of external goods, with others a religion of nationalism or a religion of the superman, and with still others a cult of science.

The first of these, in its organized form, is represented by materialistic communism and to some extent by capitalism. It makes its appeal to man's sensuous nature and finds the real value of life in the physical side of his being. The so-called spiritual element in his nature it regards as wholly secondary, if not entirely illusory. " The animal functions," said Nietzsche, " are as a matter of fact a million times more important than all the beautiful states of the soul and heights of consciousness: the latter are an overflow (that is, a superfluity), insofar as they are not needed as instruments in the service of animal functions." In other words, man is in his essential nature a being with only animal needs. If these are satisfied, all the rest will take care of itself. Man lives by bread alone. " I reckon," says a somewhat unrefined devotee of this new faith, " that when the wardrobe is full and grub adorns the shelves, salvation will be plenty and souls will save themselves." As Feuerbach put it, " a man is what he eats." It is the economic and material factor that determines the real quality of one's life. Nothing else matters much, at least so far as the masses of men are concerned.

It is this conviction that lies at the heart of the Marxian philosophy; and, according to Professor Sombart of the University of Berlin, this is the only philosophy that can make a real appeal to the working classes, to the proletariat. The average man, we are told, is an economic animal. His only real interests are food, shelter, and the propagation of his kind. Beyond these he has no real needs. The only philosophy, consequently, which can mean anything to him, is one that seeks to meet his physical needs. He has no capacity for a truly spiritual life, no capacity for religion as commonly understood. Religion may be foisted upon him by others. He may be deluded into believing and supporting it. But he has no real need of it. And when he comes to himself, when he throws off the yoke of tradition and superstition, he sees clearly that religion is something foreign to his true being. So far as his own essential nature is concerned, he has no needs except those grounded in his physical constitution. Beyond them everything is illusory.

And not only, we are told, is this true of the average man, of the poorer classes. It is true of men in general, of the so-called higher classes, though they may not be willing to confess it. The rich as well as the poor are dominated by economic motives. They may profess to value the spiritual above the material, but they do not actually do so. Not even the church does that. Karl Marx, for instance, said that the English established church would more readily pardon an attack on thirty-eight of its thirty-nine articles of religion than it would an attack on one-thirty-ninth of its income.

This cynical remark is not without some basis in fact. The economic motive does often seem to be the dominant one in every sphere of human life, the religious as well as the secular. All people at times seem to worship at the shrine of Mammon. It is the only kind of worship toward which they seem to have a native inclination.

This is, at present, probably the most common form of naturalistic religion. But the second form of it, the religion of nationalism and the religion of the superman, is almost equally widespread. It has been called "man's other religion," and is based on human pride, the pride of race and the pride of personal endowment. It is represented in its more extreme form by German National Socialism and by Italian Fascism. It is opposed to democracy and manifests itself in various forms of race hatred. It glorifies war and minimizes the value of the individual on the common level of life. It substitutes for the religion of the past those qualities that make for success in brutal strife and conflict. It revives the spirit of paganism.

The philosophy that underlies it is complex and contains heterogeneous elements. But in general it bears a kinship to the teaching of Friedrich Nietzsche, as commonly understood. This extraordinary and bizarre genius deified the superman, and saw in human society simply a roundabout way of producing a few great men. The average man, he held, has no value in and of himself. He has worth only insofar as he is the tool or instrument of the great. "What," asks Nietzsche, "is the ape to man?" "A laughingstock and a thing of shame," he answers, and then adds, "That is man to the superman, a laughingstock and a thing of shame." The great alone, he averred, have intrinsic worth.

As for Christian teaching with its idealization of the average human life, he denounced it as hopelessly false and corrupt, and vented upon it his wrath in its most vitriolic form. He overflows with scorn of "the contemptible species of well-being dreamt of by shopkeepers, Christians, cows, women, Englishmen and other democrats" — or, as he elsewhere terms it, "the universal green-grazing happiness of the herd." "Christianity," he said,

is the revolt of all things that crawl on their bellies against everything that is lofty. . . . I call Christianity the one great curse, the one enormous and innermost perversion, the one great instinct of revenge, for which no means are too venomous, too underhand, too underground and too petty; I call it the one immortal blemish of mankind.

The Christian concept of God — that of the poor people's God, the sinner's God, the God of the sick — he stigmatizes as "one of the most corrupt concepts of God ever arrived at on earth." Such a God is no God. He is the product of the selfish hopes and the hypocritical ideals of the weak, the miserable, and the worthless. "These workshops where ideals are manufactured," he tells us, "verily reek with the crassest lies." The average man has no intrinsic worth. His value is purely instrumental. His function is simply to make possible the heroic careers of a few great men. He is merely cannon fodder.

The third form of naturalistic religion, above referred to, is the cult of science. This cult is also based on human pride, but pride of intellect, not personal or racial pride. We hear less about this cult today than we did before the First World War, but it is still with us. Professor R. B. Perry, for instance, tells us that "the greatest of all modern ideas in its originality, in its widespread adoption and in its far-reaching importance is the idea that man can make his own way through all the difficulties and dangers that beset him by means of applied science or technology." This idea, although it implies faith in man rather than in God, is, we are told, "the most significant religious idea of modern times." It is not limited in its application to man's progressive knowledge and control of external nature. It includes his ability to transform his own nature. Here, according to Alexis Carrell, lies the only hope of mankind. Science has shown man "how to mold his body and his soul on patterns born of his wishes. For the first time in history, humanity, helped by science, has become master of its destiny." Properly understood and properly applied, science can save mankind from "the fate common to all great civilizations of the past." But in order that this may be done, modern society needs "an intellectual focus, an immortal brain, capable of conceiving and planning its future." Such a brain might be constituted by a high council, composed of a few individuals, who would devote their entire time to contemplation of and meditation on the phenomena that have to do with the physical and mental welfare of the race. In this way sufficient knowledge would eventually be acquired "to prevent the organic and mental deterioration of civilized nations," and thus through science the only salvation possible to man would be achieved.

This cult of science obviously moves on a higher plane than do the materialistic and pagan cults previously sketched. But all three are based on the naturalistic assumption that man belongs to what is traditionally called the natural order and rises no higher. He is in his inmost being of the earth, earthy.

III.   THE DUALISTIC VIEW

The view of human nature that I have called dualistic looks upon man as primarily a sinner. From the metaphysical standpoint he does not belong to the animal world; he is a spiritual being. He was created in the image of God. But that image underwent a radical transformation. Man sinned, he fell from divine grace, and now in his inmost being is a sinner. It is this term more than any other that defines his true nature. He is separated from God by an impassable chasm. No man can cross it through any effort of his own. Every person is sinful to the very core of his being and can himself do no good thing. He has no freedom that enables him to choose the good rather than the evil. He has no native capacity for God, and in his own strength cannot take one step toward the attainment of the knowledge of God. By nature he is completely excluded from the presence of God and is evil and only evil. " Evil dwells in his personal will itself and poisons every act of will." [5]

The view thus expressed is a reaction against the self-sufficiency of the modern man; and insofar as it opposes this phase of modernism and insists on man's dependence on God and need of the divine aid, it is in harmony with the fundamental teaching of the gospel. But when it carries this reaction so far as to condemn man in the totality of his being as sinful and devoid of any capacity for knowing God, it overlooks one of the most fundamental aspects of Christian teaching and interposes a serious obstacle to the effective preaching of the gospel in our day. Man is a responsible as well as a dependent being, and the recognition of this fact with all its implications is a vital and essential part of the Christian message to our time. To say that man is in his essential nature a sinner and to make this the very signature of his being, is in my opinion to misrepresent Christian teaching and to fall into a semi-Manichean dualism.

IV. THE CHRISTIAN VIEW

By way of contrast with the three conceptions of man we have briefly outlined, the Christian conception is characterized by an unequivocal affirmation of the essential spirituality and intrinsic worth of the human soul. Jesus by word and deed, by his preaching of the gospel to the poor and by his total ministry, expressed his profound faith in man as man. He believed that men even under the most unfavorable circumstances could rise above the bare animal struggle for existence, and though " sinners " could yet be made conscious of their kinship with God. It was this faith, translated into action, that gave distinctiveness and unique significance to his ministry. Here, said Montefiore, the distinguished Jewish New Testament scholar, " is something which we have not yet heard in the Old Testament or of its heroes. . . . The virtues of repentance are gloriously praised in the rabbinical literature, but this direct search for, and appeal to, the sinner are new and moving notes of high import and significance."

Harnack said that " Jesus Christ was the first to bring the value of every human soul to light " and that " what he did no one can any more undo." But a great many, nevertheless, have been and are trying to undo it. The movement is naturally most menacing outside the church. But within the church there is also, as we have seen, a subtle tendency in the same direction, and with this tendency I am here more especially concerned. Those who represent it claim to speak in the name of simon-pure Christianity. They tell us that there is an endless qualitative difference between time and eternity, that man who is a temporal being is in his essential nature a sinner, that he has no native capacity for a spiritual life, that he has no real freedom, that he can of himself do no good thing, that he can himself contribute nothing to his own redemption or to the redemption of the world, and that everything is dependent absolutely upon the divine will. They further tell us that this is the true Reformation doctrine, that there is at present a great apostasy from the faith in the Protestant churches, that the ancient heresy of Pelagianism has been revived and is widely current in Anglo-Saxon Protestantism, that the basal doctrines of sin and repentance are to a large extent being overlooked if not discarded, that a vague humanistic idealism is rapidly taking its place, and that the Protestant church is, consequently, being bereft of its power. Utterances such as these have been increasingly common during the past ten or fifteen years, and they have led to not a little confusion of thought and to much uncertainty and indecision in matters of vital religious concern.

This state of mind, as I see it, is due to a failure to recognize two important facts. The first is that the traditional language about our absolute dependence upon God is the language of emotion and devotion. In the presence of the Infinite we instinctively acknowledge our own nothingness and ascribe to him whatever of goodness there may be in ourselves. As compared with his perfect holiness and condescending grace we can claim no righteousness for ourselves. We renounce all merit of our own. All this is intelligible as the language of emotion and devotion, and as such it is entirely proper. But when interpreted as the language of metaphysics it denies human freedom and all rational basis for responsibility and leads to what is perhaps the worst moral scandal that has appeared in the history of Christian thought. Modern freedomism has no fault to find with the biblical doctrine of the divine grace, it preaches the doctrine with fervor; but to the current attempt to reground this doctrine in the metaphysical theory of strict predestination it has an everlasting nay.

The second fact to be noted is that there is no such fundamental difference between the traditional preaching of sin and repentance, and the modern preaching of ethical idealism, as is frequently asserted. Against a background of social and political pessimism, such as prevailed in post-exilic Judaism, it was natural that men should lay stress, not on programs of social amelioration, but on the hope of a marvelous divine intervention, an intervention to be brought about on the human side by repentance for sin. The ethical life, consequently, at that time and later under similar conditions took a negative turn. It found its satisfaction in seeking forgiveness of one's sins rather than in achievement and self-realization. With us today the reverse is the case. Despite the terrible World War and the economic and other reverses of recent years we still believe that God is working through us for the establishment of his kingdom. Hence what we are primarily interested in, is the positive program in which we are engaged. Not what we omit doing or repent of doing, but what we do, is the thing that concerns us.

So with us the satisfaction of service has to no small extent taken the place of the consciousness of sin as the decisive evidence of true piety.

This, however, does not by any means necessarily indicate a decline in moral and religious earnestness. A person may be quite as religious by concentrating his attention on ethical idealism and moral progress as by concentrating his attention on sin and its forgiveness. And under varying conditions the stress will naturally shift from one side to the other. In the past for various historical reasons the primary emphasis fell on the idea of sin and its forgiveness, and religious experience was largely molded by this emphasis. But from this it does not follow that a similar emphasis is necessary today. Indeed, such an emphasis would tend to create an artificial type of religious experience, it would lead people to try to experience an alien doctrine of sin rather than to experience God himself, and it would also lead almost inevitably to a subvolitional conception of sin. In order to make sin comprehensive enough to be a necessary presupposition of the religious life the tendency would be and *is* in certain quarters to identify it not with the evil will, but with our entire nature, with our very finitude. The result is that sin ceases to be sin in the ethical sense of the term. Instead of deepening in this way the sense of sin we distort and disintegrate it. Sin to be real, to be a ground of self-condemnation, to be a condition of repentance, must have its root in human freedom. Subvolitional sin is a contradiction in terms. It grows out of the mistaken notion that religion is simply a device for overcoming sin or for saving sinners, and that if there were no sin there would be no religion. Religion does, of course, under existing circumstances have to deal with sin. That is one of its major tasks. But it has also a deeper and more inclusive aim. It has to do with man's relation to God and with the whole idea of man's place in the universe, and would exist even if there were no sin. It makes its appeal quite as truly to man's sense of dignity and worth as it does to his sense of sin. And in these days it is the former rather than the latter that stirs most deeply the hearts of men.

In this connection reference may be made to the way the revival in Wales in 1904 began or how it reached Evan Robert, the man who became its leader. One evening as he walked down to the post office in Langham he passed a gypsy woman who saluted him saying, " Good evening, sir," with the emphasis on the word " sir." That word " sir " addressed to him, a mere miner, went, he said, straight to his heart and he asked himself why he had not in return said, " Good evening, madam," to the gypsy. " From that moment," he said, " I felt my heart was full of the divine love, and that I could love the whole world, irrespective of color or creed or nationality." The conjunction of this religious experience with the gypsy's word of greeting may possibly have been accidental, but it is at least an interesting and, I think, significant fact that the two came together. The recognition of his own human dignity and that of the gypsy woman made Evan Robert feel not only the kinship of all men with one another but their common kinship with God. The sense of human worth was to him a veritable evangel.

It was such also in the Wesleyan revival of two centuries ago. John Wesley then addressed himself to the miners in Bristol and elsewhere. These people were most of them the poorest of the poor, the proletariat of their day. Many of them had not darkened the door of a church since childhood. They were swearing, drinking, God-forsaken people. Today it would be said by men like Professor Sombart that the only philosophy that could possibly appeal to such people was a materialistic philosophy similar to that of Marxian socialism. Yet John Wesley went to them, found a divine spark in them and kindled it into a flame. He recognized that back of their ignorance, their vice and the crudity of their manners there was an essentially spiritual nature. He recognized their freedom and their responsibility for their own destiny despite their sinfulness. He affirmed their own eternal worth in the sight of God, and by so doing he awakened not only a few souls here and there: he awakened the soul of the English laboring class as a whole and made spiritual religion a power in their midst. He demonstrated a century before the time of Marx the falsity of the Marxian conception of human nature; he demonstrated by the effects of his own preaching that man as man has a capacity for spiritual things.

It may also in this connection be noted that, according to Jesus' teaching, religion manifests itself in its highest and most quickening form only when it seeks the redemption of the neediest of mankind, only when it leads to self-sacrifice for others. Three different stages in the development of religion may be noted. On its earliest and broadest level it sanctifies the natural goods of life. On its second or Judaic level it links itself with the moral law, with the common conscience of men. On its third and Christian level it links itself with the *uncommon* conscience. This was the unique element in Jesus' teaching and preaching. He took the ideal of sacrifice, the uncommon, the difficult, the heroic thing in human life and made it the true, the normal expression of the religious spirit.

This was what his ministry to the poor meant. It meant that the very essence of religion, its joy and its glory, consists in bringing by word and deed a message to the poor and lowly of earth which would fill them with joy, with self-respect, and with a sense of kinship with the divine. It meant that the righting of wrong, the giving of equal opportunity to all men, is the divinest thing in the world. It meant the end of self-complacency. It meant that there can be no real peace of soul except in self-sacrificing devotion to the needy of earth.

And this for us means that religion is primarily not a social cement but a social ferment. It means that religion does not consist primarily in maintaining the existing social and political order and in rejoicing over one's own prosperity. It consists rather in correcting present evil conditions and in relieving real need wherever it is found. It expresses itself in the desire for a better order of things. It is more concerned with need than with law. Its passion is compassion.

This, it seems to me, is all involved in the Christian conception of man as an essentially spiritual and free being. It is this teaching that underlies not only the social message of the modern church but also its entire evangelistic and missionary program. Without it we should be wholly adrift. We would be out of touch with the world in which we live. If we are to preach effectively the Christian gospel as over against the illusionism of the East and the naturalism of the West, it can be only by proclaiming such an optimistic conception of human nature as we find basal in the teaching of Jesus. There is no healing in the cry, " Back to the Reformation! " We have much to learn from the reformers, but their word is not necessarily final for us. Nor need we be alarmed by the charge of " modernism " and " Pelagianism."

Appeals to the past will not solve our theological problems for us. We must solve them in the light of present-day thought and in conformity with the demands of a consistent Christian theism. Only along this line can there be theological progress.

It is this progressive and vital type of theology that Dr. Rall has represented and to which he has made contributions that give him a place in the front rank of American theologians.

NOTES

[1] Matt. 10:31; 12:12; Luke 12:7.
[2] Mark 2:27.
[3] Mark 8:36 f.
[4] Mark 12:18–27.
[5] Brunner.

FACING THE PROBLEM OF EVIL

FRANCIS JOHN McCONNELL
Bishop of the Methodist Church

IT SEEMS fitting to me that this book of essays in honor of Professor Rall should include an article on the duty of facing the problem of evil — meaning evil both in the phase of physical pain and in that of moral wrong. In his various theological discussions Dr. Rall has himself written of the problem and has, so far as concerns theoretical and practical conclusions, said about all that can be said when we come to the end of whatever thinking we try to do. It is an intellectual delight to read any of Dr. Rall's theological discussions. For fine precision in the use of words, for exact and true feeling for perspective, for recognition of the extra-philosophical elements which must be kept in mind in philosophical discussion, for range of knowledge over the whole field of which he treats, it would be hard indeed to find his superior. The limitations of his themes, however, have prevented his discussing the problem of evil except in connection with some other subject. While the conclusions to which this chapter will come are in harmony with our leader's teaching, they will follow some reflections which have no doubt at times required his attention, but about which he has not specifically written.

There is no need of arguing much as to the importance of the fact of physical and moral evil in human experience. This, however, is no warrant for turning away from the prob-

97

lem. It is worth while to see that some attempts at solution are not solutions at all. Moreover, since the fact of pain is a feature of all human experience, religious thinking must show at least a willingness to look at the fact if religion is to be realistic at all. There can be no escaping pain in actual experience. In one form or another it is omnipresent. At the famous Edinburgh conference in 1937 a distinguished English bishop sought to get the conference to make some statement which would at least show the world that the leaders of Protestant religion recognize the problem of pain and the mystery of evil in the universe. He did not succeed because, as one of the leaders said, the preparation of such a statement " would take too much time." No doubt the search for a solution would take all the time that is ever to be, but not so the statement of a recognition of the problem. The fact of evil itself — in the broad meaning — is the parent of about all the serious skepticism of religion in the world — the younger skeptics in all eras think that religion will not face the problem and the older skeptics think that religion has nothing to say. Take one consideration as to the welfare of human individuals. It will probably be agreed that, since man first appeared on the earth, the majority of men have lain down to rest every night without having had through the day the satisfaction of enough to eat. As to the history of mankind as a whole, we do not have to be Marxians to accept Marx's statement that the true history of the human race has not yet begun. The majority of the population of the earth thus far have not had the conditions of a genuine human existence. The definite attempts at explanation of these facts are too often not serious at all. Within the memory of men now teaching, a prominent theologian disposed of the problem of distress-causing features of the physical universe by the pontifical declaration that because man sinned nature goes "like a limping king." This would mean that nature began to limp long before man sinned — though my remark is irrelevant, for the theologian expected his utterance to be accepted and not questioned. I refer to this because it is an instance of the unconsciously frivolous treatment of the theme by not a few theologians.

Suppose we look at some serious attempts to deal with the problem today. We glance first at the more optimistic spirit which has come into philosophic thinking with the passing of the older type of materialism. As Dr. Rall himself says: "Materialism is dead." It is dead — the old-fashioned lump materialism, matter conceived of as hard little bits of stuff indivisible and eternal. Now we have matter thought of as a form of energy — the atoms as systems of protons and electrons moving after the fashion of solar systems. The newer view is indeed a relief from the older. That certainly gave us an opaque universe, when we had to think of the old-time material atoms as the basic physical reality. If the new idea is hard to conceive, it is not as hard as the old, and is moreover more respectable intellectually, for the new weaves mathematics more essentially into the constitution of the universe. Atoms as indivisible matter, in a universe in which everything spatial was divisible, represented nothing but the inability of thinkers to think beyond or below a certain point. Perhaps it would be better to say that the atomic theory was a blind alley beyond which men could not go, and so had to work at the end of the alley.

The new view gives us a finer type of universe in which

to live, but does it help us much with the fact of evil? I cannot see that it does. Forces, to any imagination at all lively, may be more terrifying than material particles. To believe that my body is a center of miniature solar systems, that it is the center too of atomic potencies which, if they could be released, would be more destructive than any explosive ever yet devised, may increase my awe and wonder but hardly my conviction of being at home in the universe. Much has been made by theists of the now famous word of a contemporary scientist that God is a mathematician. This thought itself is as old as Plato, but its force in terms of religious efficiency is limited to the mathematically inclined. Of course mathematics implies mind, and mind back of the universe implies purpose, but what the purpose is in spiritual quality is not revealed to us by the substitution of energy for matter in our contemplation of the universe.

We may look next at something very similar to the argument of Leibniz that, if we are to have a system, the parts must be fitted into a harmony — prearranged or otherwise — for the good of the whole. This naturally implies that no part can be treated by itself alone. The theory of this universe as the "best possible world" has not been quite fairly dealt with by critics of the Voltaire stamp. Probably though Leibniz would have agreed with Voltaire's final word in *Candide* that, at the conclusion of all our reasoning, we had better "cultivate the garden." If we are to lay stress on the surrenders of the parts of the universe for the good of the whole, we might better say, "The best possible world *under the circumstances.*"

In somewhat more practical form than the classic statement, this thought of system falls in with the mood of the time. We hear that all our troubles would be solved by a closer getting together. In enforcing this claim its advocates tell us that system rules throughout the entire universe, that the most distant stars are composed of the same chemical elements with which we are acquainted here on earth — and so on and on.

This emphasis on system has, of course, much to commend it, but not as a good-in-itself. From the point of view of Christianity the individuals are of supreme worth in the sight of God. All these movements toward cooperation, about which I can speak more appropriately later, tend toward minimizing the worth of individuals. There is not much help for an individual in an army in having a Bonaparte tell him that the private carries a field marshal's baton in his knapsack if he knows that that same leader thinks of soldiers by the million as cannon fodder. It does not help much to tell this individual soldier that he is fighting for liberty, equality and fraternity which neither he nor his children will ever see. So likewise with the worship of the state as a mystic something above and beyond the individuals that compose the state. Up to date these movements toward togetherness have tended to lose sight of the true units whose larger life the togetherness is to serve. All organizational forms have to serve the welfare of the people for whom the organizations exist. The organizations have not yet done much more than to supply men with a dream of better days — for a posterity of a remote future, which leaves individuals here and now about as they are, except as they share in the dream for the future. There is something pathetic in the extent to which dreamers of secular utopias today hold up their utopias as a relief from the evils of the world. I shall have something to say later about the struggle for a future when that struggle is conditioned by Christian conceptions, but I am thinking now of the purely secular setting of much social idealism. Men have in the past labored and died for what to them was a picture or a vision of posterity. In a measure we of today are the posterity for which they died. If the Old Testament prophet who told so gloriously of the posterity which would beat its swords into plowshares and its spears into pruning hooks could have foreseen that after two thousand years posterity would beat its plowshares into swords and its pruning hooks into spears, he would have felt warranted in declaring himself disillusioned — and disillusionment is itself part of the world's evil. All this, of course, on altogether secular assumptions. On those assumptions there is not much relief in the " togetherness" consideration of our problem except the dream of a good time coming, without any numerous signs of its coming.

Equally pathetic is the welcome given to some ideas of today which rather loosely cluster around the theory of relativity. An acute philosopher was once discussing in my hearing the strange phenomenon of the boisterous reception given Albert Einstein when he first visited this country after the theory of relativity had become famous. " Of course," said the philosopher, " some of the excitement has been due to irrational curiosity over a celebrity, but some of it is a symptom of an almost universal weariness over the absolutes of one kind and another which have been preached to us for three generations, especially the absolutes of scientific law." Relativity seemed to break things open and to let in the free air. The mind of man was pulling loose from this overtight scheme of laws.

There could not have been quite this process of deliberate reasoning in the minds of many of those who welcomed relativity. Moreover, those who had read even a little of Einstein knew that what Einstein was fundamentally seeking was an absolute something which he called the "interval," which would be the same for everybody. Nevertheless, there is something in this passionate protest against philosophic and scientific absolutism. A genuine impulse toward freedom is back of it. It is to be doubted, however, whether any theory as highly mathematical as relativity — or even such emphasis as modern teachers are putting on indeterminism in physical forces — can be of much help in the direction toward which religious thought has to direct its effort. While we all admit that the most abstract theories in the end have an effect on religious attitudes, we cannot depend heavily on theories which require high mathematical proficiency for their comprehension.

I have mentioned in this sketchy fashion two or three attempts in current theory to deal with the question before us. We can, however, best say what we have in mind by looking at what can be set out as, in general at least, the Christian position, with some suggestions as to the strength and limitations of this position.

We begin with moral evil inasmuch as so much of physical evil is bound up with that. The summary and compendious putting is that moral evil comes into the world through human freedom, and that evil is here because men choose to have it here. Then the conscious sin is repeated deliberately or unconsciously by others and leads to pain and injury of the physical system itself — though this is admittedly not the cause of all pain and injury.

Most Christian theology states the Christian position as above and lets it go at that, with more or less elaboration as to specific features of the problem.

Now the amount of pain introduced into the universe is too large to be the effect of a wrong human choice. The way theological thinking meets this objection is to dilate upon the enormity of human sin, but this reply is not altogether convincing. To hear some teachers talk one would think that human freedom is a tremendous energy on its own account, capable of lunging about as a dreadful monster under no control, leading to consequences that omniscience could hardly have been expected to foresee. The actual fact is that freedom is freedom of choice — choice between alternatives. One choice leads in one direction, and another in a different direction. Freedom pulls a trigger, and releases and sets to work forces already in existence. It is not creative in the physical realm except in making new combinations or uses of forces already there. To say that an evil choice is responsible for all the evil consequences of that choice, is going too far. Bad as an evil will may be, even a limited administrative God could cancel out evil effects of choices or neutralize the workings of the forces so that after a time — and a brief time at that — the physical result might be about the same as if the choice had been good. We all see evil men making evil choices and yet by ordinary shrewdness, or extraordinary scientific skill, guarding themselves against harmful physical results. I am not saying this to minimize in any degree the " wrath of God " against evil but to enforce the idea that in this universe of ours the emphasis on the presence and extent of physical pain because of evil choices is overdone. If, to use the old expression, " moral law is woven into the fiber

of the universe," that universe can be expected to extermi-
nate evil, not by long continuance of the consequences of
evil, but by eliminating those consequences. Jonathan Ed-
wards once said, with notable grittiness, that God shows his
presence in the universe in that sinners are acted on and disposed of. However it may be with the sinners, we may well
believe that the forces set at work by sinners are acted on
and disposed of.

There have been at times other deliverances about the fact
of freedom as involving possibility of physical distress to
others than the actual wrongdoers which seem convincing
on first phrasing but which are not so transparent on second
glance. They become clouded over on closer examination.
The general statement seems sound enough, but the actual
facts are more of a mystery than almost anything else in
the range of human experience. That the good have to
suffer with the bad may be sun-clear as an abstract statement, but the concrete experiences of those who have to do
the suffering seem very largely to be matters of happen-so.
There is no trace of just proportion, judged by human standards, in what might be called the distribution of the suffering. To say that by the fact that we live together in groups,
the good must suffer with the evil seems a mockery in dealing with a concrete case — especially when the good may
be suffering more than the evil themselves by the misdeeds
of the evil. Again what seems like an evil use of freedom
may not be freedom at all in any exact use of terms. Some
suffering comes out of the well-intentioned deeds of persons
choosing the best course they know. They do not know
any better, not because of culpable ignorance of their own
but because nobody in their day knows any better. Or the

conditions under which men live overweight the scales against what the onlooker calls a moral choice. In common justice we maintain that a course acted upon under duress is one for which the actor is not to be held accountable. The actions of hosts upon hosts of human beings living under earthly conditions are actions under duress.

Some attempt to meet the problem of distress by reminding us that the power to feel pleasure involves the possibility of feeling pain. No doubt, but here again the puzzle is at the point of the concrete, where the pain is so much more poignant than the pleasure. The mystics have told us, some of them, that in the moment of vision they were rapt in such ecstasy that they thought they would surely die. Well, none of them died, and the pain of joy is called pain only to give a hint of its intensity. Beyond a certain point pain is weakening and deadening and even degrading.

Coming back to the word "relativity" again, we find an approach to our problem undertaken by some who remind us that pain and woe may be — indeed must be — quite dependent on a point of view which is necessarily relative to ourselves. Many of the physically destructive forces of the world, for example, are hideous to us because we think of their destructiveness. In themselves they may not be hideous at all, and from a different point of view they may not be destructive in any evil sense. Our lenses may be out of focus. This, however, merely shifts the question. The problem of evil may then be posed in the query: How does it happen that there is so much in our experience which is out of focus?

We may well be grateful that some interpretations of evil have met with definite negatives in the course of Christian thinking — negatives not on account of their philosophical inadequacy but because of their religious shortcoming, not to say erring. They have fallen by the way, dropped out, but they are worthy of a moment's notice if merely as showing the lengths to which men have gone in their irresistible impulse to deal with an insoluble problem. Take the idea that pain comes to men because their fathers have sinned before the children were born. The fathers have eaten sour grapes and the teeth of the children are set on edge. The Lord has been conceived of as visiting the sins of the father upon the children to the third and fourth generations. It is to the vast credit of religious thinking that, accepting the workings of physical heredity which have to be recognized as binding the generations more or less loosely together, the teachers of Christendom will not hold to this idea of the pain of one generation as caused by the sins of a preceding in any phrasing that implies moral fault on the part of the suffering generation. No argument has changed this view, but moral insight. Likewise with the belief that men live through successive existences and are punished in one life for what they did in the preceding — though the insight which rejects this view obtains effectively only in Christendom. Probably a quarter of the human race, insofar as they speculate on religion at all, hold to this explanation of human distress. In a word Christianity, both among professed Christians and among those who live in the atmosphere of Christianity, rejects outright the idea that suffering is a sign of guilt, except in a limited degree. The total of suffering is too great — thinking of suffering chiefly in physical forms, the phase of the enigma which most concerns us just now. If any statement on the problem is desired, the Book of Job is as nearly final as any.

It is high time, however, to get clear of the view of some of the disagreeable and painful aspects of the universe and at least glance at some features which of themselves do afford a measure of relief. There is always danger of loss of perspective in conceiving of the universe as good, and likewise danger in looking at it as bad. Between the realization that in detail the human spheres of existence are centers of pain and the general claim of the universe as good, there lies a middle territory of which we ought to take account.

In looking at the distress of the world, we can get into an awful plight by adding together the woes of men into one overwhelming total. Take it on the side of physical illness. When we think of the amount of sorrow due to sickness and bodily injury, and look at the whole incalculable sum in itself, there is hardly any escape from the judgment against the worth-whileness of the universe. We wonder that the race can exist at all. In fact, however, it does exist. The human race is in fair health, fair enough not only to exist but to increase, and to get the work of the world — such as it is — done, after a fashion. When we are appalled at the wide distribution of evil, we must remember that it is distributed — not at all equitably by our scales of justice, but distributed. If we pick out one dreadful disease germ, let us say, and realize that that germ can multiply at such a rate that in an incredibly short period it could sweep off the race, we can get over the panic by looking at the steadying truth that the germ is not the only factor in our situation, and that deadly forces do have a way of neutralizing one another. While we may not know why they are here, we know something of how they get here and how to deal with them, at least in a measure.

As to freedom: We have said that freedom as an explanation is of limited value. Still we do have some freedom, though even in our own choices no one of us knows just how much. Now whatever measure we have is practically possible because of the great regularities in our universe. Let us not be switched off the track here by the absolutist who complains that no law works with absolute regularity. Admittedly the sun rises with variations which require scientific skill for their calculation — variations which, though they are subject to law, are nevertheless quite wide. Yet they are not wide enough to hinder us from building upon the fact that the sun does rise every day. Now if there were not dependable regularities like this in the processes of nature, we could not be free, or what freedom we might have would be of no consequence. There could not be reason in the universe without these regularities, and possibly not sanity.

Bertrand Russell has somewhere pointed out that it is an advantage to us that we can deal with the physical universe without getting our emotions involved as we do with something personal. We do not blame lightning and wind and floods for the damage they do us. Probably we should have to make some exception to this summary statement, for the savage may still think of natural forces as manifestations of hostile or friendly spirits, and the nature-mystic may virtually endow stones and flowers and stars with souls, and a well-known type of interpreter of Providence seeks to interpret almost every natural occurrence as a specific and intelligible utterance of the Divine. Most of us, however, can readily see that it is important for our mental and moral development to be related to forces against whose action we cannot reasonably feel resentment. Conceding here again the problem of the harassed individual who feels that the world's hand has been indeed rough to him, we have to recognize the importance of a system with which we can work in this passionless spirit.

In other words, if we are to get far in the development of personalism, we have to build on a system that we can — for purposes of our daily experience at least — regard as impersonal — some fixities with laws with which we can deal without explaining anything to them, or apologizing to them (if I may be pardoned so grotesque a phrasing). We may do with these forces whatever we can. We can get rid of our forms of human slavery by harnessing them, if we can. We can so fashion them into tools that they all but automatically carry out our orders. They release us from slavery to drudgery and monotony and inexactitude. They do some things better than men ever can. They make that contribution to human leisure without which the higher human freedom in science and art and in religion is not possible.

Here someone may say that we are falling into that old notion that the world was made chiefly for man, that man is the center of all things. We are told that Copernicus settled all that. Of course we have all heard of Copernicus and none of us are thinking in the old Ptolemaic terms of the earth as the center of our physical system. Without regard to either Copernicus or Ptolemy, we do not hold to the belief that the physical universe was made solely or chiefly for the benefit of man. So far as we can see, the universe need not at all be thought of as created chiefly for man. It would accord far better with at least the appearance of things to believe that the world may be fitted to be a training ground for man, while it has other purposes and perhaps loftier ones.

From another angle the objection is thrown at us that now we are minimizing man because we are overawed by the spatial vastness of the universe — that we are overwhelmed, not to say bullied, by those who tell us that the earth is an insignificant speck in an out-of-the-way corner of space and who resort to all the other rhetorical devices which pronounce the insignificance of the planet on which we live. No, we are not surrendering to mere material size. We believe that even if the earth is thus physically of minor consequence, it is the mind of man that has found out this material insignificance. It is man's scales, devised by man himself, that have weighed the immense bodies which seem so much more important than the earth. Herbert Spencer was supposed to have made an excellent hit when he remarked that, swift as is the movement of human thought, light is faster. Well, mind is swift enough to seize light and to devise a system of measures of time and space to tell how fast light is flying. The earth may not be great as compared with suns and stars but it is on the earth that the superiority of mind to mere mass is established. If man is of limited power, it is man who himself has discovered that fact. He is greater when he insists that he is not necessarily the chief object of the activity of the universe than when he was avowing that he was the center of all creation. He does not think of the universe as sheer material mass. It may well have lordly spiritual significance for mind — a significance that is at least at present far beyond anything that mind can now attain. A somewhat rough-and-ready philosopher once remarked that perhaps we can get relief from the problem and mystery of pain by reminding ourselves that in many of its aspects the universe is none of our business. It is clearly our business where it touches us, but there is force in the rough-and-ready utterance nevertheless. The size of the universe does not mean the supremacy of matter; it means that the size has in all likelihood a significance beyond us. We are manifestly in a universe not intended primarily for us. Nevertheless we are free to make what we can of it. In many ways it is plastic in our hands. We are certainly not to fear it. It is independent of us — with an independence that often seems entirely self-sufficient and indifferent.

To some this will appear almost a total surrender on our part. The problem grows faster than we can even state it. Still there is some advantage in being face-to-face with a system which is not ours but which we can use. It may be just as well for us to have to deal with forces to which after all we are secondary. We can make what we will of such forces, but we need not think of them as intended primarily for us. Perhaps in dealing with them we may just as well assume that their chief purpose has little or nothing to do with us. We are most fortunate that the stars help our ships to find their paths across the seas, but we should hardly be warranted in assuming that such aid to us is the primary purpose of the stars. We are in a universe in which we can go to any length in making ourselves at home, but the home must have other purposes than the human. Of course the relief here is not large, for the question still arises as to why we are in a universe like this. Such reflections as I here suggest, however, have some value in hinting to us not to take ourselves too seriously. Much of our distress at the

problem of evil — still using the word in the broad sense —
may arise out of our taking ourselves too seriously.

Some daring religious thinkers push this question back
into the nature of God, insisting that God himself has to
deal with unideal situations which he is striving to make
ideal; that a conflict goes on, if not in the nature of God, at
least in the conditions in which God exists at all, with God
under the compulsion of working onward and upward toward nobler manifestations of the good, the true and the
beautiful. Few theologians would make this struggle moral
as implying evil in the divine nature, but it would have to
be, one would think, in some sense a struggle from a lower
to a higher — from a lower intellectual to a higher, or from
a lower beauty to a higher. This is all fine-spun. Probably
moral quality would be shown in the devotion to the higher,
or in the unwillingness to acquiesce in the lower. Of course
it does not quite meet the force of this argument to say that
a time-process is not part of the Divine Mind in itself for,
even if time be " nothing to God " in himself, it must be
something when translated into another type of experience
than the human, unless we are going to say that the form
of all human experience has no significance for God. If
time means anything for God, we ask whether it means that
God is under the necessity of successive development or
whether time means that one phase of his nature is revealed
now and another later, with the phases actually on the same
plane. Probably the former is what the holders of the belief
in a finite God mean.

Since this theory is wholly in the stratosphere of the nth
degree abstract, we may be permitted to leap for a moment
into the realm of rare atmosphere, or the realm where there

is no atmosphere at all. The theory is willing to look upon the material universe as the outcome of what might be called trial and error in the divine method. Trial and error we might agree to in the use of materials already existing, especially in the production of plant and animal forms. Much of nature looks as if it had come to be as the outcome of experimentation. Indeed some theologically minded evolutionists tell us that all we need as an explanation of the problem before us is the recognition that the woes of the universe come from the carrying along of survivals of outworn forms, especially in the organic world. This explanation does suggest experimentation but, if it is all that can be said, it makes the problem worse than before as suggesting a creative process which cannot " clean up " after itself, but which leaves useless and in some instances explosive factors behind it.

The inadequacy of this theory of intractable factors which have to be brought to smooth harmony appears in what it must assume at the start. In a spatial system it has to start with some form of organization which works according to mathematical laws. No matter how far back we push the beginning of the creative process, we cannot conceive of a period when the struggling Mind was ignorant of the laws of mathematics. If we can conceive of such a time, we have then to imagine a development of the Creative Mind from a state of ignorance of mathematics to one of knowledge of mathematics, which, if we are to conceive of creation in terms of intelligence at all, leaves us in a melancholy plight, or a humorous plight if we prefer. The scientists tell us that the study of physics shows that the highest forms of mathematics now and again reveal in the most astonishing fashion their bearing on material processes — as the fitness of the square root of minus one for our handling of a phase of an electric current. We must not rely too much on imagination at this juncture and think of a formless void out of which matter was led along to its present atomic structure — the atom today a miniature solar system so performing that its activities cannot be fully caught in any equations we now possess. In the lowest forms conceivable by us matter must have had definite structure. Creation may have consisted in rearrangement of atoms, but that would have implied a sum total of knowledge and a control of forces which would have meant that, so far as force and fundamental principles of order were concerned, there was as much of each at the beginning as there is now. The progress would not have been from lower to higher at all, except in the unfolding in successive manifestations of what was implicit from the beginning.

Nevertheless, this theory of a God wrestling seriously with creative problems has unmistakable merit — chiefly the merit of taking the problem seriously. The virtue of speaking of God as finite is that the instant we say "infinite power" or "omnipotence" we go far toward emptying the problem of all seriousness for the Divine. Infinity is not intelligible to men in any case. To close the discussion by declaring that God is infinite is like saying that God can solve all problems, and leaving it at that.

By the way, the use of many of the conventional terms about God does not lend us much comfort for the subject we are considering. For a generation or so we talked about the immanence of God. That appeared to bring God nearer but to the ordinary imagination made the difficulties all the more acute, not to say terrifying. After a generation or two had been told that God was in all things, there was a violent swing toward the transcendence of God, which was no better so far as the problem of evil was concerned. Transcendence seemed to give a God who is either indifferent or trying to find an " escape." However we may accept any form of " escape " teaching for men, we cannot provide any escape for God if we are to preserve religious values at all.

It is difficult to keep the problems of physical pain and moral evil separate from each other. We have to pass so quickly now and again from one to the other. This enigma as to a something against which God himself must contend appears in Reinhold Niebuhr's moral man in an immoral society in much more plausible form than in the claim that in all aspects of his activity God is seeking to overcome forces warring against himself. Only, the evil in society is that of the selfish will which, according to Christian thinking, calls for all the redemptive forces of the Divine. Some who have not thought much about Niebuhr's position beyond the striking phrase which expresses it, have assumed that, if all men could be transformed from evil to good in their inner lives, our difficulties would all be solved. The difficulties would be much less after such conversion or transformation, but enough would remain to keep our questions before us. We would still have moral men, moral at least in purpose, in an imperfect society. If there are differences of moral attainment at all, some are in advance of others. Out of the differences tensions and strains and conflicts inevitably arise. Or we may take account of the fact that there may always be strain between the new generation of human beings and that arriving at maturity and beyond. Here is the possibility of conflict, not necessarily outer indeed, but certainly carrying with it anguish of spirit, misunderstanding and friction. It is hard to see how this could be avoided under any system.

All that I have been trying to say implies that whatever help we get on the problem of evil depends on the character of the God in whom we believe — a God who must in any Christian attitude be accepted on faith. We may remind ourselves that one vast moral achievement of our day is the recognition that in any control by men over their fellows, or in any activities in which men touch the lives of their fellows, power and responsibility must be yoked together. There must not be irresponsible exercise of power in government, in industry, in education, in the family — anywhere. We are not to blind our eyes to the lamentable truth that power is today used without responsibility, but we recognize that the ideal calls for responsibility in such use.

If we follow the path along which we have enlarged and improved our ideas of God, we see the importance of this reflection for the theme in hand. Christianity teaches that God has made a revelation of himself, that the revelation is a veritable gift from God himself and not an intellectual creation of our own. Nevertheless we attain to better understanding and appreciation of the gift through the growth of our own mental and moral discernment and insight. Out of the growing realization that we cannot conduct our own affairs without an awareness of social responsibility, we step up to the belief that God cannot conduct his dealings with us without acting under the heaviest moral obligation. The old word comes down to us just as pertinent now as in the days of Abraham: " Shall not the judge of all the earth do right? "

Without going into details of human existence, we think

of the responsibility assumed by the Creator in creating us at all. We did not ask to be created. The race is here without having any vote on the matter. This being so, the tremendous responsibility of creation begins to dawn on us. We dare think that the Creator is responsible to us for our creation. Having once firm hold of this belief, and conceiving of God as revealed in Christ, we rest in the conviction that we can trust all these problems in his hands.

It will no doubt seem to some that we might have said all this at the beginning, and have saved all our effort in discussion for something else. We do not think so. Even if the intellectual signboard says, "No thoroughfare," we are warranted in going every inch of the way we can, and we are entitled to find out for ourselves that there is no thoroughfare.

In all reverence be it said that we need to keep alive in religious thinking an inquiring, not to say a critical spirit. If those who are believers do not exercise such a spirit, we may be perfectly certain that the nonbelievers or the doubters will. Nothing could be worse for the church than to let those outside the church suppose that religious leaders do not face this question. Again, in the practical as well as in the intellectual ministry of the church there has been a vast mass of attempted explanation of God's dealing with men which has only aggravated the distress. As a shrewd thinker once said: "Attempts to solve the problem of evil are contributions, not to the solution of the problem, but to the problem itself."

Professor Rall has rendered noble service in making it clear that, on the basis that God is what Christianity teaches, we can find in many of the forces of what we call evil in the world bases for order, fellowship, pain which leads to fruit-ful result, freedom, and productive toil. Many of the hard features of the universe to which I referred in the earlier part of this essay are not so hard when we look at them from the Christian point of view, under the Christian sky and through the Christian atmosphere.

For example, take labor from the Christian angle. Labor has been so heavy through all ages of the world's history that we can well understand that the church called it a curse. It did not need any Scripture interpretation to reach that con-clusion. Yet we have seen labor progressively conceived of as a blessing, altogether apart from the material returns granted to it. We have gone far enough along this path to catch the promise of a day when men will find noble self-expression in work, and will work for the joy of the working.

Or look at the possibilities in human sympathy. We talk rather conclusively about crowd contagion — as if men could be touched through such contagion only for evil. The sym-pathy of a group for one of their number in distress however is a high form of group contagion, if one cares to call it that. The sting of much suffering is that the sufferer bears it alone. If sympathy could be a commoner fact among men, the burden of pain thus lifted would be incalculable. So also with the everyday virtues of common honesty, common fairness, common sincerity.

Still it will be maintained that we have not thrown much light on our problem. Admittedly not, but light is light and what we have of it is good. We concede, as at the beginning, that some of the mystery is utterly beyond us. The presence and extent of animal pain, for example, is utterly blank and black to our understanding. The tender mercies of nature are cruel. There is no human wisdom which can help us here. Again, the individual is, so far as his own plight is concerned, left without much direct aid, though with considerable sound, practical advice. No matter how puzzling some of our pain, it can best be ignored. The evil is indeed not soluble by our understanding but is tolerable by our wills.

The path to Christian certainty is through doing the will of God. Through deliberately facing our problem and doing the best possible with it we attain, not to illumination, but to moral will-adjustment. In many features it is not so bad when we actually get at it. Professor Nathaniel Shaler, for many years a professor at Harvard University, used to tell of a boyhood experience of his own during the Civil War. Shaler lived in Kentucky during the war and as a youth of seventeen years once came unexpectedly upon a battle at its height. It seems that the Northern and Southern armies had met early one morning near the farm on which Shaler lived. At the sound of the firing the boy ran from his home down a road without any definite idea of what he was doing, and at a turn of the road came upon the rear of a regiment of the fighting Northern army. The first spectacle that met his eyes was a surgeon at the dreadful tasks of a field hospital. The boy became dizzy and was about to faint when the surgeon called to him, " Here, take hold." Dr. Shaler used to declare that the instant his own hand touched the stricken bodies which the surgeon was trying to help the dizziness and the faintness vanished, and that he worked through hours, which seemed minutes, with a strength that came welling up from somewhere within him, a strength that seemed at times veritably to flow over into the torn and riddled flesh of the wounded. This experience does not throw light on the suffering of the stricken but it is suggestive for those striving practically to lighten the world's woe.

It sums up at the end in the belief that we are in the hands of God who works under responsibility, under bonds, under trusteeship for the right use even of pain and death. By the " right use of death " I mean not merely death as a beneficent feature of the race's existence, without which social advance would be impossible, but death of individual lives cut short without any discernible or imaginable reason whatsoever. The belief does not answer our questions but it makes it possible for us to wait for the answer. Life is its own witness to itself. Mind is an aspect of life and mind will insist on asking the type of question which has concerned us in this paper. When living mind does begin to ask, it has to move toward the territories here traversed. As long as life shows itself in questioning at all it will insist upon setting out upon this journey. In the end it is likely to show its vitality by adjusting itself to problems which it cannot solve. The mind's surpassing achievement in this realm is the recognition of the limitations within which it must move — and the place it must make for faith.

Some will say that a better summing-up would be an emphasis upon personal immortality in a redeemed human society, an eternal kingdom of God. Even here all depends on the character of God. If we cannot assume the Christian character of God, immortality, redemption, and kingdom mean nothing, or worse than nothing.

THE REALISTIC MOVEMENT IN RELIGIOUS PHILOSOPHY

EUGENE WILLIAM LYMAN
Union Theological Seminary

THERE IS a movement towards realism in religious philosophy which is worthy of consideration by those for whom the interpretation of religion is an important philosophic interest. How far the movement is a coherent and unified one is, to be sure, an open question; for the use of the terms " realism " and " realistic " in religious thought today springs from diverse situations and causes, and the terms are used in antithesis to positions which are dissimilar in themselves. Sometimes " realism " stands for disillusionment in regard to certain meanings and grounds for religious faith which until recently have been regarded as satisfactory. Sometimes the term stands for the recognition of firmer and more objective grounds for faith than the prevailing ones. Again, realism may denote a positive valuation of scientific methods and results as being indispensable for religion, or it may denote reals which are not susceptible of scientific treatment and which are basic for religion. In some uses realism expresses a protest against idealism, in others against pragmatism, in still others against materialism. The possibility of an inner unity among these different uses of the term " realism " is a matter for inquiry after we have surveyed some of the more important religious thinkers who are employing the term.

William James used to protest against the tradition that rationalism, especially in the form of absolute idealism, was the true philosophic sponsor of religion, and to contend that empiricism, if it were sufficiently pragmatic, stood closer to the essential nature of religion and was its more adequate interpreter. Yet he did not intend a sharp antithesis between the two systems. In protesting against a tight rationalistic monism he said: " Let God have the least infinitesimal *other* of any kind beside him, and empiricism and rationalism might strike hands in a lasting treaty of peace." [1]

Subsequent developments have shown pragmatism to be, not the sole and sufficient theory of truth, but a method and a movement which has influenced idealists and realists and the various departments of philosophy in fruitful ways, and provided a better appreciation of important aspects of religion.

The official realists have not, as far as I know, been at pains to commend realism because of its suitability for the interpretation of religion, although a number among them have made important contributions in this field. But the adoption of a realistic point of view by those for whom the teaching of religion is a vocation will doubtless be welcome to them, if that point of view is congruous with the basic meaning of realism. Perhaps in the long run realism will turn out to be a principle and a movement which does not displace idealism or pragmatism, or the critical philosophy and other philosophies, but corrects and supplements each at one point or another, and so furthers philosophy as a whole in its task of interpreting the universe and man's place therein.

Such a general question about realism, however, can only be touched on obliquely in this essay, which is concerned with a quite limited survey of the realistic movement in religious philosophy. I propose to deal briefly with four subtopics: the reaction from romanticism to a realistic view of history and of man's nature; the reaction from subjectivism and relativism to an objectivist view of religious reality and of standards of truth and value; the revival of cosmology and its theological interpretation; personal realism and the union of critical realism with mysticism. The thinkers to be considered are mainly theologians, or philosophers representing movements which have been influencing theology.

I

First, let us take up the reaction from romanticism to a realistic view of history and of man's nature. Here Reinhold Niebuhr and Paul Tillich are the thinkers mainly to be considered.

Niebuhr criticizes the belief in progress, which prevailed so widely in the nineteenth century and the first decades of the twentieth, as being the result of a romantic view of history. This romanticism was nourished by the continued and accelerated expansion of the middle class in power and privilege. This situation prompted leaders of thought, both religious and secular, to the belief that there was, immanent in history, a law of progress, which would become more and more efficacious the more it was recognized. This law might be conceived naturalistically, by a combination of the doctrines of economic competition, and of laissez faire in government, with Darwinism. Or it might be conceived idealistically as the dialectic process by which the Absolute Reason is unfolding itself. Or it might be conceived in specifically Christian terms by so far identifying faith in God with faith in man that one could envisage the kingdom of God as being rapidly realized on earth through man's growth in intelligence and good will. In any case this belief in a law of progress was the ideology of the prosperous expanding middle class, which saw in its own general increase of well-being, economic and cultural, a disclosure of the meaning of history and its goal — always a flying goal.

This belief in progress Niebuhr considers to be unrealistic because all the time a class struggle has been going on. This class struggle does not fit into the scheme of evolutionary progress. The middle class has gained its privileged position by exploiting the proletariat, and to a large extent it retains that position by using coercive measures, overt or covert. Social justice requires that the proletariat should have full opportunity to improve its status as the middle class has done. But to believe that such improvement of status can come about solely by the democratic process is another instance of romanticism. History, says Niebuhr, shows no instance of a class relinquishing privileges without being subjected to coercion from the class below. Hence his outlook is revolutionary rather than evolutionary, though he would seek, so far as possible, to avoid violent revolution. One who seeks greater social justice must be prepared for radical political policies reinforced by economic pressure, whether by strikes or by more effective organization for collective bargaining; and one must not be disaffected by outbreaks of violence from the side of the underprivileged — realizing instead how often these outbreaks are provoked by covert coercive measures from the other side.

Niebuhr's realism leads him to read history largely in Marxian terms. He does not espouse the doctrine of complete economic determinism, but sometimes says that doctrine is ninety per cent true. However, he directs his realistic criticism against the utopianism of the Marxian philosophy. One must not assume that socialism on an equalitarian basis will establish so completely a just and cooperative society that the political state can be sloughed off, and that an expanding production of wealth and cultural goods, and their equitable distribution, will thereafter go on harmoniously together. On the contrary there is a kind of fatal dialectic process according to which the power that a cultural development establishes corrupts the culture from which it springs. Niebuhr also subjects the other prevalent form of utopianism — namely, that of liberalistic pacifism — to the same kind of criticism. Because of the above-mentioned dialectical law we have no right to envisage a time within history when reason and good will will have so far prevailed that all coercion, whether actual or potential, can safely be dispensed with.

At the present juncture in history Niebuhr holds that a realistic view of events will perceive us to be at the end of an era. He frequently gave warning of the outbreak of the present war in Europe, which may prove to be the debacle of Western civilization. But apart from any such forecast the First World War and subsequent events have shown that the dominant collective forces of our time, nationalism, imperialism and capitalism, are now working for the arrest and disintegration of our bourgeois society. Contradictions inherent in these characteristics of bourgeois society are reinforced in their disintegrating effect by the increasing claims of exploited classes and peoples. The transition from bourgeois society to the next era may proceed at a slower or a faster rate, but in general it will be analogous to that from feudalism to the era of bourgeois domination. Niebuhr would implement the aspiration for greater social justice by various forms of political action. But he holds that our present political democracy is so far a product of middle class ideology that it cannot be relied upon to guarantee social progress by orderly evolution.

Niebuhr's realistic criticism of progressivism and utopianism is reinforced by a pessimistic view of human nature. He deprecates the reliance on reason and the native potencies of good in man as being an adequate grounding of the hope for deliverance from human ills. The teachings of the Enlightenment concerning the power of reason and the perfectibility of man are another instance of unrealistic dogma. Religious doctrines of perfectionism have shown, on a different basis, a similar lack of realism. Niebuhr would replace these views of human nature and its possibilities by the doctrines of the fall and of original sin, only he insists that these doctrines be taken in a mythical rather than in a historical sense. They stand, not for a primeval event which involved the race in disaster, but for the inevitability of sin due to the fact that man partakes of both " nature " and " spirit." More particularly, it is man's ineradicable " egocentricity " which corrupts man's reason and introduces hypocrisy into his virtues, and which renders illusory the hope of full salvation, whether for society or for the individual, within the limits of history.

With this pessimistic view of human nature Niebuhr combines an ultimate religious optimism. He calls his final world view the prophetic-mythical view, which he sets in contrast to the rational-mystical view. " Mysticism," he says, " is really a self-devouring rationalism which begins by abstracting rational forms from concrete reality and ends by positing an ultimate reality beyond forms." [2]   The result is a dualistic otherworldliness which does not grapple with the issues of history.   Idealistic monism, on the other hand, seeks "to comprehend the unity of the world within the living flux of history." [3]   Hence it makes an optimistic identification of the Absolute with the totality of things.   The prophetic-mythical view avoids both such monism and such dualism and maintains a fruitful tension between the historical and the transcendent.   The myth of God as creator expresses God's " organic relation to the world and his distinction from the world." [4]   Content for God's transcendence is given by the absolute love-ethic of Jesus.   From this point of view man, with his ineradicable self-centeredness and his corruptibility by power, will always stand under the divine judgment and will be able to maintain hope and responsible moral effort only through the gospel of divine grace.   From this point of view, too, man can realistically recognize the demonic forces in history and his own implication in them, and yet can look for a fulfillment "beyond history," because God and the kingdom of God transcend history, while remaining always relevant to historic situations.

Since the prophetic-mythical view of the world holds man responsible for social action, it seems necessary that it should supply some principles for guidance in such action.   At this juncture in his thought Niebuhr adopts a pragmatic, relative ethics which seems hardly derivable from his prophetic-mythical view.   For example, he makes a pragmatic defense of democracy, in spite of its bearing the stamp of bourgeois ideology, because it is "a necessary check upon the imperialism of oligarchs, whether communistic or capitalistic." [5]

Similarly he defends nonviolence pragmatically, as against complete pacifism and also as against "romantic appeals to violence on the part of the forces of radicalism." For, he says, "when resort is taken to armed conflict, the possessors may have more deadly instruments than the dispossessed." [6]

The outcome of Niebuhr's realism is similar in this respect of ethics to that of Tillich, by whose thought he has been in general very greatly influenced. Let us, then, go on to take note of certain of the outstanding features of Tillich's position.

Tillich calls his position "beliefful realism." It is realism in contrast to idealism, which spiritualizes its objects in illegitimate, romantic fashion. It is beliefful in contrast to unqualified realism, which rejects any transcending of experienceable reality. "Faith is an attitude which transcends every conceivable and experienceable reality." [7] Tillich considers idealism also to be beliefful but in a too immanental fashion. Faith and realism are always in a state of tension with respect to each other. But this tension overcomes, in the only rightful way, the most fundamental of all dualisms — the dualism between the temporal and the eternal.

A significant manifestation of this beliefful realism Tillich finds in the recent developments in art. The end of the nineteenth century produced a naturalistic realism in art which fitted the spirit of bourgeois society. With the twentieth century came in an expressionism which showed great form-breaking creative power. In this movement symbolism and mysticism are at work destroying the naturalistic realism of the bourgeois spirit. As representative of the movement Van Gogh may be cited in painting, and Thomas Mann in literature. But a new realism has begun

to appear. Here the rediscovery of Dostoievski is sympto-
matic. This new realism, " with objective and metaphysical
intuition, . . . has uncovered the demonism of the present
social world," and because of the tension which it thus develops gives promise of becoming a belieful realism.[8]

But more important for the affiliation between Niebuhr
and Tillich are certain traits of Tillich's philosophy of history. Here belieful realism stands for responsibility for
present historic action, with a faith which is a direction toward the Unconditioned, and with a realism which is alive
to the demonic forces at work in the world. This position
is defined negatively because it abandons the belief in progress. To be sure, the idea of progress retains a limited meaning which can be applied in three directions: that of technical progress; that of political unification; and that of the
gradual humanization of human relationships.

But there is no progress with respect to the creative works of culture or with respect to the morality of mankind. The first is impossible because creativity is a matter of grace, not of growth; the
second is impossible because morality is a matter of free decision,
and consequently not a matter of delivery and tradition.[9]

What is rejected, then, is the idea of " an infinite approxima-
tion to a fulfillment which can never be reached."

But since Tillich stresses so much the importance of decision and historic action for any significant philosophy of
history, one is impelled to ask what result is hoped for if not
that of progress? His answer is given in terms of his doctrine of καιρός. The word καιρός is frequently used in the
New Testament as meaning " the fullness of time." For
example, Christ came in the fullness of time. The word has

a general use with the meaning of "season," "the right time," "a critical juncture." It is to be contrasted with the word χρόνος, which means evenly onflowing time. Now the idea of καιρός stands for a possible momentous breaking-in of God into history by which there is a new realization of eternal meaning. But the counterpart of this possibility is the responsibility of man for decision and action. Hence καιρός may stand for an actual fulfillment, or for a possible fulfillment which was missed. Tillich would probably say that Luther perceived his day as a καιρός and so acted that a new breaking-in of the Divine came with the Reformation. He believes that there was a ρόsκαι in the post-war period which has been missed. That is, the disarmament of central Europe might have led to a much more general disarmament. Momentous issues were trembling in the balance at that time, and right decisive action might have ushered in a new day of divine grace.

The counterpart of Tillich's conception of the irruption of the Divine into history is his conception of demonic forces in history. Creative energies in human life bring forth a variety of goods which in turn enhance the power of the dynamic individuals or groups that produce them. This mounting development of power in a group almost inevitably makes it turn destructively upon other groups. In the end these demonic forces become self-destructive, but they sweep away an immense amount of good in their downfall. The rise of National Socialism in Germany is an instance of a demonic force with which Tillich has had ample first-hand acquaintance. More generally, he sees three main forms of demonic force in our modern world: nationalism, capitalism, and dictatorship. These forces are now working in a self-destructive way and bringing our present epoch to an end.

Tillich's realistic view of these demonic forces in history involves a large degree of pessimism in his conception of human nature. There is a dialectical law by which the increase of cultural goods increases the demonic forces which then threaten to rob human existence of its meaning. Accordingly he embraces the doctrine of the fall and original sin as a mythical expression of that opposition to the Divine which will always persist in human history. History is " a battlefield of the divine and the demonic."

Tillich's final interpretation of history is in terms of the beliefful pole of his bipolar beliefful realism. For this interpretation he employs the idea of the kingdom of God. " In the symbol of the kingdom of God," he says, " the final victory over the demonic powers in existence generally and in history especially is implied." The kingdom " expresses that ' God is a living God,' entering history, struggling in history, fulfilling history and is not the unity of eternal essences." [10] At the same time the fulfillment and the final victory which are the kingdom of God are never realized in history. Their realization is beyond history. The significance of belief in the kingdom of God for us is that it maintains the dynamic tension between the temporal and the eternal.

This dynamic tension between the temporal and the eternal is applied by Tillich to the question of knowledge, and the result is what he calls " beliefful relativism " in knowledge. There is an ambiguity in all concrete situations which requires the recognition of an element of decision in knowledge. What then is the status of the Unconditioned, which

plays so large a role in Tillich's thought? It is a " guardian " conception which prevents any knowledge from pre-
tensions to unconditioned validity. But how is a beliefful
relativism, with its insistence upon the inevitable relativity
of all knowledge, different from just plain relativism? Tillich answers that the judgment which affirms the Unconditioned is not merely one judgment among others, but is
the expression of a basic metaphysical attitude. " It is the
judgment which constitutes truth as truth." It expresses
" the metaphysical meaning implied in judging." [11] " True
knowledge," says Tillich, " is not absolute knowledge. The
guardian puts an end to that arrogance; on the contrary, true
knowledge is knowledge born of the καιρός, that is, of the
fate of the time, of the point at which time is disturbed by
eternity." [12]

If we pause, now, to consider the general purport of this
realistic reaction against the too romantic views of history
and of human nature which were so widely prevalent for a
century or more before the World War, we can hardly help
noting how much more articulate are the negative criticisms
than the constructive positions. This is perhaps inevitable
so far as a movement is new, and so far as it is being worked
out under the pressure of momentous and baffling events.
Yet it is on the positive positions, in part at least, that the
significance of the negative criticisms turns. If, then, we
press for greater articulateness for the constructive positions,
we may well do so at two points. The first point concerns
the ultimate significance of faith. Is the meaning of faith
sufficiently expressed in terms of a perpetual tension between
the temporal and the eternal? Does not faith attain to an
objective content of meaning which is less abstract than the

idea of the Unconditioned as a guardian conception? Tillich and Niebuhr, to be sure, give additional content to the eternal but always in terms of myth. Does not this treatment give the faith in the eternal a too subjectivist status — a status which is hardly an adequate counterpart for their historical realism?

The second point concerns the principles for historical, moral and religious judgments and decisions. Are these principles to be treated in relativistic and pragmatic terms, subject only to the reservation that the guardian conception of the Unconditioned is to be maintained? Or may these principles be given a more objective and realistic significance? Tillich himself, in a brief paragraph on pragmatism, remarks that one might undertake to speak of a religious pragmatism, but that then one would find that pragmatism had transcended itself because one would be appealing to the Unconditioned. But may it not be that this transcending takes place only when a more realistic basis is recognized for the principles of moral and religious decision?

II

These two questions bring us to the phase of the realistic movement in religious philosophy defined as our second subtopic; namely, the reaction from subjectivism and relativism to an objectivist view of religious reality and of standards of truth and value. Perhaps in this phase of the movement we may find elements which will serve in part to criticize and in part to supplement the phase which we have been considering.

In 1931 there appeared the volume entitled *Religious Realism,* edited by D. C. Macintosh of Yale and written by him and fourteen other American writers.[13] In the preface religious realism was defined as

the view that a religious Object, such as may appropriately be called God, exists independently of our consciousness thereof, and is yet related to us in such a way that through reflection on experience in general and religious experience in particular, and without any dependence upon the familiar arguments of epistemological idealism, it is possible for us to gain either . . . adequately verified knowledge or . . . a practically valuable and theoretically permissible faith not only that that religious Object exists but also, within whatever limits, as to what its nature is.[14]

The general background and presupposition of the essays in this volume is a critical realism in epistemology. The editor, Macintosh, indeed discusses the whole epistemological question in outline, arriving at the form of realism which he terms "critical monism." Richard Niebuhr, to be sure, ranges Tillich's position, and even that of the theology of crisis, with the religious realism of this group as a whole, although admitting that epistemologically they do not belong there. Tillich's position, at least, is one of critical idealism rather than critical realism, while the affirmation of the wholly transcendent God and of his objective supernatural revelation in Christ is a matter of pure fideism.

Because of their critical realism in the general field of knowledge the American religious realists tend to revive the cosmological and the teleological arguments for the existence of God, in contrast to the epistemological argument of modern idealism, and to the too exclusive dependence of much modern theology on philosophies of faith and value alone. At the same time it is not as separate syllogistic arguments, in the form criticized by Kant, that this group would

employ cosmological and teleological reasoning with respect
to God. Rather, the cosmological and teleological arguments,
together with the moral argument and the appeal to the objective significance of religious experience, become various
strands which are woven together into one single argument.
Or better, these strands are interwoven so as to give a unified
interpretation of the different areas of experience, taken on
a realistic basis, in terms of the objective reality of God.
This is what is done in the essays by Macintosh, Wright of
Dartmouth, and others. It is what is done also, in suggestive
and very original form, by Professor Montague in the concluding essay, entitled "The Trinity — A Speculation."

My own essay in this volume concerned the objective significance of religious experience. Its thesis was "that religious experience affords us intuitions of truth and of reality,
which are important and irreplaceable contributions to the
philosophical interpretation of reality and life as a whole."[15]
First I showed the large part which intuition plays in the
actual religious experience of the prophet, the saint, and the
humble believer as well. Then I pointed out the indispensableness of a perceptive intuition in the apprehension of selves
as unique individuals and a like indispensableness of synthetic
intuition for the interpretation of reality in terms of value
and so for the knowledge of the Divine. Intuitions in religion are not infallible nor withdrawn from criticism, but
when made the subject of critical reflection they may grow
into a body of intuitive insight. Kant's dictum concerning
perception and conception may be paraphrased in this connection by saying that intuition without reflection is arbitrary,
reflection without intuition is sterile.

But the synthetic intuitions of religion, even though reflected on and organized in their own sphere, will need to be brought into relation with the generalized results from other spheres of experience, if an idea of God is to be arrived at which has the meaning and validity which religion itself affirms. Hence the importance of cosmological and teleological reasoning for religious realism. The procedure of religious realism at this point can be discussed further in connection with the third topic mentioned at the beginning of this essay. But before passing to another aspect of our present topic let me suggest that the abstractness and subjectivity which we found clinging to Tillich's idea of the Unconditioned might be overcome if he were to join the American religious realists in the field of cosmological and teleological thinking.

But the movement represented by the volume, *Religious Realism,* has also reacted against relativism to an objectivist view of standards of truth and value. Two essays in the volume in question especially represent this character of the movement: one by Professor Bixler, now of Harvard, who expounds German phenomenology, and one by Professor Calhoun of Yale, who writes on " Plato as a Religious Realist."

Bixler esteems phenomenology highly because, over against " psychologism " and " historicism," it maintains the autonomy of knowledge, of value, and of religion. Psychologism is unable to deal with the objectivity of knowledge. " There is no psychological explanation when a man believes that two plus two equals four, but there is if he thinks the answer is five." [16] Knowledge here depends upon an intuition of essential relationships, which are valid in themselves and which apply to all existences. Similarly in the sphere of value: intuitions of essences are attainable, which then are normative for determining the valuable in existence and in action. Moreover, essential values stand in essential relations to one another and form a hierarchy, the climax of which is love. It is the thought of Scheler which Bixler chiefly sets forth, and he goes on to show how Scheler maintains an autonomy for religion.[17] The religious consciousness, like all other consciousness, is determined by its " intentional " character, and the intentional object of religion is God as the ground of all existence and all value. The religious consciousness of God denotes an object which is constitutive of reality itself. Here " we are arguing not from man's empirical need of God, but from the fact that an analysis of pure consciousness discloses Absolute Reality on the one hand, and on the other the religious act in which it is grasped." [18] According to this phase of religious realism, then, there are objective standards of truth and value in the form of essences which are inherent in these very ranges of conscious experience.

While Bixler writes with approval concerning the phenomenological doctrine of essences, he finds phenomenology weak because of its division between phenomenological truth and empirical conditions. The philosophy seems to imply " a belief in the fundamental consistency of our entire world of experience," [19] which it fails to justify. This difficulty is met in the volume, *Religious Realism,* by Calhoun's interpretation of Plato. Calhoun warns against reading Plato with the eyes of Aristotle, and makes the following statement of his own reading:

There are not two separate worlds, realms, substantial orders, one of intelligible or noumenal things, the other of perceptible

or phenomenal things, standing over against each other in re-
ciprocal relation. Forms and things are present together in one
world, in which each is logically distinguishable from the other;
in which there are complex, systematic interrelations among
things, among forms, and between forms and things; and in
which more ultimate factors than either things or forms are discoverable by systematic analysis, which tests every ostensible ultimate, and seeks to press even further its search for " the natural
lines of cleavage " and of unification in the actual world.[20]

Those more ultimate factors in Plato's thought are that the
Good is the goal of the cosmic order and that " Mind is the
orderer." [21]

With this last thought we come to the teleological view of
the universe which is the predominant view of the American
religious realists, and which could meet the difficulty raised
by Bixler concerning phenomenology. Going back to Tillich's " beliefful relativism " for a moment, I would ask why
he, who derives a good deal from the phenomenologists,
should not find significant standards in terms of the essences of truth and value, thus transcending relativism; and
why, at least in terms of essences, we do not have a knowledge of the being of God which is more than myth and symbol? For God and his kingdom would not need to be understood as merely a system of timeless essentialities, if one
conceived His relation to the universe to be teleological — a
view which is no less biblical than Platonic.

III

Let us now pass to the third subtopic proposed at the outset, to which several of our previous considerations have led
up; namely, the revival of cosmology and its theological in-

terpretation. We must content ourselves, however, with treating this topic only in very summary fashion.

A revival of cosmology has taken place, notwithstanding the indifference to the subject which characterizes both positivism and idealism. The most notable expressions of it are to be found in the systems of Alexander and Whitehead. But the newer philosophies of evolution also present constructions in this field. Such, for example, are those of Bergson, Lloyd Morgan, Hobhouse, and Boodin. The movement is also furthered by the third Copernican revolution introduced by Einstein and the new physics.

Let us take the philosophy of Whitehead as the most developed expression of this movement. His *Process and Reality* bears the subtitle, *An Essay in Cosmology*. He has described his position as that of a provisional realism. Although the outcome of his thought, he says, is in many respects not far from that of Bradley, the kindred doctrines are maintained on a realistic basis. He is also concerned, he tells us, to rescue the type of thought represented by Bergson, James, and Dewey from the charge of anti-intellectualism.

What are some of the aspects of Whitehead's cosmology which may be regarded as relevant by religious philosophy? He rejects the bifurcation of nature according to which what Fechner called the " night view " of nature expresses its objective reality; and he upholds the " day view " according to which the qualities of things are no less objective than their quantitative aspects. He finds for spontaneity and creativity an ultimate ontological status. He holds that forms or essences are " eternal objects " and not just generalizations from the universal flux. But they do not constitute for him a superior realm of being; rather, they have their signifi-

cance only in relation to actuality. Because of the " fallacy
of simple location" and the reality of the time-dimension,
he maintains that wholes determine parts as truly as parts
determine wholes; and ultimately he comes to a doctrine of
the interrelation between microcosm and macrocosm. He
insists that any cosmology must involve the interweaving of
efficient causation and final causation. The doctrine that
the laws of efficient causation are statistical averages permits
this interweaving. He finds that the presence of forms and
values in the world is due to God. God is " the actual but
nontemporal entity whereby the indetermination of mere
creativity is transmuted into a determinate freedom." [22] He
is " the ordering entity. . . . His nature remains self-con-
sistent in relation to all change. . . . The purpose of God is
the attainment of value in the temporal world." [23] Finally,
the universe as a whole is characterized by creative advance.
The law of entropy — itself a statistical law — may mean
the termination of this epoch of the universe, but this epoch
will be followed by other epochs for which this one will have
prepared the way.

We can do no more than give this brief summary of some
of the characteristics of Whitehead's cosmology because our
concern here is mainly with its theological interpretation.
Considerable irony, both from within and from without the
ranks of theology, has been expended on such an undertaking. It implies, some say, the position that now at last we
may believe in God because the cosmologist permits. What
will happen when this new cosmology gives place to another? Must the humble believer wait on the reconstruction of the cosmological argument? What kind of God, it
is said, is arrived at by such an argument? The principle of
concretion is hardly sufficient as a Being to whom prayer

should be addressed. Others say that a cosmological interest means a diverting of religious thought from human relations and the interior life, which are its only proper sphere. This last objection, of course, really requires religion to withdraw from metaphysics altogether. The other objections would have more force if realism applied only to the fields of science, logic, aesthetics, and ethics, but not to that of religion. But to deny to faith, intuition and mysticism any capacity for metaphysical knowledge is to fail to perceive what the phenomenologist calls their "intentional" character. The religious realist should not do this. His position requires him to accord an autonomy to the religious consciousness in respect to the gaining of metaphysical truth. Therefore it is a distortion of his position to represent that he holds the idea of God as objectively real only on sufferance—by grace of cosmology. At the same time the religious realist recognizes the other autonomies too and considers all of these, and religious autonomy as well, as being relative to one another, like the different relative authorities within a constitutional political system. He may even use the conception of *primus inter pares* to define the status of religious autonomy, but he will not seek for it any detachment from the other relatively autonomous fields of experience.

At all events, belief in God as creator properly implies an interest in the creation according to our other knowledge of it—that is, in cosmology—just as belief in God as redeemer implies an interest in the careers of men and of societies in time according to our other knowledge—that is, an interest in the philosophy of history.

Archbishop Temple's Gifford Lectures, *Nature, Man and God,* is an important theological interpretation of the new cosmology. He announces his point of view and method as that of " dialectical realism." He acknowledges much dependence upon Whitehead and, rejecting Cartesian dualism, takes as a realistic premise Whitehead's doctrine that " consciousness presupposes experience, not experience consciousness." The process which is the objective world of experience displays continuity and organic character and — most significantly of all — the emergence of mind. Mind, in the form of personality, becomes our supreme explanatory principle for two reasons: it is an originative principle and it is capable of orientation towards transcendent values. Temple criticizes Whitehead's conception of God because it is not fully personal. This appears in the latter's distinction between God's primordial nature, which is unconscious, and his consequent nature, which is conscious. This leads to the conception of thoroughgoing polarity between God and the world, which Temple considers to be no explanation at all. The personal God and his purpose, then, furnish the supreme explanatory principle, the validity of which rests not only upon its explanatory significance but also upon its dynamic meanings and upon revelation. The supreme purpose Temple defines — again referring to Whitehead — as " the Commonwealth of Value." " Its Christian name is the Communion of the Saints; its perfection is in eternity, but to bring its divided and warring members into that Harmony and Peace wherein it alone is actual is the purpose which gives meaning to History." [24]

Another theologian who has undertaken a theological interpretation of the new cosmology — a task in which I also have joined in my book, *The Meaning and Truth of Religion* — is Calhoun, whose position may be very briefly indicated here. Calhoun says that Whitehead's later writings came to him as " a kind of revelation." In his *God and the Common Life* he presents a world view which is arrived at by a union between the principle of sufficient reason, critical realism, and faith. He builds on the organic character of the universe, the fact of emergent evolution, the reality of pure forms, and man as " critic, creator, and worshiper." On the basis of analogical argument he holds that the most adequate explanation of the universe having these characters is God as primordial Mind and purposeful Spirit. This argument is not a coercive proof, but it brings support to faith and in turn is supported by faith. I quote the following summary of Calhoun's total position:

Every natural event is the result of God's working *and* other factors, formal, material and dynamic. Not merely in some, but in all the concrete situations men must live with, the hand of God is at its creative, reconciling work. Every human self lives under the persuasive influence of saving Power that confronts him upon all sides, and cannot be avoided; that he can deny, but never leave behind.[25]

If one links the two foregoing interpretations of cosmology with the positions of Macintosh, Wright, and other writers in the volume *Religious Realism,* one sees a definite tendency to hold that the organic character of the universe is subordinate to a more comprehensive teleological character, and that the purpose of the universe is one whose full meaning can be realized only through freedom and redemption.

IV

Our last subtopic can be taken up only in the form of a brief conclusion to this too wide-ranging discussion. It was defined as: Personal realism and the union of critical realism with mysticism.

Professor Pratt, in his contribution to *Religious Realism,* characterized his general metaphysical position as that of "personal realism." By this term he meant the doctrine that persons, as conscious, unitary centers of spontaneous activity, are fully real in their own right and are not mere derivatives from the system of physical nature. In contrast to that system they are supernatural and they establish the reality of the realm of the spirit with which religion has always been concerned. Last year appeared his own volume, *Personal Realism,* in which the system of his thought is presented. There he maintains the reality of a world of things and of selves. The reality of things is based on the general principles of critical realism. The reality of selves is a matter of direct intuition. As they are intuited, selves have the characters which call for a doctrine of interaction as concerns the relations between mind and body, and for an acknowledgment of teleological causation as really operative in nature, so far as human minds are concerned. Such an ontological status for personality as Pratt presents is essential, not only for the teleological cosmology which we have just been discussing, but also for the realistic philosophy of history with which our first topic was concerned.

Pratt's development of his conception of the realm of the spirit is given in his final chapter, entitled "Ultimate Guesses" — a somewhat disconcerting title from the standpoint of religious realism. There he develops a view of the whole of reality in terms of the hypothesis of "spiritual pantheism" which, he says, might quite as well be denominated "immanent theism." This view he does not offer as a mere

guess but as a reasonable overbelief. His procedure is first
to compare it with four other cosmic hypotheses: materialistic naturalism; dualistic and atheistic pluralism; deism or
transcendental theism and the conception of a finite God;
and absolute idealism. To all of these he considers spiritual
pantheism to be superior, in view of the major aspects of the
universe which must be taken into account. In giving reasons for the superior claim of his view he draws upon arguments such as we have been surveying under our preceding
topic, namely, the organic character of the cosmos as a whole,
the doctrine of emergent evolution, immanent purposive-
ness in nature, and a conscious cosmic purposefulness as the
only principle which makes these other characters fully intelligible.

Finally Pratt appeals to the facts of mysticism. And here
he says he refers "not so much to ecstasies and visions, as
to the widespread milder type of religious consciousness, to
the sense of a More, of a reservoir of spiritual life akin to our
own, upon which we may draw." [26]

According to his concluding portrayal, God is the World
Soul and the physical world is his body. He is the Cosmic
Artist, who "eternally is Being or Life, Consciousness, and
Joy." [27] At the same time "his life is full of finite death, his
delight includes sorrow and anguish." [28] Yet all the actuali-
ties in his nature may be so united "that were our minds
great enough to comprehend them together, we should find
the Whole an overwhelming and unspeakable beauty, a bea-
tific vision." [29]

But there are other realists who would give to mysticism a
less tentative place than is the case with Pratt. I am inclined
to think that this is true of Professor Montague. Episte-

mologically, at least, he treats mysticism as one of " the ways of knowing." Its method is that of intuition, which is the method that creates and discovers, whereas reason confirms or confutes. And " in the real mystic intuition the inner self in its entirety is the controlling factor." [30]

More positive still in respect to the cognitive significance of mysticism is Baron Friedrich von Hügel, who is the last thinker that I shall introduce into this discussion. Von Hügel was in reaction against the subjectivism in modern philosophy. His first series of Gifford Lectures, which he did not deliver nor fully prepare, was to have been entitled: " Concerning the Reality of Finites and the Reality of God: a Study of their Interrelations and their Effects and Requirements within the Human Mind." In *The Reality of God,* which contains the material prepared for these lectures and published after his death, he adopts an epistemological position which he calls " critical realism," though — as Pratt notes — without referring to the earlier use of the term by the American group of writers. He means that we have " apprehensions of realities [which are] independent of our apprehensions of them." [31] He finds " Intimations of the Reality of God in Nature and in the Human Mind." [32] He will not admit a pantheistic inclusion of evil in the being or life of God, with the result that evil becomes essentially unreal, and so he rejects a merely immanent God. [33]

He then goes on to give a veridical function to mystical experience. Speaking of himself at the age of five or six years he writes:

The religion which was already so strong was of the mystical type, in so far, at least, that its thirst and support was not drawn from Ethics, at least of the elementary kind, but from existence, and the sense of existence, in the sense of various realities penetrated and supported by the Supreme Reality, God. . . . I remember vividly how my delight was precisely in the fact that, beautiful as the external nature was, God did not consist even in its full totality, but was a Life, an Intelligence, a Love distinct from it all, in spite of His close penetration of it all. Thus Otherness was as [much a] part of the outlook as was Reality. . . . The moral sense required a strong and sustained awakening to full vigor and aimfulness; and a large part correspondingly, the historical element in religion, above all the detailed earthly life of Our Lord, had to come as a Convention of God, as the power to lift us out of the dust. Yet certain general peculiarities remain with me still, and they are, I take it, the peculiarities of the Moderate, Theistic, Christian Mystic.[34]

In this mysticism of von Hügel's the intuition of God has a cognitive significance in no wise inferior to the intuition of personality or to the organized knowledge of finite things in nature. Each form of knowledge requires criticism and interpretation in the light of the other forms — a view of knowledge which is quite consistent with the conviction that the transcendent God is also immanent in all finite existence.

v

Is there an inner unity between the different realisms that we have surveyed, which have been evoked by different situations? This was a question raised at the outset of this paper and deferred to the end. Some continuities between the different realisms we have noted as we went along. On the other hand some of the views are indifferent to, or skeptical about, matters which other views present with positive conviction. Perhaps a positive solution of these differences could be secured through the development of a *pan-realism*[35] according to which each of the areas of experience would serve to criticize and to supplement all the others, on the basis of a parity in respect to the claim to be a commerce with reality yielding metaphysical insight.

NOTES

[1] *A Pluralistic Universe* (New York: Longmans, Green & Co., 1909), p. 312.

[2] *An Interpretation of Christian Ethics* (New York: Harper & Bros., 1935), p. 24.

[3] *Ibid.*

[4] *Ibid.*, p. 26.

[5] *Ibid.*, p. 191.

[6] *Ibid.*, p. 189.

[7] *Religiöse Verwirklichung*, p. 67; see the translation, *The Religious Situation* (New York: Henry Holt & Co., 1933), p. xii.

[8] *The Religious Situation*, pp. 53, 70.

[9] Tillich's essay in the Oxford Conference volume, *The Kingdom of God and History* (Chicago: Willett, Clark & Co., 1938), pp. 113–14.

[10] *Ibid.*, p. 118.

[11] *The Interpretation of History* (New York: Charles Scribner's Sons, 1936), pp. 169–71.

[12] *Ibid.*, p. 174. "Fate," in Tillich's usage, is a term for "time's being supported by the eternal."

[13] For a more recent expression of the realistic attitude, in relation to practical religious problems, see *The Quest for Religious Realism*, by Paul Arthur Schilpp (New York: Harper & Bros., 1938). Compare also *Realistic Theology*, by Walter M. Horton (New York: Harper & Bros., 1934).

[14] *Religious Realism*, p. v.

[15] *Ibid.*, p. 260.

[16] *Ibid.*, p. 80.

[17] Cf. Paul Arthur Schilpp's article, "Max Scheler, 1872–1928," in the *Philosophical Review*, XXXVIII, 574 ff.

[18] *Religious Realism*, p. 81.

[19] *Ibid.*, p. 92.

[20] *Ibid.*, p. 231.

[21] *Ibid.*, pp. 233, 234.

[22] *Religion in the Making* (New York: The Macmillan Co., 1926), p. 90.

[23] *Ibid.*, pp. 99, 100, 104.

[24] *Nature, Man and God* (London: The Macmillan Co., Ltd., 1934), p. 426.

[25] *God and the Common Life* (New York: Charles Scribner's Sons, 1935), p. xxiv.

[26] *Personal Realism* (New York: The Macmillan Co., 1937), p. 366.

[27] *Ibid.,* p. 377.

[28] *Ibid.,* p. 379.

[29] *Ibid.,* pp. 379, 380.

[30] *Ways of Knowing* (New York: The Macmillan Co., 1925), p. 57.

[31] *The Reality of God* (New York: E. P. Dutton & Co., 1931), p. 41.

[32] *Ibid.,* p. 53.

[33] *Ibid.,* pp. 67, 68.

[34] *Ibid.,* p. 81.

[35] I owe this concept to Professor Joseph Haroutunian, of Wellesley College.

THE MEANING OF RATIONAL FAITH

PAUL ARTHUR SCHILPP

Northwestern University

I T IS, I take it, impossible for any religion to get on without *faith*. At the same time it is equally true that under the cloak of " faith " religionists of all time have managed to hide almost anything, not excluding lamentable credulity, positive absurdity, and sheer magic. Sixteen years ago, therefore, I ventured to demand a rational basis for any faith that could legitimately be held by rational minds.[1] More recently [2] I have made an attempt to distinguish religious faith from metaphysical speculation on the one side and from empirical knowledge on the other. My contentions, especially in this latter connection, have been repeatedly challenged,[3] and in any case I must admit that I have never made myself explicitly clear on the question as to the precise distinction between " rational faith " and empirical knowledge. I rather welcome the opportunity, therefore, of making a more careful analysis of this problem. All the more so because this issue seems to be of the utmost importance for religion, if religion is to be freed from the continuing charges that, if it is not actually nothing more than " the opiate of the people," then it is at any rate nothing more than wishful thinking, or even sheer credulity and blind superstition.

An analysis of this problem appears, moreover, to be particularly appropriate in a volume published in honor of Harris Franklin Rall. For not only was it Professor Rall's early volume on *A Working Faith* [4] which first attracted me to him as a religious thinker and later caused me to enroll under him as my teacher in the philosophy of religion, but his profound faith in God and faith in men have, without a doubt, been the most characteristic aspects of his work as a contemporary theologian of the first magnitude.   From first to last Dr. Rall's faith has been " a *working* faith; " that is to say, not primarily a set of doctrines or dogmas to be asserted and to be " believed in," but rather a way of life to be " lived by." With him it has been a living faith, the validity of which has been proved by him in action.   Nothing, therefore, could be more fitting than to subject this notion of religious faith to critical analysis in a volume which is humbly dedicated to him.

I

Let us begin at the beginning.   If the word " faith " is to have any identifiable meaning, it would seem to me to stand to reason that the word cannot be used equivalently with the word " knowledge."   Where there is knowledge in any significant — i.e., empirically testable and verifiable — sense, faith is not only no longer necessary but becomes actually a weapon of deceit.   Or is it really fair and just, in some specific instance which calls for action, for myself to act on privately gotten information (which gives me actual knowledge in the situation), while I permit my neighbor, who has not been fortunate enough to have had access to this private information, to " take a leap in the dark," i.e., to act on faith? The answer to this question is, I think, quite obvious and would be almost universally identical.   Accordingly, in concrete, everyday life, all of us are quite used to making a real and meaningful distinction between knowledge and faith. To obliterate or obfuscate this distinction can only lead to endless confusion.

Lest, however, I be misunderstood at this point, I need at once to speak a word of warning. Nothing I have said thus far is to be interpreted as implying that by knowledge I mean absolute certainty. In fact, nothing could be farther from my mind than to make such a claim.[5] The human mind and organism being, after all, only a *finite* mind and organism, it hardly would be reasonable to expect that mind to have infinite or absolute knowledge; and obviously only such knowledge could lay claim to absolute certainty. Knowledge of no situation, fact, or event is so complete and full that the possibility of error is completely ruled out.[6] It may not be comfortable for man to have to accept this fact, but we are concerned with the analysis of facts, not with the desires of fancy.

Although I agree, then, that knowledge is still by no means the same thing as absolute certainty, it does seem to me that knowledge has an assignable meaning which is not at all the equivalent of faith. It is, of course, quite possible that something like faith is itself a necessary ingredient of anything which passes as knowledge; but even though this should be the case, that would hardly, in itself, be sufficient reason to equate the meaning of the two terms. It is possible, that is to say, that both in the initial stages of the process which leads to the getting of knowledge as well as in the final claim to knowledge as had, the element of faith enters in. Since — as I have already insisted — certainty seems to be beyond the pale of human possibility, it is perhaps only natural that no kind of significant knowledge can be achieved without an initial bent of man (more particularly of the specific individual

who happens to be in search of some definite bit of knowledge), by which man is inclined to " believe " whatever it
happens to be that he wants to know. And it is equally possible that no final — so-called — possession of any particular
bit of knowledge would be considered as such by its possessor
without, again, this same sort of bent towards it, i.e., without
the tendency on his part to " believe " that what he thinks
or says is so, really is so, and is not otherwise. All of which
may have to be granted, and may lead to the proposition that
knowledge itself — in a certain sense — must always rest on
faith. I repeat, however, that none of these considerations
justify the assumption that there is no difference at all between knowledge and faith. Even though it could be proved
that faith is a necessary prerequisite of knowledge, it still
needs to be seen that knowledge — if the word is to have any
assignable meaning in the context of everyday life — still has
some other requisites. Real knowledge, to put the matter almost inexcusably briefly, must be capable of being tested and,
in some sense at least, verified. Without that the word would
lose whatever significant meaning it may have.[7]

Here the fundamental distinction between knowledge and
faith seems to me to lie. Knowledge must be capable of being tested and verified. Whereas faith — if it is to be distinguished from knowledge — is essentially speculative. It is,
obviously, this hypothetical and speculative aspect of faith
which has laid it open to the repeated charges that it is either
nothing more than idle wish-thinking or — what is even
worse — just superstition.

It is not, however, necessary — on any analytical or reasonable grounds — to make such identifications or reductions.
For, as everyone knows, even natural science makes signifi-

cant and necessary use of hypotheses, without thereby laying itself open to the charge of wish-thinking or superstition. It is a well-known fact that all real scientific progress depends upon the scientist's willingness to venture out into the areas not only of hypotheses but of actual speculation. The speculative and projective element in faith need not, therefore, be regarded as cause either for surprise or for suppression. This aspect of faith is more than peripheral. The construction of new ends and objectives is an essential characteristic of faith, whereas the framing of hypotheses is only one tool among others in the sciences.

It is, of course, true enough that if no reins are put on man's speculative enterprises, if his imagination is allowed to run wild, he may — and usually does — end up in all sorts of vagaries, both intellectual and otherwise. Within the realm of historic religion there certainly has been entirely too much justification for the answer of the Sunday school boy who, when asked by his teacher, " What is faith? " replied: " Faith is believin' what you know ain't so." In fact, it would be useless to deny what appears to the present writer at least to be an obvious fact, namely, that much of what specific religious institutions have historically required to be believed by their adherents belongs all too uncomfortably in the category so well characterized by that Sunday school boy's reply. And it is, clearly, this very fact which has brought to too many historic manifestations of religion not merely reproach, but the active irony and scorn of increasingly large classes of thoughtful people. So it ought! If specific religious institutions are going to keep on insisting that believing the unbelievable and uncritically accepting that which runs counter to man's every past experience and against all his best rational judgments — I say, if they keep on insisting that such beliefs are of the essence of religious faith, then it will not be long before religion — thus interpreted — will be completely discredited before the enlightened conscience and understanding of mankind. Again I say: such fate would be highly deserved. If God be the creator of man as well as of the universe, it stands to reason to accept the proposition that he did not endow man with the capacity and function of rational judgment only to ask him afterwards to betray this very capacity and function. It is unnecessary to argue this point; it is self-evident to every rational creature.

Faith, then, though only speculative and hypothetical and therefore not quite amenable to the tests of immediate verification, can be significant for conscious rational creatures only if it does no violence to man's actual or possible experience and to his considered rational judgment.[8] It may not be amenable to immediate tests of verification; but it is nonetheless subject to the canons of reason and to the rationale and test of past human experience.

In fact, faith — in distinction from mere " belief " — is an active principle, an attitude or principle of action as much as it is one of " acceptance " or of " assertion." This, it would seem, is true of faith in any area; in none more so, however, than in that of religion. What we may mean by rational faith, then, is something like the following: Devotion to a worthy object, to a reasonable objective; such devotion expressing itself in considered action and conduct; action and conduct which are in line with the respective objective and which are laden with the emotion and richness of sentiment that would be appropriate to that object.

In this statement all three essentials of a rational faith are clearly in evidence; namely, (1) rational consideration, (2) emotional commitment, and (3) action. With any one of these three essentials omitted faith is something less than worthy of the rational-moral-spiritual being which man is. We have already observed that so-called "faith" which is blind, which, in other words, is not rationally considered, is sheer credulity, blissful wish-thinking, or silly superstition. And any so-called "faith" which lacks the emotional dynamic of a personal dedication to ends, of loyalty and commitment, may indeed be a series of accepted beliefs, of dogmas assented to, but it can hardly be called "faith." After these two points are clearly envisaged it is easy to see the inevitability with which they lead to the third: action, conduct. The ends, objectives, loyalties, to which a man commits himself after he himself has set them up, created them by the power of his own best rational judgment and considered deliberation, simply cannot fall short of having their inevitable effect upon action and conduct. Tell me what a man ultimately has faith in, and I shall tell you what kind of man he is!

Nowhere does the difference between a set of beliefs merely accepted or assented to and a vital living faith become more immediately obvious than when faith is thus seen as a rational commitment to rationally considered and worthy ends. In comparison with such faith most historical "credos" of the orthodox religions sink into mere nothingness. For, all too universally, those historical credos concern themselves with the asserted belief of the so-called "believer" in what are said to be historical events in the life-history of this or that founder of this or that religion. Any rational mind finds it difficult to see what difference such belief could possibly make either in the actual sequence of events as they actually may or may not have occurred in the past, or in the lives and conduct of those who today assert their belief in those alleged historical happenings. If the events actually did happen, neither belief nor disbelief in them can change anything in the historical facts. And if they did *not* occur, no amount of belief in them — though the belief be shared by millions of people through millennia of time — can make them actual. In either case it is impossible to see what particular efficacy they should have for the actual life of today. The whole force of such beliefs is obviously directed towards the past. Whereas faith, as I have been delineating it, is in the very nature of the case not backward- but forward-looking. Its ends, its goals, its objectives are to be striven for, they lie ahead and are objects still to be reached, objectives still to be achieved. Nor can these objectives be achieved unless we *do* something about it. What a man really has faith in he is willing to work, labor, and if necessary to suffer for. That is why such faith is always an active principle.

II

I realize, of course, that such an activistic formulation of the nature of faith is bound to encounter a number of objections. We shall be asked: Are there not objects of faith — particularly of religious faith — which are quite beyond us? Are there not objects of faith, that is to say, concerning which "acceptance" is the only possible attitude on the part of finite man; objects which are totally beyond our control and for which, therefore, a formulation in terms of our own ends of action would be irrelevant, if not indeed impious? As pointed illustrations, we would, for example, be asked: Do we ourselves create God? or, Are we ourselves the inventors of immortality?

There is a sense in which this objection is well taken. In any case, a consideration of it will serve to bring out our meaning. It is, of course, obvious that, if God really exists, we did not create him. The same principle, clearly, holds in the case of immortality: if man actually does survive the shock of bodily death — well, then, he does, and the fact is not of our own making. Moreover, among the objects of faith one may distinguish a whole range — from one extreme in which things are given, are quite beyond our powers, to the other extreme in which, as a limit, they may be totally under our control. In between these two extremes lie probably the vast majority of the objects of faith, such as the building of better communities, the development of international understanding and good will, and the achievement of world brotherhood — these and millions of other worthy objects of faith are partly within our own power and partly dependent upon forces beyond our immediate control.

But let us take a look even at the two extremes, at the ideal limits. It is clear, of course, that towards that which is entirely within our control — if such there be — we stand in the relationship of creators, fully responsible for existence or nonexistence. The final justification of faith at this point occurs only in the actual bringing into being of the object of faith, followed by the realization of its promise as previously contemplated. Yet, although to such an object as God or any other purely " given " — such, for example, as the " beauty of holiness " in another person — it is obvious that we do not stand in any position of actual or even of potential creators, it is by no means true that faith at this point contains no activistic aspects. The appropriate response of faith here lies in the determination and commitment of one's self to *become* a certain kind of being so as to be able to sustain a satisfactory kind of relationship to the divine (or to any specific instance of divine characteristics). This process of *becoming* is very much of an activity. So that even at this extreme limit of an object of faith which may be said not at all to be within our control it is still true that vital faith in that object issues in definite action and conduct on the part of the believer; provided, all the time, that it is real living faith that we are talking about and not just the mere assent of the head to the judgmental proposition that such a being as a God exists (although I fear that most so-called religious people's belief in God really is exhausted by this latter type).

Rational faith, therefore, does not by any means preclude the inclusion of acts of worship. Only it is to be remembered that in such experiences of worship (or of appreciation) as those to which allusion has just been made we are (1) not only engaging in an act and are (2) not only re-forming ourselves in the light of an ideal thus apprehended (or to put it into the old familiar phrase, " transformed by the renewing of our spirit "), but (3) our sensitivity to such an ideal will also disclose the obligation to further actions in order to bring other, still unregenerated, raw materials of experience and of existence " into subjection " to the ideal. This kind of worship, therefore, is very much of an act [9] of faith. And it is, of course, perfectly possible that, especially on certain occasions, the sense of the richness and depth of an appropriate sentiment may appear to be the dominant feature of an act of worship. Yet even on those occasions I must insist that, if that act of worship is not to be a mere orgy of emotion, it is bound to issue in activity and conduct continuous with and appropriate to itself.

Let us now, however, return to the above first-mentioned objection raised against our activistic interpretation of the nature of rational faith. There is another sense in which we may quite accept that purported " objection." For there is, after all, *a sense* in which — whether God exists independently of us or not — we do create God as well as immortality or, indeed, any other object of devotion or of faith. Any *conception* of God which any human being has had, has today, or ever will have must have come out of human experience and out of human reflection.[10] So that, *in this sense,* even those objects of faith whose independent existence itself is wholly beyond our control, are still in a most significant way the objects of our creation. For objects of faith must be conceptual in nature, and our concepts are, obviously, to a large degree matters of our own creation.

Moreover, it is at this point of the creative construction of the objectives of rational faith that judgments of fact (whether clearly perceived — and to that extent held to be more or less certain — or only probable) enter. For the constructions of rational faith can be created only with reference to actual events and experiences. True, such judgments of facts are not — alone and by themselves *qua* cognitive judgments — determinative of faith; they are determinative only of further judgments of fact subsumed under them. Whereas faith is a venturing out beyond the mere limits of judgments of fact. Nonetheless, a reasonable faith cannot be built without due regard for judgments of fact. As has already been repeatedly remarked above, to have " faith " in what we are reasonably sure is not true, requires an act of insult not only towards our own rational mind but towards any divine Creator who may be the responsible agent for the existence of finite minds. Nor is this all. To have such " faith " is also to invite the collapse of any and all institutions which address themselves to the maintenance of such pseudo-faith; since in a rational and moral universe no institutions erected upon untruths can, in the long run, expect to survive. But even that is not yet the worst. To advocate such " faith " in the name of morality and spirituality is to introduce corruption into the very fountains and foundations of life.

III

In brief, then, faith, in order to be rational, must take account of knowledge. It cannot labor in an epistemological vacuum. At the same time, it may rightly be asserted that faith lies in a somewhat different dimension from knowledge. What this dimension of faith is, has, in what has already been said, quite definitely been hinted at. For it must already have become clear to the reader that not only are judgments of fact pertinent to a rational faith, but even more essential to it are judgments of value. The framing, judging, selection, and creation of ends and objectives worthy of commitments are, obviously, *evaluative* processes. Religious faith, therefore, is quite unthinkable without value-judgments.

Without entering here into a detailed discussion of the multitudinous problems of a value-theory, it can be asserted, without fear of serious contradiction, that men do in fact make value-judgments. More than that: in most areas of everyday life value-judgments are felt to be more significant than and perhaps at least quite as numerous as judgments of fact, if not indeed more so. That such value-judgments themselves are, for the most part, not merely based upon judgments of fact but also intend to have some factual reference need not be denied. The fact remains, nonetheless, that judgments of value can definitely be distinguished from judgments of fact. Whereas these latter are statements intended to be purely descriptive or existential in character, value-judgments are judgments of appraisal, of worthfulness, of significance.

That is to say, value-judgments are concerned, in the main, with human purposes, interests, preferences, ideals, demands; whereas judgments of fact are much more nearly descriptive or assertive in character. This must not be taken to mean that value-orientation has nothing whatever to do with judgments of fact. Far from it. It is, in fact, quite true — as I am in the habit of saying to my students — that " all facts are selected facts," i.e., that human preference (which is of the nature of a value-judgment) has already entered into the process by which we happen to pick out one specific fact rather than another. Factual judgments may therefore be granted to be value-oriented. But this is by no means to admit that judgments of fact are logically dependent upon value-judgments. The difference between logical dependence (or rather *in*dependence) and psychological succession of events at this point needs to be kept clearly in mind. And the close relationship thus admitted to exist between judgments of fact and value-judgments, so far from slurring over the distinction between them, would only seem further to bring out their fundamental difference.

With these facts in mind, it may be said that one has faith in what one decides *ought* to be, whereas one merely believes that something is so and so, or actually knows it to be thus. Objects of *knowledge,* as has already been insisted, can be tested, demonstrated, and verified. Objects of *belief,* insofar as they are or claim to be assertions of fact, are really in the last analysis objects of knowledge and as such subject to the tests, demonstrations, and verifications of such objects. Objects of belief in the sense of objects of *faith,* on the other hand, are objects whose validity as speculative or projective commitments may perhaps yield to a certain kind of testing also, but not — so long as they are objects of faith and not of knowledge — to verification. Once an object of faith is capable of yielding to actual verification it has ceased being an object of faith and has become an object of knowledge.

That is why faith has to do with ought- or value-judgments. Faith boldly asserts that so and so ought to be! In this sense it is — literally — concerned with demanding that which, as yet at any rate, may not exist (except, perhaps, potentially). Faith, in other words, is a definitely creative capacity. As such it presents one of the most powerful of human functions. For what boundaries are to be set to such creative capacities? Who is to say: This far and no further!

The answer to this last question is: Nothing and no one, *if not* the only arbiters man can use at any time, namely human experience and reason! It is not merely possible and conceivable, but has actually happened numberless times in human history, that men have pinned their faith to the impossible, not to say at times even to the worthless and absurd. It is this fact which requires even for the creative work of faith that it remain still under the control of the critical faculties of human intelligence. In other words, even the ideal ends and objectives created by faith need still subject themselves to the question: Is what I desire or demand truly reasonable and meaningful; or is it merely the idle creation of a rambling, unsteady, and uncontrolled mind?

Even a value-judgment, that is to say, is still subject to the canons of reason and must yield to the criticism of rational thought, analysis, judgment, and reflection. If it proceeds without consideration for the possibilities of human experience, it can do so only at the risk of being idle and useless imagining. These latter may be interesting human phenomena from a merely psychological point of view; but they lose all significance from the standpoint of meeting human need, or of affecting human achievement and progress.

This last statement must not, however, be interpreted to mean that an ought- or value-judgment is merely another kind of descriptive or existential judgment (of fact). Not at all. Faith is the assertion of what is, in general, *not yet*. But the point is: in order to be reasonable faith, it must not assert what is — in the nature of the case — altogether impossible. Rational faith is the assertion of and the demand and working for that which not only *ought* to be but which, by every rational consideration, *can* be — if only we (and enough of us) shall actually be willing to demonstrate our faith by working for the achievement of the ideal thus set before us. Here we see again the activistic element in such faith. What a man is not willing to work for, he does not *really* have faith in. Faith, therefore, so far from being supposed to be something opposed to works, demonstrates its reality and vitality precisely in and through works. At the same time, it is just this fact of faith expressing its reality in work which also stresses the necessity — indeed the practical inevitability — of the reasonableness of such faith. For it is certainly *un*reasonable to expect any normally rational creature seriously to engage in work which is either held to be actually futile, if not definitely absurd, or the end of which is at any rate considered to be quite unachievable, and that not merely within any foreseeable future but at any imaginable time. To be specific: it is perfectly conceivable even for a rational mind to be committed to what may, at the time at least, appear to be a losing cause, so long as one is sure of at least two considerations, namely (1) that the cause is inherently felt to be worthwhile, and (2) that, though its immediate chance of success may seem remote, it actually is felt to have a real chance in the long run.

To put this more specifically, let us take a concrete example. Suppose the end sought be that of universal peace. Certainly this is a goal which, in the light not merely of the actually devastating character of present events, but also in that of the all too clearly discernible trends of the times, would appear to be foredoomed to miserable failure. Yet it would be readily admitted by most rational men (and such glorifiers of war and slaughter as Hitler and Mussolini could hardly, of course, qualify as "rational men," at least not in this particular area) that universal peace is an end greatly to be desired. Moreover, even on the second ground, namely that of the question of the ultimate possibility of achievement, it would be difficult to maintain the proposition that universal peace is — in the nature of the case! — beyond the realm of possibility. Granted, thus far such a state of affairs has never yet been achieved by mankind — an argument which does of course have the weight of previous experience. But by virtue of such argument any novel human experience would be ruled out — a proposition which obviously proves too much, since it has in innumerable specific instances (as in the successful flight of heavier than air machines) been disproved. The prospects for the accomplishment of universal peace may be ever so remote; it could nonetheless hardly be demonstrated or even rationally made plausible that its ultimate achievement lay beyond the pale of possible realization. Quite the contrary! For it could very well be pointed out that even on grounds of purely selfish and economic interest, the method of settling international disputes by recourse to war is irrational and self-defeating. In other words, it would seem to be a comparatively simple matter to demonstrate to almost any reasonably normal human being that war is not only wholly unnecessary, but actually precludes dedication to any worthy ends; quite apart from the additional fact that it is a means which is itself almost without exception destructive of all higher human values and therefore stands condemned before any enlightened moral consciousness, regardless of whatever ends it may be asserted to be serving. That being the case, it would seem that faith in universal peace is, as such, a quite rational faith, all present indications to the contrary notwithstanding. But again I repeat: no man had better claim to have *faith* in a warless world, who, in the very midst of the present chaotic world situation, is not moving a finger in order to make that dream of the sages and seers of mankind come closer to realization.

Specific objects of rational faith are thus objects which come out of the crucible of experience, projected, interpreted, and tested by a reflective mind envisaging a better state of affairs — both within and without. A man of rational faith is one who is guided by such commitment. His mind is made up in advance *only* on its dedication to the use of the method of rational reflection, and *not* to that of any specifically given or previously accepted end.[11]   The goals, ideals, purposes, ends, which he constructs and to the realization of which he bends his every effort, must seem inherently worthy of pursuit and promise to carry forward not merely the progressive achievement of a morally more mature personality but also the enhancement of the community of which he is an integral part.   Here it can again be seen how such a faith expresses and also engenders (1) a carefully reflecting mind, (2) the emotional warmth which naturally goes with the envisioning of and commitment to what is "felt" to be a great and worthy object or end, and (3) an active procedure working towards the realization of such an end or cause or towards conduct worthy of such an object — the same three features which we have previously stressed as essential ingredients of any faith which could significantly be called rational.

IV

The call of the hour, then, is not for less faith, but for more faith.   We still need to "walk by faith."   But the faith that is needed, so far from being a mere affirmation of a stated historical creed, is the faith that Jesus talked about: faith that "moves mountains."   Look at the mountainous difficulties which confront humanity in this tragic hour of her history! The breakup of the family and the confusion in morals.   The dissolution of the community into the loneliness of crowded cities.   The corruption of politics and the nationalizing of the state.   The aimlessness of education and the helplessness of science.   Unemployment.   Too much wealth for too few people.   Too much poverty and despair for too many people. Increased race-consciousness and race-antipathy. Nationalism, militarism, imperialism. Communism and fascism. War — "the world's greatest collective sin." Churchianity. And — religionism which, when not magical, superstitious, or pagan, seems at least to be hopelessly futile. Mountains of difficulties? Yes, too many of them.

Knowledge, by itself, has not and cannot remove these mountains. There is hardly an area here named in which the necessary *knowledge* for the solution of our problems is not available at this very moment. And such knowledge is, of course, of the utmost importance. But it is still true that "without *vision* the people perish." Knowledge, like patriotism, is not enough. It needs to be implemented by a faith that can move those mountains, by a vision the compelling power of which will send men out on a new quest and a new crusade: to build that world of human society wherein men shall at last have a chance to prove themselves to be children of God and brothers to one another. Faith thus enacted *is* rational faith.

NOTES

[1] In an article on "A Rational Basis Demanded for Faith," *Journal of Philosophy*, Vol. XXI, No. 8 (April 10, 1924), pp. 209–12.

[2] First in an article on "Can God Be Known?" in the *Personalist*, Vol. XVI, No. 3 (Summer 1935), pp. 216–26, and then in a revised form in the chapter "Can God Be 'Wholly Other' and *Our* God?" in my Mendenhall **Lectures of** 1938, which have appeared under the title, *The Quest for Religious Realism* (New York, 1938), especially pp. 167–78.

[3] In print more particularly by Professor Jared S. Moore in his "The Empirical Knowledge of God," the *Personalist*, Vol. XVI, No. 4 (Autumn 1935), p. 383.

[4] New York and Cincinnati, 1914.

[5] I have, in fact, previously broken my lance for the proposition that cer-

tainty is not even achievable within the area of the natural sciences; that the best of which the (finite) human mind is capable is a high degree of probability. Cf. my discussion of this point in my reply to Homer H. Dubs' "The Paradox of Certainty," under the same title (as his article) in the *Philosophical Review*, Vol. XLIV, No. 3 (May 1935), pp. 480–82.

6 There is, I think, only one exception to this rule and that is in the realm of mathematics. We can achieve absolute certainty in mathematics. But there is a (good and sufficient) reason for this fact. We can have certainty in mathematics because mathematics is itself a game invented and manufactured by man. Man himself having laid down the rules of the game is of course capable of reaching absolutely certain conclusions, so long as he scrupulously plays the game according to his own rules. The moment, however, that he *applies* that game to any situation, fact, or event in the physically existing universe, that moment he has left the realm of absolute certainty and can, at best, achieve only a high degree of probability. Under the leadership of the foremost living physicists, all of the natural sciences have, within recent decades, had to come to and accept this conclusion.

7 It stands to reason, of course, that, within the very circumscribed limitations of a brief essay, it is impossible to develop an entire epistemology. Yet, I suppose, nothing less than a complete theory of knowledge could really suffice for a precise denotation and connotation of the words "knowing" and "knowledge." Under the present limitations of space and propriety I can do no more than throw out a few broad hints.

8 It should be added at once that this is *not* to be taken to mean that the new projection, with which faith is always concerned, may not be violently in conflict with previously *established* ways of thinking or living. The fact is, very often it will be just that. What I do mean to assert at this point is simply the fact that even the demands of faith cannot — in reason — fall outside the realities and possibilities of human experience and must, in principle, not run counter to the considered judgments of rational reflection.

9 It is interesting, in this connection, to observe the acuteness with which the very habit of our (English) language has caught the reality of the *activistic* aspect of faith, as in the phrase, "an *act* of faith." On the other hand, we need to guard against the tendency to let the frequent repetition of such "acts of faith" make of them only an empty — and therefore no longer really "active" — habit. Let acts of faith be acts, not *mere* repetitions!

10 There is, of course, no better proof of this point than the fact that humanity has harbored a vast multitude and an almost infinitely great variety of God-concepts; and that even within the Hebraic-Christian tradition there has been an interesting evolution of the God-concept, an evolution, moreover, the end of which is by no means in sight. In fact, at this very moment it would be possible to point to a considerable number of — sometimes at least — widely divergent God-concepts, many of which would lay claim to being "Christian."

11 More detailed arguments for this point, from the standpoint of a more

technical discussion of the philosophical issues involved in the interpretation of an ethical position agreeing with the point of view here advanced, the interested reader may find in the following essays:

1. Henry W. Stuart, " Valuation As a Logical Process," in John Dewey's *Studies in Logical Theory*, Chicago, 1903.

2. Henry W. Stuart, " A Preface to Ethics," *College of the Pacific Publications in Philosophy*, Vol. III, Stockton, Calif., 1934.

3. Paul A. Schilpp, " On the Nature of the Ethical Problem," *International Journal of Ethics*, Vol. XLVII, No. 1, 1936.

4. Henry W. Stuart, " Dewey's Ethical Theory," in Paul A. Schilpp's (ed.) *The Philosophy of John Dewey*, Evanston and Chicago, 1939.

INTERPRETING THE RELIGIOUS SITUATION

IRL GOLDWIN WHITCHURCH
Garrett Biblical Institute

I

ALL HUMAN experience becomes in fact an ongoing argument with reality. In the process the significant questions resolve themselves finally about two foci: the nature of reality and the dependability of human knowledge. Religious experience cannot ask exemption from facing squarely these two questions. Too often interpreters of religion have claimed such release, presuming a direct and certain access to the divine. In doing this they have only transposed a presupposition about religious faith into a misleading conclusion. The first refers to the fact of a God; the second deals with his nature. The one forms an indispensable condition of any experience; the other constitutes the object to be investigated, not assumed. All experience begins with a presupposition that reality is meaningful to us; in religious language: that God, the ultimately real, initiates a significant divine-human relationship. But the minimum conditions of our experience must be clearly distinguished from the actual achievements of experience in which its meanings have become actualized and understood.

The two questions about the nature of reality and the dependability of human knowledge are really one and inseparable. Always religion — and indeed all experience —

makes a double claim: a claim to a significant degree of knowledge, and a claim that this knowledge discloses the nature of reality or the divine. In an eagerness to verify the experience of communion with God religious persons often presume to be able to ignore the conditions necessary for the understanding that is implied in their claim to communion. In that case, they mistake their own religious reactions for the literal word of the Most High. On second thought it becomes clear that such eagerness defeats itself. For religious experience on its many levels always implicitly acknowledges that dependable knowledge is an indispensable requirement. Begin, for example, with one-way revelationism, with religion at its most elementary level. What is revelation taken to mean? At least two basic presuppositions are involved. One says that a man dependably knows; the other, that the actual nature of the divine is thereby disclosed. But is revelation a one-way deposit of truth and without price to the receiver? Authoritarianism first conceals the explicit nature of these two claims, and then goes on to assimilate the content of divine revelation with a very human tradition about it.

Even today in the Christian movement entirely too much thinking goes on at that level. That is an index to the belated character of much of our religious thinking. One would naturally suppose that Christian thought might have learned something from those conditions of careful investigation which make possible the better elements of modern culture. But no. Common-sense obviousness, native indolence, traditional conservatism, medieval institutionalism, and many other elements, all combine to retard the normal developmental processes in this all-important area of human experience. Too often religious thought consists in a credulous assent to a set of predigested opinions. Faith then becomes a meritorious act, although what is involved may amount to self-deception about the most vital of all human concerns. Sometimes this approach is openly encouraged and officially approved. More often, it lives on as an insidious parasitic growth. Hence unexamined authority usurps the function of careful examination into all relevant evidence. Who can fail to recognize the manner in which Protestant theologians have allowed themselves to be victimized by an abstract authoritarian method? Much time is consumed in propping up dogmas whose chief claim to consideration is that they have been entrenched in a tradition. Our direct appeal to the Christian consciousness, under its many names, has surely revealed itself as a threat to the integrity of a healthy spirit. By it the objectivity-seeking spirit of the Christian religion is stifled in the house of its friends. In precisely this atmosphere some variety of theological rash will continue to break out sporadically until the religious climate is changed for the better. Until then noisy declarations of faith will continue to be mistaken for courageous thinking.

II

Whenever the appeal to external authority has weakened, Christian thinking reflects a sensitivity to contemporaneous settings of the knowledge problem. This is only natural, since the religious person lives in an actual world, not in paradise or in a vacuum. Religious experience is organic to the whole of living. What is taken to be true in religion must continue to verify its truthfulness within an ever more comprehensive and pervasive mode of living. What is generally known as the medieval standpoint failed just here. According to it reason is by nature a captive of revelation. Religious faith begins with certain originally revealed and untouchable propositions. Reason properly operates as the handmaid and defender of the established faith. In brief, after reason's back has been broken, it has full liberty. Thus an initial negative reaction of religion was crystallized against the experimental outlook of the modern mind. It is nurtured still in a certain confidence generated by appeal to established authority and in a fear of what the future may bring. No prophetic insight is required to see that this temper of mind will be here when and if our planet congeals in ice.

The questing soul, however, will find a more significant supplement to the story of religious faith as it participates in the ageless adventures of the human spirit. On its deeper side the Christian religion is not content to claim historical continuity, or even utility value. Its inner compulsion lives by coming to terms with its world, and in the spirit of truth-seeking. In this sense religious faith intends to be a theory of human understanding and a theory of reality in its wholeness. During the Middle Ages, penetrative minds like Anselm of Canterbury, Abélard, Hugo of St. Victor, and especially Thomas of Aquin, gave expression to that deeper spirit by which religion comes to grips with an enlarging world of facts. Call this philosophical-mindedness, if you will; it is no less scientific and religious, and even more characteristically human, than any such specific expressions suggest.

With the coming of the sciences the religious spirit was destined to find itself in a radically changing world. The intellectual climate had shifted. Within organized Christian-

ity the dogma of the congenital limitations of reason continued to be proclaimed, and reasoning continued to be used
to destroy the integrity of reason. Nevertheless, a reality-
oriented human spirit was on the march and fixed theological fences could not finally bar the road to freedom. Very
soon the outmoded Aristotelian science with which religious
thought had encumbered itself began to be replaced. In the
new environment orthodox Christianity found itself in a precarious situation. A statement by Whitehead invites much reflection: " The sixteenth century of our era saw the disruption
of Western Christianity and the rise of modern science." [1]
Subsequently religious thinking faced at once a double problem of orientation toward the sciences, and of the increasing
tensions within the spiritual climate created by our applications of them. The intellectual ferment was straightway
accelerated by two major philosophical tendencies. In continental rationalism and English empiricism the growing scientific outlook received significant formulation. Caught in
the welter of these new historical settings Christian thought
embarked upon decisive experiments. Scientific methodology laid out the new course. Philosophy meant only to ex-
plicate scientific ideas and collaborate in their metaphysical
implications.

III

On the whole the attempts of Christian thought to make
itself at home with the modern mind have thus far proved
an unhappy experiment. Not that the venture could have
been avoided. Scientific methodology has rather completely
leavened modern thinking. The religious outlook simply
had to take that fact into account. But from our vantage

point of over three centuries it appears that the experiment
goes on haltingly. Pronouncements of reconciliation to the
contrary, the so-called conflict between science and religion
will continue for centuries.

The grounds for that continued struggle can be briefly indicated. On one side, the sheer fact of the ascendancy of
scientific method has operated to compress the human situation essentially into *the question of the dependability of
knowledge*. Among the first results of this reorientation
was the posing of the issue as a tension between scientific
knowledge and religious faith. At various times that tension has been relieved or disguised by the use of numerous
expedients. From the side of religion, two elements have
been especially active. Christian faith operates under a dual
compulsion: to maintain a genuine historical continuity, and
also to explore the deeper possibilities of human life under
the nisus of religion's incurably ontological spirit. These
two elements are never quite compatible. Yet they operate
in conjunction so as to draw attention away from the crucial
issues of religious knowledge. It has been too easy to assume
the solution of these latter problems by some doctrine of
revelation. And so a concern with historical dogmas shifts
from a secondary position to the center of faith. Grave consequences follow this treatment of religious knowledge. In
the last analysis Christianity takes very seriously its historical continuity because of the belief that its traditional doctrines present a valid account concerning the nature of reality. In short, Christianity claims to be a *true* interpretation
of the divine. Meanwhile, from the other side, the phenomenal development of the sciences instilled an equally
uncritical confidence that knowledge comes by the scientific

method. Before long this proposition was expanded into the doubtful contention that only through the sciences can valid knowledge be attained.

The stage is now set for a head-on collision. The conflict, however, is inadequately conceived as one between science and religion. It actually generates about two radically different theories of knowledge and of reality. Instead, therefore, of falling back upon the device of assessing praise and blame upon scientists or religionists, let us by the help of historical reference try to improve our understanding of this epoch-making controversy. To begin with, we must bear in mind the different primary emphases of the religious and of the scientific mind. Such a difference of accent arises very naturally from the work which each undertakes to perform. As of old, religion concentrates upon the problem of human values in their ultimate significance. The sciences, on the other hand, seek to understand the order of nature, its laws and their meaning for human behavior. "Knowledge is power," said Bacon. "To see in order to foresee," wrote Comte, the inaugurator of the era of the social sciences. In our historical perspective the religionist has been bent upon coming to terms with deity, with human destiny. Hence the issue of dependable knowledge never got out into the open on the same level of concern. Likewise, the scientist has been so extensively absorbed in checking observation and experiment — in the extension of one kind of knowledge — that he has scarcely seen the human problem in its total context.

Just this intensification and specialization of interest has characterized the vitality of both religion and the sciences. But just as surely has it opened the door to abuse in both directions. With most of us concentration of interest means constriction, if not outright distortion, of perspective. During the modern era, in respect of both religious and scientific development, one principle has gradually emerged with increasing clarity. So far it has received scant recognition. The principle can be stated briefly: A discussion of knowledge theory implicates a theory of reality and vice versa. The two problems are logically inseparable and their solutions mutually qualifying. As one problem is set and interpreted, so is the other, *by implication*. We have been too slow at seeing this principle clearly enough, during these centuries so fateful for our Western world. If, on one hand, the sciences have kept to the fore questions about the nature, extent, and dependability of human knowledge, they were also and at the same time by implication working at a theory of reality. If, on the other hand, Christian thinkers proclaimed a faith in the nature and purposes of God in respect of the cosmos, human history, and man's destiny, they were also and implicitly claiming a solution of the problem of human understanding. Now, in view of the peculiar character of the solutions to these two problems which have been formulated during these centuries, it is perfectly clear why the so-called conflict between religion and the sciences has become steadily more acute. Until the outlook of each of these great disciplines has been modified by a clearer understanding of what is logically involved, the warfare of these ideologies will go on.[2] Otherwise, only by the mutilation of the one or the other can the conflict be resolved. Is there any doubt about which course is being taken by Western civilizations?

IV

Historically considered the incompatibility of scientific knowledge and religious faith remains deep-seated. Simple solutions which continue to fail are a commonplace. We are not now concerned with them. Our attention must be given to the basal commitments of modern ways of thinking. Above all, the modern mind registers the impact of the sciences. It moves ahead in confidence that in principle a method of dependable knowledge has been worked out. What remains, according to this view, consists primarily in the extensive application of scientific method. All experience awaits its illumination. If religious faith fails or refuses to march in order, the responsibility lies not with the sciences.

There is doubtless much truth in this main contention. Is there not also much ambiguity? If we watch closely, it will become apparent that scientific method shuttles between the meaning of attitude and the meaning of technique; between method employed by the sciences and conclusions offered by a naturalistic philosophy. Let us make a beginning by turning to prominent historic tendencies. The first extensive expression of religious thinking under the direction of scientific method was the view finally worked out in eighteenth century English deism. Encouraged by Newton and Descartes educated minds conceived the physical universe as a vast machine, mathematically accurate in structure and functioning. Going thus through scientific nature to God, they arrived at God, the First Great Cause. Only a kind of intoxication produced by a passion for scientific method could have concealed the self-contradictory nature of this procedure. But it remained for the reasoning of Hume to disclose how impossible it is to associate the Christian God with a mathematical neutralism developed as an illegitimate extension of scientific methodology. Little did Hume realize what he contributed to the integrity of modern thought in his demolishing stroke at natural theology. " The whole of natural theology," he wrote, " resolves itself into one simple, though somewhat ambiguous, at least undefined, proposition: That the cause or causes of order in the universe probably bear some remote analogy to human intelligence." [3] At any rate, he added, the proposition signifies little or nothing for the human conduct of life.

Confronted by the scheme of natural religion, the greatest of the apologists, Bishop Butler, sought to eke out some consolation by dilating upon the moral government of the world. That approach was only propaedeutic to his main theme. Christianity contains also " a revelation to a particular dispensation of Providence, carrying on by his Son and Spirit, for the recovery and salvation of mankind." No one, I take it, would willingly undertake to defend in detail this eighteenth century version of Christianity. It has, however, two notable merits. First, it recognizes the relevance of a scientific theory of nature within a religious philosophy of life. Second, it disputes the claim of a naturalistic philosophy to give an adequate account of spiritual man and of reality as a whole.

Under these double attacks, from within and from without, natural religion, constituting the triumph of scientific method, was destined to revamp its outlook. What had actually happened was that a scientific outlook had first become transposed into a naturalistic philosophy, and so lost its standing as science; and then, as it developed a critical analysis of its epistemology, headed straight into agnosticism. As Windelband has so appropriately remarked: "The natural religion of the eighteenth century sought in morals the support which a metaphysics of the natural-science sort could not permanently afford it." [4] Backward toward medievalism it could not go, for there reason was laced in the straitjacket of a revealed faith. Now reason had been liberated once and for all from those ingenious uses of reasoning as a means of destroying reason. Within that standpoint of untouchable dogmas it is a travesty to speak of a philosophy of religion. So with reason still partially enslaved now by a specific development of scientific methodology, natural religion sought escape via the newer Religion of Humanity. Heretofore religion had been regarded as a relationship to an ontologically objective order. In the new context of the positive philosophy, religion is redefined as devotion, with the character of the object left undetermined. This nineteenth century development, however, carries us ahead of our story. In order to understand more fully this historical development, we must go back and pick up threads of the logic which operated in scientific epistemology and in metaphysical theory.

v

When Christian thinking became the agreeable companion of the sciences of the eighteenth century it embarked upon a self-defeating experiment. What were some of the more salient reasons for the outcome? Historical developments only illustrate an implicit logic fundamental to the so-called scientific mind. That mind obtained its most significant philosophical formulation in two major tend-encies: First, in the rationalism of Descartes and Spinoza; second, by the empiricism of Locke and Hume. The two tendencies have much more in common than is usually rec-ognized. Their boundary lines were surveyed and estab-lished by the scientific method. Philosophy meant to expli-cate scientific ideas and to collaborate in their metaphysical implications. Let us summarize these developments in the briefest manner possible, beginning with rationalism.

Descartes and Spinoza made rationalism the philosophi-cal embodiment of the logic of contemporary science. This setup began with the Cartesian dictum: " All knowledge is of the same nature throughout, and consists solely in com-bining what is self-evident." To the huge assumptions not indicated in this statement, there was added a theory of di-rect perception as a medium of knowledge about nature. As a matter of course rationalism ended in a philosophical neutralism, from which all values had been excluded by hy-pothesis. Four main steps sufficed to accomplish this result. First, philosophy became transposed into a restricted epis-temology, a pure cognitionism. Second, the whole proce-dure was dominated by a mathematical logic. Third, the knowledge problem was set so as to isolate the mind from reality. On one side of a chasm was located a bottomless well of ideas; on the other, entity objects were posited. Sub-sequently, mind spent its ingenuity in trying to bridge the artificial barrier. Fourth, rationalism proceeded, surrepti-tiously or otherwise, to leave the scientist-philosopher out-side of the scheme of nature so interpreted. Within this contextual neutralism rationalism could continue to use the language of religion only because the terms had acquired an entirely new meaning. With admirable candor Spinoza spoke of religion as contemplation of the mathematical world order. But plainly, the term God, used as a name for logical stability, the geometrical necessity from which all events flow, differs radically from the object of religious devotion.

In respect of form, empiricism stands opposed to rationalism. Intentionally it was that, as Locke's famous indictment of innate ideas reminds us. All knowledge, he said, originates in experience. But what is meant by experience? Essentially the answer is found in the proposition: *the ultimate in experience is a perception.* That basal idea Hume accepted from the Lockean tradition. With allowance for shift in accent, empiricism is now encamped next to rationalism. First, philosophy means a restricted epistemology. It is based upon infallible intuition in sensation and in reflection. Second, the mathematical method and ideal of certainty remained in full charge. Third, a fundamental breach between the knower and the object was assumed and left unbridged. Hume's skepticism arrived in due course mainly because primary dependence was located on the subject side of experience. Accordingly empiricism transposed theory of knowledge into a psychological relativism. On that basis Hume questioned our knowledge of nature and sought to reduce the principle of causality to psychological association. Finally, the nature and status of man was radically changed. Theoretically he became more completely immersed in " scientific nature," whereas functionally the scientific philosopher remained outside the scheme in order to make experience possible.

Following through on the same general line, Hartleyan

psychology and utilitarian ethics grafted on to empiricism the valuation aspect of experience. Grafted is the word, because of the two incompatible logics involved. Evolutionism eked out the laws of association and carried forward the naturalization of conscience. Gradually the ideal of scientific understanding shifted toward prediction and operational control of human affairs. An economic, social, and political liberalism joined with the spirit of revolt expressed in romanticism. Conditions were ripening for a rejuvenated empiricism under the name of positivism. Metaphysics in the old sense was discarded. The function and scope of the sciences were immensely enlarged for the nineteenth century perspective. Human values, no longer excluded from the purview of the scientific understanding, are reinterpreted in terms of a thoroughgoing naturalistic philosophy. Indeed, religion now functions as the handmaid of scientific theory.

Christianity within the context of the modern mind as formulated by continental rationalism, English empiricism, and nineteenth century positivism can be characterized by four successive shifts in point of view. First, many of its orthodox dogmas about God's relation to the world order and about revelation were rendered definitely passé. The old science with which religious views had been associated was once for all displaced. Second, deism as the scientific religious outlook of the enlightened mind first achieved the status of orthodoxy, and then succumbed to a combination of agnosticism and philosophical neutralism. Comte only disclosed its nakedness when he pointed out that such a religious view means the substitution of the social sciences for Newtonian science as the locus of dependable religious knowledge. This shift represented sufficient gain in perspective to conceal what had actually taken place. Third, religion was by agnostic tendencies brought nearer to the human scene. By the same process it was transformed into a devotionism, with an indefinite status for the object of devotion. Intensity of commitment is what counts for most. Recent nontheistic humanism embodies the newer logic in its mature form. So-called religions of science, of nationalism, of professional skill, or of business efficiency are only cheap imitations. Finally, with the coming of the historical-evolutionary point of view, Christianity was forced in dead earnest to re-evaluate its entire historic tradition. Biblical criticism was followed by interpretations in terms of the sciences of anthropology, psychology, and sociology. Consequently Christianity as a way of living has faced increasingly a chaotic world — a world made inhospitable mainly by the misuse of the sciences. Today dogmatism, confusion, self-contradiction, and evasion are all juggling for position. Meantime Christianity is growing older. It is by no means certain that Christians are growing up. The hot winds of naturalistic philosophies of life sweep across the entire field. To what extent are we aware of what is actually going on?

VI

In this discussion I am assuming that our religious situation has been shaped in large part by the basal scientific thought-forms of the past three hundred years. During that time the sciences have developed, expanded, and come into their own. We are still trying to understand them, and so learn to use them relevantly. One thing is plain: the sciences have accentuated the problems both of knowledge and of the nature of reality. Philosophies have developed divergent tendencies within this climate of a scientific age. Religious thinking as a matter of course participates in the ongoing argument.

Having sketched briefly the impact of the scientific modes of thought upon the Christian religion, and noted some of the demands made for its reinterpretation in the temper of conformity to the logic of the sciences, we must now turn to one of the greatest liberating influences in the entire situation. With Kant the most thoroughgoing Copernican revolution in modern thought gathered momentum. Kant was, first of all, and in terms of his own age, a great scientist. Although educated as a rationalist, he was thoroughly captivated by the magic of scientific methodology in the new turn which empiricism gave to it. Incidentally his enthusiasm helped to crystallize one of the most unfortunate dogmas of the modern mind; namely, that scientific method yields the only form of valid knowledge possible. But Kant was also a great seminal thinker. He drove a wedge into knowledge theory and at length made room for value-judgments alongside and on a logical parity with cognitional judgment.[5] In its attempts to understand our cosmos, the mind has been forced to construct two fundamentally different sets of categories. We may not draw the lines exactly where Kant did. Yet the distinction is required of every mind sufficiently awake to see the absurdity of forcing human values into molds designed to deal with physical-mathematical objects. If one harbors a prejudice against all forms of dualism, he must still reckon with the structure of experience. After Kant had turned nature over to the working principles of mathematical physics, he undertook to work out another set of categories for the spiritual side of human experience. In short, he inaugurated a critical philosophy of scientific method. He paved the way for a treatment of values and of valuation on a parity with nature and cognition. In these two steps Kant opened a way for spiritual man to escape the prison house of "scientific nature," where a reductionistic naturalism had confined him. Not that Kant realized fully the implications of what he started. Indeed, in the first *Critique,* he repeatedly emphasized the purely "regulative" function of the "ideas of reason." Nevertheless, Kant sees clearly that certain "regulative ideas of reason" must be employed, symbolically of course, as necessary co-implicates of experience. So much is required if we are to speak meaningfully about such things as knowledge, morality, religion. In principle Kant is here recognizing the inadequacy of *experience* in the restricted sense of English empiricism. What he makes abundantly clear is that the mind employs two radically different sets of concepts in dealing with the double aspects of experience. By emphasizing the new freedom or significance of mind, Kant made inroads upon the territory of naturalistic thinking that were destined to do it irreparable damage. Henceforth valuation is to be recognized as bona fide judgment. It may remain for our century to claim distinction by clarifying this Kantian insight with respect to the status of values.

After Kant, the reverberations in the religious world gradually accumulated about two tendencies. First, a wave of consternation and even despair swept the field; and second, mainly through Kant, men began to build a truly empirical faith. With respect to the first count, three main reasons operate. On one side of his thinking Kant appeared to confirm a growing mountain of evidence, which two centuries of uncritical use of scientific methodology had built, in favor of a naturalistic metaphysics. In the second place, Kant's doctrine of regulative ideas apparently demolished two of Christianity's cardinal doctrines. Seemingly, after the manner of Hume, Kant had rocketed God and immortality beyond the reach of scientific understanding. The great difference was that Kant knew what he was about. When he " destroyed knowledge to make room for faith," he only pointed out the fundamental error of trying to interpret religion exclusively in terms of a restricted scientific understanding. This is the fundamental error of all naturalistic philosophies of religion. Their truncated notions of religion are strewn across the centuries. In our time one living variety remains pre-eminent. William James, a typical product of scientific methodology, with just a measure of the Kantian genius, trained Christians of his generation to poise on the springboard of passionate belief and leap into the beautiful isle of nowhere. Why? Because he saw only one-half of what Kant understood. He partly realized the inappropriateness of trying to go all the way through religious experience with the categories of the sciences. But for James these scientific concepts alone yielded valid knowledge. Hence religion had to be content with a second-rate " practical knowledge," whereas Kant had recourse to another kind of genuine knowledge. The vast difference between these positions is suggested by a thought-provoking sentence from Morris R. Cohen: " The pragmatic glorification of belief contains the deep poison of scepticism as to what really exists, and thus like a Nessus shirt will destroy any religious belief that puts it on." [6]   Finally the Kantian antithesis between naturalistic metaphysics and religion appeared to isolate religion from the modern mind.

With respect to the Kantian attempt to found religious faith upon an "empirical" base, a second and very different type of reaction emerged. Kant was right, as Hume was right, in rejecting every current empirical approach to religion that was restricted to a manipulation of sense perceptions within a methodology designed by eighteenth century rationalism. To such a naturalistic metaphysical theory the spirit of religion stands unalterably opposed. Deism and a religion of positivistic humanism are counterfeit products of a scientific imagination gone astray. Accordingly, Kant repudiated prevailing scientific interpretations of religion. They were no more acceptable than speculative orthodoxy. He saw through them all, and beyond. Kant's fresh start followed the empirical road of an ethical theology. First, he reversed the order of dependence between ethics and theology. A theological ethics he held to be wrong in principle. It deduced ethics from a speculative theological tradition in which moral experience has functioned incidentally or not at all. Besides, the road to certainty in religion starts with the datum of moral experience. In the second place, Kant repudiated the religious outlook which later found a voice in positivistic humanism. There moral principles are at bottom a form of human agreement. Morality means mores. In it man is a child of organic nature, with an added flair for social discontent. Oddly enough, man is captivated by an ideal called universal ethical community, social welfare, the good of humanity, et cetera. Combine social good with a vague evolutionism and the appeal seems irresistible.

That outlook on Kantian principles comprises an unintelligible view of morality, and hence involves a counterfeit religion.

Kant's own version of moral experience stood at the opposite pole from utilitarianism. He began by assuming the competence of moral judgment in respect of reality. If duty is a rational command, one that is categorically binding, then reality is of such a nature as to support the moral quest and justify it. There are two reasons why Kant thought this position sound. First, the moral law lays hold upon our rational as against our sensuous nature. Second, moral achievement implicates a relationship with a trans-natural environment of objective moral values. Religion is at least " the recognition of all duties as divine commands." Epistemologically, moral facts come first. Logically, the spiritual order which generates morality has priority. Morality and religion are two ways of stating the cosmic significance of human life on its spiritual side. The taproot of this view is found in the primacy of practical reason, our valuational consciousness. Here lies the beginning of the view in which spiritual value takes priority over " existence." Religious thought then carries the cosmocentric accent of historic Christianity, divested of its unscientific and unphilosophical accretions. Experience is taken in its full-orbed meanings. With man's moral restlessness begins the surest empirical road to God. For Kant, God is primarily and essentially the author and maintainer of the universal moral order.

VII

In Kant's idea of man as an intrinsic moral personality, and of intrinsic value as the frame of reference for interpreting reality, we find the fundamental contention of subsequent idealistic philosophy. Its liberating influence upon the modern mind has been incalculable, yet insufficient to dislodge a prevailingly dominant naturalistic outlook. In the main, then, the carry-over of naturalism has been potent enough to spread a bias over the religious situation in our time. Current interpretations of Christianity should be evaluated with this fact clearly in mind. That fact, too, should be reflected in the form which discussions of the religious problem assume. Modern naturalism engages religion in a life-and-death struggle precisely because each takes a different category as primary. Naturalism sets out to delineate the world as " existence." Religion construes the world as a value-order with existence as a subordinate category. Whether in its symbolism of act or of thought, religion sets out with a fundamental distinction between existence and value, and with the primacy conceded to the spiritual. And this claim launches not only a psychological value-consciousness, but also and more especially an epistemological interpretation of reality as a spiritual whole. Indeed, religion in its deepest aspect is incurably metaphysical in character. Let us examine these ideas more carefully by looking at the three types of propositions which religion employs.

To begin with, religion contains a doctrine of the world order. Even a cursory study of religious symbolism shows how naturally and profoundly the religious man acknowledges his kinship with nature. His first lesson appears to be that of dependence upon his cosmic surroundings. Nature marks at least the beginnings of his environment. For him nature is a life-giving and a death-dealing power. Sun worship, for instance, constitutes a center for a widely diffused ritual. In conjunction with earth, the sun comes to be regarded as a main source of fertility. Its light and warmth suggest the source of life-giving spirits. Further expression of the principle of fertility abounds in the fecundity of sex relations on both the animal and the human levels. Evidences of phallic worship are found as indigenous expressions of the life-giving principle among grazing and agricultural peoples. At length the gods are symbolized in terms of parenthood. Accordingly, myths of creation assume a variety of form. One of the most penetrating expressions is found in the Christian doctrine of *creatio ex nihilo*. Greek and Hebrew myth, for example, lingered at the level where the gods were at most instigators of order in the cosmos. Some of the later Hebrew prophets stopped at the threshold of outright creation. Isaiah declared, "I am Jehovah and there is none else. I form the light and create darkness; I make peace and create evil; I am Jehovah that doeth all these things." [7] Centuries later, in opposition to the dualism of the Gnostics, Irenaeus formulated a very definite and advanced notion: "While men indeed cannot make anything out of nothing but only out of matter already existing, yet God is in this point pre-eminently superior to men, that he himself called into being the substance of his creation, when previously it had no existence." Augustine proceeded to make the conception of absolute creation, "out of nothing," a central doctrine. Making allowance for linguistics, we have here one of the cardinal ideas of a Christian theism.

Clearly, the interest of the doctrine of creation out of nothing is the religious and philosophical idea of the relation of

God to the world order. The manner in which it has been misapplied as a scientific theory through the centuries falls little short of tragedy. Within the tradition of Christianity creation became associated with the biblical account taken in its literal and temporal meaning. Modern theories of organic evolution have practically added the stroke of mercy to this process, mainly by forcing a recognition of the double nature of the creation idea. Creation as a chapter in methodological explanation is one thing; as a philosophical principle by which the order of nature becomes an integral part of the universe in its entirety, it has a very different connotation. Religious symbolism looks in the latter direction. It represents a distinctive attempt to interpret nature as a *dependent* aspect of a universal spiritual life. God's creatorship simply declares that nature is not a self-sufficient and self-explanatory absolute, but rather finds its ground and meaning in an ultimate value or purposeful order.

The second type of proposition deals with divine acts in history and in relation to human destiny. In Christianity the symbolism of creation finds its inseparable counterpart in what theologians have called providence. Although the religious person recognizes his kinship with nature, he is unable to segmentize the universe so as to isolate the natural order from the course of history and from the entire human adventure. In providence, then, creationism goes the limit in making God responsible for the world. The main difference appears when in providential history God accepts a new status for man within the created order. Man is essentially a will related to divine willing. Creation now becomes an activity at least analogous to willing. Purpose, freedom, communication of meaning, cooperation and persuasion are elements in a divine-human adventure. At this level the creature, in opposition to the doctrine of emanation, stands in relation to God as alienated or reconciled. The shift or elevation is clearly from power unqualified, not only toward will, but especially toward benevolent will.

Within this context the time element recedes. History becomes more genuinely the march of God's purposefulness. Dispensations and "the fullness of time" are rather more meaningful. Augustine's quip about what God was doing before he began to create the world has special point, when we see that "making a hell for the inquisitive" stresses purposeful activity, and not the matter of a local when. Two sets of concepts are here involved and they move in two different worlds of discourse. Kant's first antinomy about creation rests upon their confusion. History is less a succession of events and more a spiritual process within which the meaningful purposes of God are working out his will. For that reason early Christians very appropriately looked upon the incarnation of Jesus as at once the true beginning of history and also its culmination. "God was in Christ Jesus reconciling the world. . . ." Reconciliation marks the new level of relationship. Hebraic messianism, apocalypticism and Christologies are versions of the one idea which seeks to interpret the special kind of divine immanence present in the acts of history. And history becomes par excellence a relationship with perfect personality who is also *ens realissimum*.

We are now confronted with a most difficult problem: the consummation of history as divine purpose. To some degree, we have seen, the ideas of creation and of providence tend to merge. When that happens the idea of destiny

makes its appearance. For man destiny is commonly symbolized in the idea of immortality, or better, in an eternal
and divine kingdom of life. Most important is the idea that
when reality is construed on the plane of history as a purposive or value whole, the question of finality necessarily
comes up. Process and goal are inseparable aspects of one
meaningful life. Religious symbolism seeks to convey the
idea that internal finality is a truncated notion. The events
of human history constitute only the stage for the divine
drama. This is not a puppet show, however. For, as we saw,
the relationship at the level of providence in history expresses
all the freedom of willing — benevolent or otherwise. Only
through the idea of incarnation Christianity affirms the final
consummation of the world in and through a perfectly
righteous will of God. Finality is transcendent or it is
nothing.[8]

Already we have penetrated to the third type of religious
judgment, namely, that concerning the nature of God. Why
not? If our approach has been in the best sense empirical,[9]
questions about the nature of God are directly implicated in
the doctrines of creation and providence. Epistemologically,
at least, we always begin with phenomena, with reality in
its manifold expressions. That principle holds in religion.
We know only the God who meets us through the fragments
of experience. While the God-concept represents religion's
attempt to interpret the ultimate meaning of reality, we do
not begin at the destination of religious thinking. And if
our steps are to mark advance they must be taken with due
caution.

If that be true, then the question concerns not the " existence " of God, but his nature. Strictly, it is meaningless

to ask, Is there a God? All thinking presupposes, in a minimum sense, that reality is a meaningful order. The only rational question becomes, What is the nature of that order? In religious terms, What is the *nature* of God? A reference to the familiar cosmological and teleological arguments will illustrate. The former avowedly sought to establish the existence of God. By the accepted principle of causality it moved to God as the First Great Cause of the world order. Questions of validity are aside. Within the context of a given world of discourse, the argument set out to find an end to the chain of causation, to find an " existent " God. Our interest lies in the discovery of the inseparability of the " existence " and the nature of God. Even as " existence " God had to assume the character of omnipotence, and at least a measure of intelligence. Just this shift in the real issue is exemplified by its proximity to the teleological argument. As a complement to the cosmological argument the central point in question became, What characteristics or attributes can properly be applied to God? Quite unintentionally the problem had carried these apologists beyond their limited starting point, had in fact shifted from the existential frame of reference to the value standpoint.

That shift appears to be of the greatest importance, and that for three main reasons. In the first place, as the two traditional arguments for God remind us, the concept of experience is enlarged to include values and valuation — the spiritual activities which constitute man as a distinctive level within reality. Properly understood, the older ontological argument looks in this same direction. As modern intelligentsia we have found it too easy to echo Kant's gibes at the ontological argument. A better judgment, however, shows that the argument is trying to express a confident outreach of human experience to take the full measure of reality in its wholeness. This enlarged concept of experience, and the confidence in reason to interpret reality which underlies it, receives at our hands a different formulation. Moving away from the Kantian form of a priori, we nevertheless acknowledge trans-perceptual elements throughout all experience. "Necessary presuppositions of all thinking" may strike us as an improvement in language. Or, with Urban, the form may be improved by the phrase, "co-implicates of experience." But the significant idea is the expansion of the concept "experience" in acknowledgment of its spiritual aspect. The change, be it noted, is not merely one of inclusiveness, but stresses an order of significance. The fact that these spiritual elements, which we call "values," are disclosed as indispensable conditions for the understanding of experience in the more restricted senses, points to a certain logical primacy that belongs to them within the ordered whole of experience. Here we have come upon the prime characteristic alike of the spirit of philosophy and of religion. God becomes that most significant concept in religious thinking, in recognition of the continuous expansiveness of experience and more especially of its essentially spiritual character.

The second reason why the transition from the existential to the value standpoint marks an advance is that the shift cuts across our common-sense bias in favor of the physical. Nowhere is that bias more plainly or persistently revealed than in the restricted view of experience as perceptual experience. That tradition was first formulated clearly in the Lockean interpretation. It has formed the core of "empiricism" throughout the entire range of the history of the sciences and of scientific philosophy. In many areas its provisional use has been fully justified. Its final indictment, however, is to be sought in the fact that empiricism in that restricted sense and as a philosophical principle cannot account for itself; it must always draw upon excluded principles or remain unintelligible. The absurd length to which such thinking can go finds ample illustration in the closing sentences of Hume's *Enquiry Concerning the Human Understanding*. They memorialize in a simple manner the self-stultification process in human thinking at this level:

If we take in our hand any volume of divinity or school metaphysics, for instance, let us ask, does it contain any abstract reasoning concerning quantity or number? No. Does it contain any experimental reasoning concerning matter of fact and existence? No. Commit it to the flames, for it can contain nothing but sophistry and illusion.

It takes the candor of a Hume to unmask the bias involved in such an idea of experience.

In the third place, the movement from the existential to the value standpoint emphasizes the necessarily symbolic character of religious language.[10] Consequently all our thought on the nature of God as the supreme value which is also ultimate reality must be carried on through the use of symbolic terms. When we speak of the wisdom or grace or goodness of God we employ symbols which, as it were, say, "God is not wholly in me, I only point the direction." For it is characteristic of a symbol that it both does and does not claim to be adequate to the truth about its object. It stands on the advanced threshold of human understanding and points up the highway toward completeness. In this respect religious symbolism stands on a parity with scientific and philosophical symbols. By reason of the spiritual nature of its object, religion has come to be more frankly and avowedly open in its use of them. In this it has seemed to part company with the sciences which dote on "existence." For the same reason religion must break with naturalism as an "existential" construction of reality. Along with certain philosophies religious thought has transcended strict adherence to the limits of existential experience in favor of a value-oriented construction.

Since the work of Kant no thinker should have been indiscreet enough to insist upon the *literal* character of religious terms. The reason has become plain. Our language is constructed on the contour of things — in Bergson's phrase, on the "pattern of solids." Shall we, then, after extending our concept of experience to make room for religious values, cancel the process and reverse ourselves to the extent of translating values into existential terms? Thereby God, for instance, is made in the image of things in a space-time causal order. That is what literalism proposes. Another alternative view hesitates to perpetrate that kind of absurdity. Instead it proposes one of two solutions. According to one version, language expresses nothing but emotion. In that case religious sentences cannot be taken literally, or even symbolically, because they are not bona fide judgments, being purely emotive in character. Religious activities are therefore an emotional cleansing. A second version of reductionistic positivism suggests that the object of religious experience is not *the* Deity, but a certain "quality of deity," a kind of pervading presence in the phenomenal world or a special way of looking at "experience." This notion of deity as an emergent quality, on the one hand, only thinly disguises its nature as a name for an aspect of the natural order; on the other, its qualitative character hints at the transcendent nature of the divine. Hereabout lie sound reasons for suspecting many so-called empirical approaches to religion. They consort with a variety of truncated theories of religious language such as: literalism, the emotive theory, the behavior theory, conceptualism, value-nominalism, or some variety of self-authenticating mysticism. The situation will in all probability be unimproved until our slavery to the "existential" concepts has been abolished.

VIII

The patent inadequacy of these alternative proposals leaves us confronted with the datum of religious values, with a claim to a trans-perceptual dimension of human experience. Consequently, the old double-edged question returns in all its urgency. What is the nature of reality, and can our knowledge of it attain validity? If the symbolic nature of religious language be granted, we are better prepared to deal with the spiritual side of human experience. As we have pointed out, God is the highest (moral) perfection that is also ultimately real. Such appears to be the claim of the religious consciousness. That idea the stubborn vitality of the ontological argument endeavors to reach and to clarify. Symbolism is made necessary as a way of articulating the drive of the religious consciousness to come to terms with reality in its perfect wholeness. For that role of interpretation empiricism in the usually restricted sense has shown itself wholly inadequate. As Kant made abundantly clear, so-called "empirical" proofs for God can go only a little way, and when illegitimately applied, border on the absurd.

Still, the rejection of traditionally empirical proofs is not enough. Two most formidable issues remain. If with the aid of religious symbols we endeavor to interpret the divine, the trans-perceptual or metempirical aspect of experience, with what evidence shall the interpretation proceed? Upon what sort of foundation does it rest? What is to prevent symbolic interpretation from degenerating into unrestricted fancy? A second closely associated type of question presses for an answer. Is religious symbolism unique? If so, how does it differ from other types of value symbolism? What is its relationship to moral symbolism, for example? In short, in what terms may the divine be most adequately characterized?

At least four alternative ways of answering the first type of question are possible. First, one might attempt to rehabilitate some form of empirical knowledge by employing the traditional concepts of restrictive empiricism. In it religious symbols are transposed into the concomitant perceptual elements of experience. This procedure betrays a bias in favor of the actual in which values are reduced to the existential. Throughout history attempts of this kind have assaulted the religious life. Always their inadequacies have brought distortion of the facts. If our previous discussion has been at all going in the right direction, this way is closed to us.

A second alternative follows a current notion among religionists to the effect that religious faith has no need of "natural or logical witness." Outside evidence is not desirable. Religion is rooted in an act of faith. The judgments of faith validate themselves in terms of practical consequences. The appeal to consequences takes many forms: renewed confidence in life, a certain buoyancy of spirit, an emotional glow, more satisfactory social, business, or professional adjustments, a certain kind of moral transformation. Now, on closer examination the plausibility of this approach evaporates, and for many reasons. To begin with, it appears to identify evidence with "natural or logical witness," while at the same time it implies that religious faith is self-authenticating. Nevertheless an appeal is made to ambiguous varieties of evidence which in turn opens the door to all the fallacies of false attribution. Then, too, a religion that rests upon an act of faith should arouse suspicion. On the face of it, the whole procedure looks like evading the bothersome feature of evidence. At any rate such faith is subject to barometric changes, made dependent upon the general conditions of the liver. Here the door to subjective determination of the knowledge process stands wide open. The divine may be fashioned in the image of man's prudential wishes. The objective conditions of human understanding are minimized, if not overlooked. Against this setting of the situation the so-called argument from consequences avails little. Drugs cautiously administered would produce effects similar to, in some cases identical with, those attributed to religious faith. Finally, this "act of faith" plausibly begins with a minimal proposition "that God exists," that the religious consciousness embodies a meaningful distinction or judgment. To this assumption assent might readily be given. Certainly it is true that religious faith constitutes a claim to be investigated. Properly understood the contention is of one piece with a presupposition of all experience whatsoever, viz., that the universe or reality is a rationally ordered or meaningful whole. But incautious religionists surreptitiously inject a second and very different proposition which says that God is righteous love. The two propositions are by no means identical. The first presupposes a real object of genuine faith; the second claims to have discovered the basal content of faith. The second claim may be substantiated only by exploring the nature of the object of that faith. It must not be simply taken for granted.

A third alternative bearing upon the verification of religious judgment appeals to the testimony and authority of distinguished religious persons. A note of authenticity rings through the " Thus saith the Lord " of the prophetic mind. Throughout the Christian tradition the idea of a divine initiative has prevailed. Men were to wait and hear what the divine seeks to communicate. Woe to the man whose eyes are holden that he may not see, whose ears are dulled that he cannot hear and whose heart is hardened that he understands not at all! The divine initiative speaks in creation, providence, the incarnation, and last but not least, in " the witness of the Holy Spirit " as an inseparable companion of the sensitive and questing soul. Undoubtedly the value of this approach is very great, when employed with proper safeguards. It lies open to abuse in two directions. First, it has been used as the pretext of false prophets and pseudo-saints. The witness of the Holy Spirit in a man must be tested. Second, organized religion ofttimes usurps the authority of divine revelation by exploiting the words of the prophet. In this direction lies authoritarianism of the lowest variety. But more especially, let it be clearly understood that the testimony of the prophet or saint carries proper authority only when and because his word obtains validation in critical experience, not because the word is *his*. Except God speaks, *his* word will be in vain.

We have now come to a fourth alternative. From Plato on a notable line of thinkers have pointed out how, in its deeper logic, experience discloses a unitary nature. This nisus toward a coherent unity expresses more than a subjective bias of the human mind. In it our thinking has rather submitted to a constraint that is cosmic in import. If this be something like the truth about our situation, then religious judgment becomes a strand within the whole fabric of experience, and religious faith or knowledge must submit to the same critical, slow, and gradual processes by which any fragment of human understanding acquires validation. In which case a religious judgment stands poles apart from a self-authenticating or mysterious intuition. Rather does it constitute, like any other judgment, a rational claim to interpret the meaning of its object. Every judgment of faith continually submits itself to correction and supplementation first by other religious judgments, and then, in principle, by all fragments of human knowledge whatsoever. The process of mutual correction sets out from phenomena next of kin, and proceeds in appropriate degree in the direction of complete comprehensiveness. Hence religious knowledge dawns by degrees, submits, with proper qualifications, to the general conditions of the knowledge-process, and never comes to self-stultification by reaching a wooden finality. It is then prepared to profit by all relevant evidence by which it is confronted. No genuine fragment of human understanding can be altogether foreign to it. In short, faith constitutes a claim to a specific kind of knowledge, and accepts withal the consequences of that claim. Accordingly the three methods of religious knowledge just mentioned are not so much false as they are fragmentary conclusions which are set in a false perspective.

The one question about which we need some illumination is at once the most difficult and the most important. Is there a limiting or compulsory element within religious symbolism? What arrests the imaginative tendencies of the religious mind and holds it to the hard task of interpreting wholly under the constraint of what constitutes the ineluctable data within experience? In other words, what prevents religious symbolism from degenerating into wish-thinking, and constrains it to be guided wholly by the nature of the divine as objectively given? Frankly I do not see how that question can be discussed with any degree of adequacy within the limits at our disposal. I propose therefore to rest for the time being with two brief suggestions, one general and the other specific.

First of all, the question seems to be only a special form of the most decisive issue which all knowledge disciplines confront. Whether in the realm of common-sense opinion, in the sciences, or in philosophy, we employ figurative language to some degree. Or, if you choose, we think symbolically. Always, then, the issue stands before us: How control the symbolic element in human thinking so that the interpretative process yields genuine understanding of the situation? My *specific* suggestion is that the purification and control of any knowledge adventure represents a gradual achievement and is therefore not determined by a particular element, and that the process is carried on under the coherence principle. Let us take a typical example. One is introduced to an-

other person for the first time. What happens? Something
very complex. To begin with, one was introduced by a
friend. This fact in itself tells one many things about the
new acquaintance. Then, there is an occasion, social, business, or professional. That situation, too, makes a contribution. In conversation common interests are discovered. All
the while one observes the other person's facial expression,
his manner of speech, his dress and general bearing. And
so on, *ad libitum*. Human understanding employs manifold terms. The symbolic elements vary, but are always
present. All thinking has a history. It is time to recall that
scientific and philosophical symbols also have a history, even
as religious symbols have. Such history does not invalidate
them. Indeed, under the coherence principle, the enterprise
of human understanding goes forward by reason of that
history.

Our second formidable group of questions is concerned
with the distinctive nature of religious symbolism. Do religious values make a unique contribution, or are they only
a special dimension of experience in general? Here again,
in lieu of an entire volume and ability commensurate with
the task, this kind of ultimate question must go begging. I
can only recall certain significant possible alternatives. In
this connection the imposing suggestions of men like Ernst
Troeltsch and Rudolf Otto come to mind. The former proposes " the religious a priori consciousness " as an ultimate
reference for his religious epistemology. Hence for him, as
well as for Otto, religion is *sui generis*. In the language of
Otto it is a "numinous" experience, absolutely distinctive.
The divine impinges upon the soul of man as unqualified
Holiness. It awakens a sense of awe-ful-ness. Appropriate

response carries a double and contradictory current — a unique conjunction of terror and fascination. But a most interesting feature of this general standpoint of intuitionism is the manner in which this original divine-consciousness, "a qualitatively unique feeling-content, underivable and in that sense not evolvable," gradually yields its sovereign independence and becomes permeated by the rational and the moral aspects of experience.

A point of view which in some respects is very different finds notable expression in Hegel. According to this tradition religion is philosophy written in the language of parable or symbol. Perhaps I cannot do better than to quote from a kindred point of view, recently outlined by W. M. Urban in *Language and Reality*. What do religions, *as religion,* say? "In one form or another they all say the same thing. They all assert implicitly that values have cosmic significance, that value and reality are inseparable — the identity of the *summum bonum* or *ens perfectissimum* with the *ens realissimum.*" [11] What stands out for emphasis here is the innermost drive within religion to come to terms with ultimate reality. "The religious symbol is, then, in its essence — and epistemologically — metaphysical in character, although psychologically it is more akin to poetry." [12] Whatever else may properly be said about values, they have "ultimate metaphysical or ontological significance." Then, as if in the same breath, the religious spirit ventures to characterize that reality as a rational value-order. The value character of reality constitutes the first principle of intelligibility. Moreover, religion says that reality means value-perfection. The highest perfection of value realization in human experience symbolizes the nature of God. This point appears to be what Urban repeatedly stresses as "the categorical superiority of the good." [13]

Of special importance to both these points of view is the fact that they have at least three fundamental elements in common. First, both stress the ontological character of religion. Here man becomes aware that he is confronted by ultimate reality and he is determined to face it honestly. Second, the religious man lives in the assurance that genuine knowledge of the divine may somehow be obtained. The quest must and can go on in confidence. Third, both have special difficulty with the moral element. Intuitionism anxiously repudiates the relevance of morality only to be forced to retreat from that position. In somewhat the same temper Urban tries to locate the religious beyond the moral. "That the symbols function in a practical or moral context in no wise excludes the fact that their reference is beyond the human and the moral." [14] But almost immediately there follow assurances that, although religion reaches beyond our moral experience, "its authentication can take place only within that experience." [15] The reason, moreover, is plain and direct. Though not exclusively connected with the moral, it is "only in connection with the moral that the full religious quality is felt. It is only when the infinitely other fuses with the infinitely good that the full quality of deity is experienced." [16] In brief, what the history of religions seems to say is that, as Holiness comes to concretion, it is more and more bound up with moral goodness.

In Christian thinking there can be little doubt on this point. The eighth century Hebrew prophets stand out by reason of their moral elevation and accent. Jesus advances over them through excellence in moral insight and achievement. By following this line the highest characterization of God in Christianity maintains that God is perfectly righteous love. It is not necessary to argue where the richest concept of perfectly righteous love can be found. The important issue lies in the attempt thus to symbolize God.

The hesitancy which many religious thinkers express on this point and their attempts to go "beyond morality," depend largely, I believe, upon what morality is taken to be. Since the seventeenth century in the Western world there have developed influential naturalistic interpretations of morality. On that view morality means essentially a body of contractual agreements that have proven expedient under specific conditions of social life. With respect to such a restrictive view of morality Christian faith must move on "beyond." The reason is that such a truncated notion of morality falls far short of being morality, not that moral symbols are necessarily defective in relation to religion. Therefore I would like to suggest that a fusion of the ontological accent of Christianity with an adequate conception of morality might yield the very language — yes, and also the consummate experience and life — for which religious faith at its higher reaches has been seeking.

NOTES

[1] Alfred North Whitehead, *Science and the Modern World* (New York: The Macmillan Co., 1926), p. 1.

[2] " When we consider what religion is for mankind, and what science is, it is no exaggeration to say that the future course of history depends upon the decision of this generation as to the relations between them." — Whitehead, *op. cit.*, p. 260.

[3] *Dialogues Concerning Natural Religion*, Part XII.

[4] *History of Philosophy* (New York: The Macmillan Co., 1898), p. 500.

5 In the nature of the case it is impossible to follow through with Kant's discussion of this point. The distinction concerning two types of judgment is the important issue. It amounts to saying that we utilize two kinds of knowledge: cognition and valuation. That general contention appears in the following pages. Religious faith claims to be a form of knowledge which in principle stands on a parity with cognitional judgment.

6 *Reason and Nature* (New York: Harcourt, Brace & Co., 1931), p. 455.

7 Isa. 45:6–7.

8 Cf. the chapter on "Intelligible Finality" in Wilbur Marshall Urban's *The Intelligible World* (New York: The Macmillan Co., 1929), pp. 330 ff.

9 "Empirical" is a term which gives endless trouble. Usage follows a wide variety of meaning, culminating perhaps in the restricted notion of eighteenth century English empiricism and its affiliated versions of sense perceptionism.

10 See the excellent chapter in Urban's *Language and Reality* (New York: The Macmillan Co., 1939), pp. 571 ff.

11 Urban, *Language and Reality*, p. 622.

12 *Ibid.*, p. 381.

13 *Ibid.*, pp. 714 *et al.*

14 *Ibid.*, p. 603. Cf. p. 600.

15 *Ibid.*, p. 613.

16 *Ibid.*, p. 610.

THE KINGDOM OF GOD AND THE LIFE OF TODAY

CHESTER CHARLTON McCOWN

Pacific School of Religion

I. PRESENT TRENDS IN CHRISTIAN SOCIAL THINKING

A VIGOROUS reaction has set in against the social interpretation of the familiar phrase, "the kingdom of God." Whatever opinion may be held regarding the evidences of vision and leadership in the published preparatory volumes and official reports of the Oxford Conference of 1937 on church, community, and state and of the Madras Missionary Council of 1938, these publications may be taken as fairly representative of cautious and conscientious opinion within Protestantism. They indicate that a considerable body of intelligent Christians is moving backward toward the nineteenth century view that the kingdom of God is only within the soul and has no direct relation to practical social problems, while a yet larger body of extremely dogmatic conservatives is still marching around within the high stockades of Bengel's eighteenth century chiliasm in antiscientific and antisocial contempt of modern thought. The divided and uncertain mind of Protestantism could not be better illustrated.

Fortunately, when the two conferences escaped from theory and theology to face the world of today, they reached much more socially enlightened conclusions than some of the preliminary studies promised. In view of the sad retrogressions of the last decade, there is reason for hearty congratulation that both Oxford and Madras were as forward-looking as they were. Nevertheless, some of the preparatory discussions published in connection with both conferences are most disheartening exhibits of the debilitating confusion and pusillanimous defeatism from which the church now suffers.

In the Oxford Conference book on *The Kingdom of God and History* the two writers representing America, Lyman and Tillich, present the only historical and social interpretations of the kingdom of God which the book offers. The other writers conclude that in Jesus and his message the kingdom of God was fully "realized" (Dodd), that "it is the heavenly hope which is essential to Christianity" (Bevan), that, the world being totally and increasingly evil (*sic*), "the more 'Christian' the world, the more secular the church" (Wendland), that the "incarnation principle" involves, not the overthrow of evil, but "an increasing tension between the church and the world" (Dawson). In the Madras preparatory volume, Professor Kraemer wrote that "the kingdom of God is a transcendental, supra-historical order of life," while "this world is dominated by the forces of evil and is the object of divine wrath." [1]

There are not wanting statements in the Oxford volumes and the Madras report which reveal the persistence of still more naive theological notions based upon thoroughly literalistic, essentially pagan, and clearly unethical interpretations of the Scriptures. The logical outcome of the arguments of Kraemer, Wendland, Dawson, and the German delegates at Madras is the attitude which is recorded — with horror — by Professor Reinhold Niebuhr, of a German

Lutheran who had read Niebuhr's paper prepared for the Oxford Conference book on *Christian Faith and the Common Life*. The substance of this Lutheran criticism of the social application of Christianity was that human society is essentially and unavoidably opposed to Christianity. It necessarily demands the punishment of the guilty, not their forgiveness. It is built upon the " friend-enemy " relationship. The weak must not be allowed to dominate. They must be eliminated. Accordingly the Christian must witness against the world, but he is under no obligation to attempt to alter or improve it. The doctrine of " orders " allows the state to rule according to its laws, for " the powers that be are ordained of God." As Professor Niebuhr says, " If I thought for a moment that the Christian gospel meant what is implied in these words, I would prefer not to be a Christian. In such an interpretation, Christian eschatology becomes the source of moral complacency." [2]

Barthianism contributes its share toward theological obscurantism and social reaction. Its emphasis on the gulf between the church and the world inevitably implies that there is no hope of saving society. The logical outcome of its premises seems to be that the reign of God is now within the heart, in the individual life, and in the church, with no direct relation to society as such. The true, ultimate meaning of the idea is to be found in the final consummation, literally understood as depicted in the language of Jewish apocalypse.

It hardly need be said that according to the greater part of the views outlined above, the kingdom of God can have little relation to the life of today. In contrast to the vigorous social Christianity proclaimed by the official reports of the two conferences and by some of the writers in other Oxford

Conference books, especially by Archbishop Temple, Reinhold Niebuhr, and John Bennett in that on *Christian Faith and the Common Life,* it would seem that to considerable numbers of the most vocal leaders of thought in ecumenical Christianity, the good news of the imminence of the reign of God has degenerated into a *spes abscondita* resting upon a *dominus absconditus.* The Christians' Lord, as Doremus Scudder expressed it, is

> Directing campaigns grand
> On some removed coast
> Of Eternity's vast sea.

He is neither leading his hosts to wage relentless war on the demonic powers of earthly evil, " until he has put all his enemies under his feet," nor is he concerned with the conditions which cause the present catastrophic hatreds and conflicts between the classes, races, and nations of the earth. If he is present in the world at all, it is as the Comforter in men's hearts, not as the Judge of evil and injustice. The church, like the world, seems to be in the grip of an irresistible antisocial reaction.

II. CAUSES OF THE ANTISOCIAL REACTION

From three areas objections are raised to the social gospel — from the practical, the dogmatic, or theological, and the critical, or historical, sides. The objections which come from the practical side are the product of average, unregenerate human nature, of childish impatience and shortsightedness. The failure of evolution to set up the kingdom of God on earth before 1914, the inevitable post-war reaction of deceived and disillusioned altruism, and the evident inability of social service and social reform to save the world forthwith from its accumulating ills and evils, coincided to produce bitter disappointment. Events seem to have justified conservatives, cynics, and skeptics within and without the church in doubting the practicability of Christian ethics. The present world situation appears to prove that society cannot be saved.

The discredit into which social Christianity has fallen on the practical side reinforces the theoretical, or theological, objection, that, for the Christian, salvation is purely individual because man is a fallen creature and human society incurably tainted by his sinfulness. Extreme fundamentalists, adventists, and premillennialists have long insisted that all man-made schemes of social reform must wait upon the return of Christ on the clouds. Liberalism seems to be hamstrung by the present economic distress and the apparent collapse of democracy. The Calvinistic-Barthian emphasis on human depravity and the " otherness " of God has strongly reinforced the natural human propensity to avoid difficult tasks and wait for God to act. Social conservatism easily takes refuge in a dogmatic alibi and agrees that social reform is useless and hopeless because it is doctrinally discredited. Years ago Emil Brunner wrote, " Our slogan must be, . . . Away from the religion of the modern mystics, the romanticists, the practitioners of the kingdom of God " (*Reichgottespraktiker*).[3] The kingdom of God is a transcendent entity which cannot be brought to earth. Thus ethical pessimism, social disillusionment, pettifogging philosophies, and inherited creeds have combined with unchristian political and economic ideologies to discredit all attempts at saving society.

The third factor in producing the antisocial reaction within the church has resulted from historical study and scientific exegesis. Practically it may have been relatively unimportant, being as much a result as a cause. Theoretically, for the conscientious follower of Jesus, it is fundamental. Just as the social-gospel movement was acquiring its greatest influence, it suddenly received what seemed a death blow, and that at the hands of those who were supposedly its warmest friends, the liberal historical critics. The literary criticism and historical interpretation of the Gospels unexpectedly raised a Gorgon's head to petrify the " social gospeler." In the first decade of the twentieth century, when the social-gospel movement was sweeping America " like an equinoctial gale," Albert Schweitzer's " consistent eschatology " brazenly arose to shatter the Gospel authority for the " liberal Jesus " and fully to discredit — so it appeared — the current social interpretation of Jesus' teachings.

Alfred Loisy had already unmasked the unscientific science of Harnack's *Das Wesen des Christentums,* although only a few keen-sighted souls, such as Loisy's fellow modernist and martyr, George Tyrrell, realized the devastating effects of Loisy's criticism. When Schweitzer's volume, *The Quest of the Historical Jesus,* appeared in English (1910), Dean Inge, that unusually strange mixture of reaction and progress, who is anything but a " social gospeler," did see it and stigmatized the book as blasphemous. By that time interest in the social gospel was ready to ebb. Schweitzer's vigorous and self-confident arguments came like a hot blast to drive it back into the sea of lost causes and to dry up the last vestiges of the refreshment it had brought into the arid wastes of theology and ecclesiasticism. The social attitudes which it had developed have persisted, " like the perfume of an empty vase." But already in 1914 the social interpretation of the kingdom of God seemed to many to have been completely exploded. If Jesus taught a thoroughly transcendent eschatology, as Schweitzer maintained, then his was only an interim ethics intended for the short period "between the times" until the miraculous reign of God should begin. It was not only impracticable, but was never intended for use in the twentieth century.

In Germany, form history, another movement which undermines the social gospel, blossomed suddenly in 1919. Its study of the pre-Gospel stages of Palestinian Christianity apparently established the conclusion that the greater part of the traditional narratives is a precipitate of apostolic faith and missionary propaganda, and, consequently, has little proven basis in contemporary sources or authentic recollections of the ministry of Jesus. At best we can know little of his life and teachings. We know only what the church believed.

If then, so the argument runs, we can know so little about Jesus' actual words and deeds, if what is reported is largely apostolic faith about Jesus, then we have no recourse but to accept what the apostles believed and taught about him in lieu of what he taught and believed. Not the religion of Jesus but the religion about Jesus should be the basis of our faith. In this, it is urged, there is not loss, but rather gain. Let us return to the apostolic faith that conquered the Roman Empire. It was good enough for Paul; it should be good enough for us. As to the social gospel, for both Paul and "John," the two greatest New Testament writers, not the coming of the reign of God to earth, but the life of the soul in communion with God was the essence of Christianity. Therefore the social applications of Christian teachings are secondary and relatively unimportant. Thus we return to the idea that the kingdom of God is solely within, and civilization is not dough to be leavened but chaff to be burned. The thesis I wish to propound is that, not only as the successor of the great Hebrew prophets but also as a convinced apocalyptist, Jesus proclaimed a fundamentally and inescapably social message. The reign of God meant social and economic justice.

III. DID JESUS PROCLAIM THE IMMINENCE OF THE REIGN OF GOD?

The questions involved may be reduced to four: (1) Did Jesus proclaim the imminent coming of the reign of God? (2) If he did, what did he mean by it? (3) Are we bound to accept his understanding of it literally, or must we reinterpret it to fit the life of today? (4) In either case, how is the Christian's relation to the life of today affected?

The easy and banal alibi with regard to Christianity's social responsibility is to say that it is impossible to know what Jesus said about the coming of the reign of God because the records of his teachings are historically inadequate. It must be granted to form criticism that there are no first-hand, contemporary records of Jesus' words and deeds. We are dependent upon the missionary preaching of the apostolic church about him. The historian must make due allowance for these circumstances. That does not involve the abdication of criticism, but rather its enthronement. If the apostolic preaching was honest and reasonably accurate as to Jesus, criticism can discover from it what the faith of Jesus was. If it was dishonest or seriously mistaken, it is a poor basis for a religion. It is fortunate that no honest and intelligent person can claim to have *ipsissima verba* of Jesus which must be literally obeyed. The legalism he hated has no place in the Christian faith. On the other hand, the records being what they are, there is likewise no excuse for raising helpless hands to heaven to abjure our responsibilities on the ground of ignorance. If he who runs may not easily read, it is nevertheless far from impossible to learn the social implications of Jesus' message. Even if, as some leading scholars hold, Jesus did not regard himself as the Messiah, it is impossible to avoid the conclusion that the Christian movement was born of the apocalyptic expectations that were current in Judaism. Jesus must have preached the " good tidings " of the coming of the reign of God, or the Synoptic Gospels and the Book of Acts are fabrications.

IV. JESUS' CONCEPTION OF THE REIGN OF GOD

What Jesus' " gospel " of the kingdom meant is a question that is not easily answered. His intention can be understood only if, first of all, modern ideas are forgotten and every effort is made to think in terms of first century Judaism. Unfortunately— perhaps fortunately, rather, in view of man's love of literalism— Jesus never gave the phrase an explicit definition. He exhorts men to prepare for it and emphatically reiterates the demand for certain moral qualities essential to participation in its benefits. But the exact nature of these benefits he never stated in detail, doubtless because everyone agreed as to what they were.

The nearest approach to a description of the results of the coming of the reign of God appears in two passages, both taken by Matthew and Luke in varying forms from Q, the hypothetical teachings source. In reply to the question of

John the Baptist, Jesus points to his work in relief of suffering and to his preaching of good news to the poor. In the Beatitudes, again, the poor, the hungry, the unhappy, and the persecuted are promised the reversal of their conditions under the reign of God.

This is exactly what might be anticipated on the basis of innumerable documents from Egypt, Babylonia, and elsewhere in the Near East, as well as from the Old Testament and from contemporary Jewish literature which did not achieve entrance into the canon. The protest of the poor and oppressed against the injustices which they suffered runs like a sanguinary stain through all the gorgeous tapestry of Oriental history. Their cry for justice rises as a shrill discordant note above all of the choruses of adulation which salute the monarchs of antiquity. The great gods — Shamash, Aton, Amon, and Yahweh — were gods of justice, who cared for the poor. Therefore the kings, the sons and earthly representatives of the gods, were bound to give to every person, no matter how poor and insignificant, his rights. New monarchs, especially upstart usurpers and revolutionaries, from Uru-kagina (2700 B.C.) down, were constantly promising boons to the poor. Courtiers, writing of the exploits of their sovereigns, praised their release of captives, their rescue of the exiled, and their relief of the poor, along with their victories over their enemies. Amon himself appears in Egyptian courts, so we read, to plead the cause of the poor. In the Ras Shamra texts Danel (" God is Judge ") brings justice to the widow and the orphan. In the Zenjirli inscriptions King Kalamu was a benefactor of the *mushka-bîm,* the " prostrated " peasantry. Thus for two thousand years before Amos contemporary documents from Babylonia,

Syria, and Egypt disclose the reiteration of the demand for social and economic justice to the poor.

It is hardly necessary to point to the constant repetition in the Hebrew law books of commands to care for the poor, the widow, the fatherless, and the stranger. The execrations which the greatest Hebrew prophets heaped upon the luxurious rich who neglected and oppressed the poor, upon men who " sell the needy for a pair of shoes," and their demands that " justice should roll down as waters and righteousness as a mighty stream," that social righteousness, as the only service acceptable to God, should replace the sacrifices and offerings of the temple — these are commonplaces, too often ignored, of modern Christian preaching. The Psalms are, in good part, a songbook of the poor and needy, who regard their poverty and need as in themselves passports to God's special favor. One of the dominant strains in Hebrew tradition was God's hatred of the proud, the rich, and the powerful, and his compassion for the poor, the humble, and the sufferers of every description.

In the apocalypses, which, it must be remembered, form one of the most extensive sections of the Jewish literature written during the three centuries centering about the birth of Jesus, this tradition comes to its fullest expression. At times Israel as a whole, at times the faithful and persecuted remnant within Israel, was regarded as meriting God's favor, while the Day of Yahweh, the day of judgment, was, as it had been to Amos, the time of the great reversal, when all human injustices should be redressed by the mighty hand of God — a real *Umwertung aller Werte*.

The (Ethiopic) Apocalypse of Enoch, the work that gave currency to the phrase, " Son of man," in a messianic sense, repeatedly denounces " the kings, the mighty, the exalted, they who possess the earth." It pronounces a series of woes, which in bitterness far surpass those recorded in Luke, against men " who devour the finest of the wheat and drink wine in large bowls and tread under foot the lowly," against the mighty who "help oppression and slay their neighbors until the great day of judgment." It promises that the " Son of man . . . shall put down the kings and the mighty from their seats. . . . He shall be a staff to the righteous . . . and the hope of the troubled of heart." [4] Luke caught exactly the spirit of this side of the primitive gospel when he quoted, doubtless from some similar apocalypse, the proleptic proclamation of the Magnificat:

He hath scattered the proud with the machinations of their hearts.
He hath put down mighty rulers from their thrones and lifted up
    the lowly.
He hath filled the hungry with good things and sent the rich
    empty away.[5]

The indirect intimations as to the nature of the reign of God which may be derived from Jesus' moral demands agree exactly with the picture painted by his predecessors and contemporaries but trace its outlines more clearly. It was the Father's good pleasure to give the kingdom to the "little flock," to the " little people," to the childlike in spirit. Jesus gave his attention, not to the " haves," but to the " have-nots," not to the socially honored rabbis and scribes, but to the ostracized "publicans and sinners," to the sick and suffering, to the vast multitudes who did not count in synagogue and society. When, " by the finger of God," he cast out demons from the epileptic and schizophrenic, then was the

" reign of God come upon them unawares." Jesus had only condemnation for the rulers of the Gentiles who lorded it over their subjects. Among those who were seeking the narrow gate to the kingdom of God, he that was greatest was he that served, even as the Son of man came, not to be served, but to serve. But it was " easier for a rope to go through a needle's eye than for a rich man to enter into the kingdom of God."

Two inferences must not be drawn from Jesus' sayings regarding poverty and wealth. On the one hand, Jesus does not praise poverty and the spirit it engenders as moral preparations for entrance into the kingdom. Only those who have never known the inhumanly debasing poverty of the Oriental and European peasant, the Southern sharecropper, the California migrant agricultural worker, the mine and factory slave, and the city slum dweller could imagine such nonsense. Also, according to the Beatitudes, the reign of God means joy to the poor and woe to the rich. That does not promise wealth and luxury to the poor. Just as little does it mean that the rich shall be reduced to poverty and the same vicious conditions perpetuated in reverse order. The reign of God means an even-handed justice under which the virtues of love and neighborliness will flourish and " every man shall dwell under his own vine and fig tree, with none to molest or make him afraid." The apocalypses were a literature of social protest, and, as the Epistle of James witnesses, the primitive Christian gospel nobly carried on that tradition. Jewish and early Christian eschatology was thoroughly social, if that word includes righteousness and justice in social and economic relationships.

Whoever immerses himself in the literature of the ancient

Orient and tries to see the universe as the farmers and fishermen of Galilee saw it in the first century will almost certainly also come to read the Gospels as dominated by an antisocial and antihistorical notion, the idea of catastrophic eschatology. That does not mean the transcendent eschatology of the first edition of Johannes Weiss' *Predigt Jesu vom Reiche Gottes* (" The Preaching of Jesus about the Kingdom of God ") and of Schweitzer's *Quest of the Historical Jesus*. As Weiss recognized in his second edition — to the uncompromising Schweitzer's disgust — Jesus did not proclaim a completely future and thoroughly transcendent kingdom. Rather, as Ernst von Dobschütz showed in his *Eschatology of the Gospels* (1910), it was a " transmuted eschatology," or, to use the attractive, but less accurate, phrase of C. H. Dodd, a " realized eschatology." [6] For Jesus the reign of God was both present and future, both immanent and transcendent, partially " realized," yet still to come. Its powers were already at work; its final consummation was in the future.[7] In this Jesus broke with the current eschatological notions of his time and his people. But all agreed that the consummation was to be brought about, not by anything that man could do, but solely by the miraculous power of God.

Albert Schweitzer was right, then, in maintaining that Jesus' eschatology was thoroughly catastrophic and miraculous. No Jew knew any other kind. But this does not mean that it was transcendent. It is surely perverse to make Jesus' eschatology noneschatologically mystical, as C. H. Dodd does, because it was not evolutionary. " Realized eschatology " is not eschatology at all as the Jew knew it. Jewish and primitive Christian eschatology was not a doctrine of the future life and of heaven and hell, as Christians, beginning with the Apocalypse of Peter, made it, as systematic theologians of the nineteenth century understood it, and as Edwyn Bevan now would do. It was the predicted history of the " last things " at the end of the present " age " (αἰών, not γῆ, or even κοσμος). That involved also the beginning of a new age, which was to continue on the present earth according to some, or on a miraculously transformed earth according to others. It was to be a return to the primeval Eden. It seems never to have meant the beginning of a purely transcendent existence. For such an existence the resurrection of the body could have no meaning or value. To the Jew, the " age to come " did not at all mean what we mean by " the eternal world." Jesus never meant to say that, with his ministry, eternity had broken into time. To inject such a philosophical idea is a glaring anachronism and a complete misrepresentation.

Paul and his fellow Hellenists caused a decided shift in the primitive Christian conception of the reign of God. Paul was far from abandoning the idea, but it was to be realized, not on earth, but in a transformed and incorruptible world. The emphasis was no longer on the redress of immemorial social wrongs and injustices, but on individual salvation from sin and the world. Moreover, Paul's faith-mysticism was for him the dominant theme. The reign of God was of secondary importance. The first great apostasy had begun in fact, if not in appearance.[8] The Fourth Gospel introduces it explicitly and boldly into the church when it frankly substitutes for the coming of the reign of God over men's lives the coming of God's Spirit into men's hearts, instead of insisting on both. The Gospel ascribed to John has had immense value for the church and its substitution of the coming of the Comforter for the spectacular return of Christ on the clouds did much to stem the ebbing tide of Christian faith at the beginning of the second century and to save Christianity for the world when men were beginning to ask, "Where is the promise of his coming?" Nevertheless the new idea was an apostasy. It was a fundamental "modernization" of Jesus' message and made it something of which the Synoptic Gospels gave no hint.

It must be remembered that Jesus talked of a "reign of God," as Mark and Luke express it, not of a "kingdom of heaven," as Matthew has it. This phrase, as everyone should know since Gustaf Dalman's *Words of Jesus* appeared (1898), is only a periphrasis which, to the ancient Jew, meant the "reign of God," not a happy home in heaven. The Palestinian Jew of Jesus' day had no Hellenistic philosophical notions which would prevent him from believing in a reign of God on earth. Even if he was "farther off from heaven" than when his race was young, "God's arm was not shortened." If the world was full of demons, heaven was full of angels, who only awaited God's command to swarm to earth. The Gospel evidence for the belief that God's will was to be done on earth as well as in heaven is far from weak. This was in all probability the faith of Jesus. But, even if this be denied, the fact remains that Jesus believed with all the fire of the ancient prophets and the contemporary apocalyptists that social and economic injustices were the chief sins of earth, that social righteousness was the basis of the divine order, and that there was coming a great reversal of present conditions such as would punish greed and oppression and establish a just social order.

V. A LITERAL INTERPRETATION IMPOSSIBLE

If the argument outlined above is correct, Jesus preached the imminent, catastrophic, and miraculous intervention of God in the established order and the resultant coming of a new age in which God should rule, injustice be overthrown, and the deserving poor, indeed all who did God's will, should enjoy their proper share of the good things of earth. Can such a view be literally adopted and applied to the life of today? Obviously not, for many reasons. The question hardly makes sense.

First, it is an inescapable fact that the imminent change never occurred. It is highly disingenuous as well as absurd to maintain that, because Jesus disclaimed knowing the day and the hour of the coming revolution, there is no discrepancy between his reported predictions and the subsequent facts of history. His language was necessarily based upon antique, prescientific cosmological and philosophical ideas. Surely the twentieth century cannot be bound to such modes of thought. It is the ethical and religious truth back of the antiquated form that is of importance.

Second, it should be noted in passing that, as Schweitzer and the Adventists on the one hand allege, and "realistic" politicians and economists on the other gladly agree, such literalism makes Jesus' ethics merely interim rules of conduct with only an antiquarian interest for the modern world. This would be true even on the basis of a moderate interpretation of Jesus' eschatology as "transmuted." If modern Christianity were inescapably bound to a literalistic exegesis, then it would have to take the consequences, as Lutheranism is doing today in Germany. But no such radical conclusion is justified for, in the third place, Jesus himself was not a literalist. This is the fundamental fact which conservatives and fundamentalists ignore. Jesus plainly proclaimed the relativity of known truth. He quite clearly set aside some Old Testament laws. Moses had given them because of the hardness of men's hearts. In other words, all the laws and all the truth that men know have their value in relation to their own times. They are not absolute and eternal, but subject to improvement or abrogation with the growth of intelligence.

Jesus' ethical teachings, then, related to the conditions of his time, not to ours. Social and economic concepts and institutions which suited first century society cannot satisfy the twentieth century. The social and political relations of Jesus and his disciples were so different from ours that their ethical obligations were not only different but measurably smaller. The detailed applications with which he illustrated his conception of the reign of God naturally and inevitably applied to ancient society and cannot be transferred bodily to modern conditions.

Intelligent exegesis and honest theology will insist that the literalistic interpretation and legalistic application of any word of Jesus — on war, on divorce, on almsgiving, on riches, on poverty, on paying taxes, on any subject whatsoever — are entirely contrary to the spirit of Jesus' teaching. If the modern Christian would follow Jesus, he must reinterpret Jesus as Jesus reinterpreted the Old Testament. Jesus put an " I say unto you " in place of what had been " said of old time," and always with a heightening and enlargement of obligation. Surely, after two thousand years, there is no less necessity and opportunity for new interpretations.

The Spirit that leads into all truth has not ceased to speak to men. Jesus still repeats, "But I say unto you."

VI.   BASIC PRINCIPLES OF INTERPRETATION

This is far from meaning that any man whose spirit has been fired by a vision of human need and divine justice can put his thumb into the Scriptures and pull out a juicy plum which will assuage the world's hunger for righteousness. The " social gospelers " have been as constant and as blatant sinners against the laws of sane exegesis and historical method as have the dogmatists. *The Peril of Modernizing Jesus,* to use the title of Cadbury's recent volume, is one into which the socially sensitive have been most prone to fall. Not the direct application of specific words of Jesus but a broad understanding of his total spirit and purpose justify the Christian in making his religion socially significant. The application of the basic ideas involved in the expectation of the reign of God on earth is a task that demands all modern knowledge, all the sciences, physical, biological, and social, as well as common sense and spiritual insight of the highest order.

Solid progress in the inevitable reinterpretations will be possible if, instead of a pretense of conserving the old ideas, frank recognition be given to the fact that " time makes ancient good uncouth." The danger in modernizing Jesus is that his authority is claimed for ideas which he never entertained. The rabbis claimed Old Testament authority for their traditions by twisting and torturing new meanings out of the old Scriptures. Through all the succeeding ages men have done the same. There are no final, unimpeachable authorities. The classical interpreters of Jesus, such as Paul and John, St. Augustine and St. Thomas Aquinas, Luther and Calvin, are all equally inadequate. Kant and Hegel, Ritschl and Harnack, Kierkegaard and Barth are not authorities for our day.

This is far from meaning that there are no permanent truths or abiding values, least of all that Jesus can be lightly discarded. The great leaders of the past have made contributions to human thinking which it would be folly to neglect. They saw distant visions. They were leaders because they not only saw and dreamed but went forth. Above all, Jesus had insights into the fundamental problems of human nature and social relations which have never been equaled. Our slogan must be, not " Back to Jesus," but " Forward with Jesus."

To say that the teachings of Jesus are not to be modernized but are to be reinterpreted means that those words and ideas which represent merely ancient modes of thought are to be consciously and conscientiously discarded or intelligently translated into modern terms. Only the elements which now appear to square with all human experience, both ancient and modern, both social and religious, are to be retained. The question then is, What in Jesus' message can be expressed in modern language and categories of thinking so as still to be morally and religiously effective?

On the negative side I have tried to show (1) that the literalism which still expects a visible second advent cannot be retained, for it is discredited by the facts of history; (2) that all literalism is anti-Christian; (3) that a complete reaction into quietistic mysticism is likewise unjustified, because, for Jesus, the reign of God meant social justice, not an escape into a nirvana of individual bliss; (4) that it is equally unreasonable to claim that, because Jesus preached eschatology rather than evolution, he regarded the kingdom of God as purely transcendent. His eschatology had to do, not with the end of the world, not with hell and heaven, but with making the rulership of God effective over human life.

If Dodd and Bevan, Brunner and Barth wish to insist that the reign of God must be reinterpreted as a purely transcendent entity, well and good. Let them not try to prove it by quoting texts! They have no right to claim Jesus' authority for such a reinterpretation. He knew no such category of thought as " transcendent." That is not the logical escape from the dilemma which results from the fact that the reign of God on earth is an unrealizable ideal, a flying goal. There is no escape from that paradox. Paul comes near to avoiding it when he insists that Christ " must reign until he has put all his enemies under his feet." It is ridiculous, not to say blasphemous, to cry, " The more Christian society, the more secular the church." Is it evil for the world to become better? A sensitive conscience will always discover new worlds of sin and injustice to conquer. The Spirit will always lead into new truth. If society catches up with the church, so much the worse for the church. If the Christian is not " a practitioner of the kingdom of God," he is no follower of Jesus. Jesus asked men to do the will of God as if God were reigning on earth, although he knew that was not fully impossible. Allowance must be made for pedagogic and parenetic exaggeration. But it should never be forgotten that an immediately achievable ideal ceases to be an ideal.

Perhaps this argument tends toward logomachy, since the substance of what I am contending for is accepted by Dodd,

Bevan, Wendland, Kraemer, and the delegates to Oxford
and Madras. It is brilliantly set forth by Emil Brunner in
his *Divine Imperative* and by Jacques Maritain in his *True
Humanism,* who agree remarkably in their ethics, for example in their excoriation of the capitalistic system as it
now exists.[9] All of these men agree that the kingdom of
God is transcendent, but they all also agree that the Christian
church must "have a formative influence on society and
culture."[10] One of the evidences for the importance of the
point I am trying to make is the recent conversion of Karl
Barth — by the betrayal of Czechoslovakia — to a vigorous,
not to say vicious, political activism, which seems wholly in-
consistent with his former principles. He surely proves that
no true follower of Jesus can remain indifferent to social
wrong.[11] The one thing above all others that a proper reinterpretation of the term must insist upon is that the social
obligations of the Christian are not secondary; individual
salvation and social salvation stand and fall together.[12] No
better expression than the "reign of God," none more terse
and meaningful, can be found to express the ideal of Jesus
for men and for society.

On the positive side, then, the first conviction necessary
to a proper reinterpretation and modern application of the
phrase, "the reign of God," is that the world moves, physically, socially, and spiritually. Nothing that lives is static.
In spite of the Jonahs who forever cry, "Yet forty days and
civilization shall be destroyed," in spite of the old men who
in all ages have insisted that the best has been and the worst
is yet to be, the human race has improved. Jesus had faith
in men.

Jesus had faith also in God. We cannot believe, as he and

his fellows did, that God worked from without to create the world and will, in the end, step in from without to transform it. God worked within the universe to create it, not in six days, but in uncounted millions of years; God is at work to transform the world of humanity, not in one great " day of the Lord," but through long and patient millenniums, not with a steady and irresistible upward sweep, but through many a catastrophe, in spite of many a retrogression.

Since Jesus had faith in man and God, the modern believer is justified in assuming that the reign of God is to come, not by some divine magic, but by the miraculous forces that God has planted in human nature and human society. The reign of God can come only as men by their own free choices put themselves within it. Even God does not do that for them. He has chosen to let men work out their own social salvation. Men and society are to be saved, neither by man's self-sufficient reason nor by God's unilateral grace, but by man's self-denying devotion to the right and his intelligent use of the resources that God has made available in nature and in society. Everything hangs upon men's decisions in the repeated crises of history, whether for God or against him.

The outstanding conviction of Jesus was that ethical values are paramount. In face of the denials of political and theological totalitarians, this truth still stands. The terms in which these values are expressed will change, but individual and social righteousness will never cease to be necessary to a progressive civilization. Man must have food, whether he buys it with dinars or dollars, and man lives not by bread alone. The reign of God is first of all righteousness, whether or not Paul intended the order of his words to imply it. The area to which righteousness applies has gradually, all too gradually, enlarged since the days of Uru-kagina and the Eloquent Peasant. That the reign of God will ever be realized is too much to claim. The eschatology of Jesus has not been realized but is forever being realized.

Properly understood and reinterpreted to successive generations even as he reinterpreted the Old Testament, Jesus will never cease to be the Messiah who brings in the kingdom. In his life and death, because of his sincerity, devotion, and courage, in his teachings, because of his insight, simplicity, and concreteness, age after age can discover the basic truths that society needs and the basic impulses that keep it alive and growing. The best-selling novel ever written is *In His Steps*. The kingdom of God has meaning for the life of today and every day as man after man and generation after generation rewrite that story.

May I claim that there is a peculiar appropriateness in defending such a thesis as this in a volume honoring Harris Franklin Rall? His theology, unlike much that is now current, has never questioned the central importance of the social element in Christian thought. He has long taught — to use his own phrases — " the prophetic religion, that ethical monotheism which was proclaimed by the Hebrew prophets and consummated in Jesus," and Christianity as " a religion of redemptive good will . . . , the way of individual and social redemption." [13]

NOTES

[1] *The Christian Message in a Non-Christian World* (London: Edinburgh House Press, 1938), pp. 93, 92, 25.

[2] *Christian Faith and the Common Life* (Chicago: Willett, Clark & Co., 1938), p. 88. Cf. p. 142.

[3] *Erlebnis, Erkenntnis und Glaube* (2nd and 3rd ed.; Tübingen: 1923), p. 4.

[4] 1 En. 94; 96; 99; 46:4; 48:4.

[5] Luke 1:51 ff.

[6] See Dodd, *Parables of the Kingdom* (New York: Charles Scribner's Sons, 1936); McCown, *The Promise of His Coming* (New York: The Macmillan Co., 1921), pp. 146–53.

[7] See McCown, "The Eschatology of Jesus Reconsidered," *Journal of Religion*, XVI (1936), 30–46; R. Otto, *The Kingdom of God and the Son of Man*, tr. by Floyd V. Filson and Bertram Lee Woolf (London: Lutterworth Press, 1938).

[8] See the article, "The First Great Apostasy," in *Christendom*, I (1936), 792–99.

[9] *Divine Imperative* (London: Lutterworth Press, 1937), pp. 217 f., 617, 209, 287, 426; *True Humanism* (New York: Charles Scribner's Sons, 1938), pp. 88–104, 107 f., 131. Cf. William Ernest Hocking, *The Lasting Elements of Individualism* (New Haven: Yale University Press, 1937), pp. 47–51, 163–66, 169 f. — a similar attitude in a different area.

[10] Wendland in the Oxford Conference volume, *The Kingdom of God and History* (Chicago: Willett, Clark & Co., 1938), p. 187.

[11] See his address at the "Assembly of the Swiss Evangelical Auxiliary of the Confession Church in Germany," delivered December 5, 1938, printed in *Die Kirche und die politische Frage von heute* (2nd ed.; Evangelische Buchhandlung Zollikon, 1939). I have to thank my colleague, Professor John C. Bennett, for the references in this paragraph to Brunner, Maritain, and Barth.

[12] See the suggestive and informative book of D. C. Macintosh, *Social Religion* (London and New York: Charles Scribner's Sons, 1939), especially pp. 85 f.

[13] His chapter on "A Social Faith" in *A Faith for Today* (New York: Abingdon Press, 1936), and that on the significance of religion for "Social Change" in *Religion and Public Affairs* (New York: The Macmillan Co., 1937), (a suggestive title), the volume he edited in honor of Bishop Francis J. McConnell, are sufficient evidence.

THE CHURCH AND SOCIAL OPTIMISM

SHAILER MATHEWS

The University of Chicago

THE AMERICAN people need social psychiatry. A neurosis of pessimism has succeeded a neurosis of optimism. Delusions of grandeur have given way to feelings of fear. A period of depression has been treated with depressants just as the period of optimism was treated with stimulants.

Economically viewed, the reason for this pathological situation is not hard to find. The optimism of 1928, like the pessimism of 1931, was a case of mob psychology. To say that one is as irrational as the other explains nothing. We have long since ceased to identify thought with rationality. The cycle of economic hysteria has made a half-revolution. The optimism of those who saw the ball fall on the red was no less intense than their pessimism when it fell on the black. Even when they hope for better luck, the prophecy of the coming of prosperity has become like the prophecy of the second coming of Christ. The date of arrival has been postponed.

The stock market has been a thermometer which men heat to prove that it is summer and pack with ice to prove that it is winter. Comrades in doom seek to become comrades in hope.

I

We expect prosperity to return. But can we administer
the optimism which prosperity will engender? Any student
of social affairs will be certain to say that we have not learned
that lesson. Periods of speculation have usually the same
general characteristics. Those who think that the halcyon
days cannot last pyramid their margin investments in the
hope that they will be able to sell out before the crash comes.
Men of affairs administer optimism by exhortations to be
more optimistic.

We have learned by experience that an economic neurosis
carries its own outcomes of suffering. But we have yet to
learn what to do when everybody is hopeful. Until we learn
how to administer optimism, we shall continue to be threatened by pessimism.

Pessimism is more than a passing emotion. We have only
to look at European countries to see that it may give rise to
revolution. When great masses of people become convinced
that no condition can be worse than that in which they are,
they need only a leader to pursue some new optimism which
involves the destruction of institutions that have failed to
socialize privileges.

The rational optimist does not believe that all things are
as good as they can be, but that they can be made better than
they are. Such healthy-mindedness resents being deceived
by those whom it has trusted. It is simple enough to believe
that it is as dishonest to lie about business conditions as it is
to lie about anything else. It is ready to forgive mistakes,
but it has grown skeptical of the sincerity of those who have
cried, "Prosperity, prosperity," when there was no prosper-

ity. A wolf who persistently wears sheep's clothing will be as much shunned as a sheep that wears wolf's clothing is laughed at.

II

In other than the economic aspects of our life, badly administered optimism is followed by equally unintelligent distrust of a previous faith. The complacency born of an imperfectly organized philosophy of evolution has resulted in cynicism. A newly discovered truth, like a newly discovered medical treatment, is likely to be treated as a panacea. It is easy to recall cases where the announcement of a new serum or radioactivity has led to unwarranted hopes that some disease has been conquered. In most such cases a limited hopefulness was thoroughly justified. But the unintelligent manipulation of such a heartening fact was the cause of many a bitter disappointment.

Similarly, in the organization of some new philosophical or religious thought, an uncritical optimism has brought indifference or cynicism. I do not know whether humanity is sufficiently reasonable to proceed in any other way than by vacillation between illusion and disillusion. It may be that we must submit to being taught progress through a bitter trial-and-error method. Personally, I am loath to believe that an intelligent world view is beyond our ability, but too many technicians who have turned philosophers generalize conclusions drawn from a highly specialized knowledge. They have exploited our ineradicable hope that truth will make us free into a propaganda that a fact will make us free. They have taught us to discredit religion as dealing with the supernatural, but they have not shown us that the behavior of birds and animals encourages us to believe that mankind is superior to glands and reflexes. The undoubted discoveries of the psychological laboratory are too often used to discount the conclusions of the social psychologists. And the social psychologist, in his present devotion to statistics and his application of a quantum theory to human action, has weakened our confidence in human freedom. Rival dogmatisms make their own myths of betterment and mutual criticism makes pessimism appear sophisticated. As a reformer needs an evil to reform, so the sophisticated man needs something hopeful to criticize.

There is in consequence a new evangel among our intelligentsia — the evangel of futility. Its heralds may not have had the rich and varied experience of the writer of Ecclesiastes, but they join in his wail, " Vanity of vanities; all is vanity! " In their opinion we live in a universe that is neither kindly nor unkindly, under the control of no purpose, caught in a wheel of life that makes karma seem like a merry-go-round, with nothing before us but frustration. They salute us as comrades in doom, and bid us therefore love one another. I must confess to a sense of logical unexpectedness in this exhortation. If the cosmos is valueless and purposeless and relentless, with neither goodness nor badness nor personal response, why worry about being kind to anyone else! Shall the clutch say to the driving rod, " Be merciful," or the cog to the wheel, "I trust you are friendly? " If we are comrades in doom, it would seem as if the real exhortation should be, "Lay on, Macduff! Since we love each other, I propose to send you to your doom before you send me to my doom."

The philosophy of frustration and futility, of course, has

no place for hope. To it the expectation of a better world is hopefulness that is mid-Victorian — than which there is nothing more anathema to the sophisticated, unless it be bourgeois. The prosperous man is said to fear that he will cease to be prosperous, or that he will not be more prosperous, whereas the poor are blessed, for, having nothing to lose, they can expect the kingdom of God. But having reduced efficiency to a search for futility, our futilitarians take away from the poor man even that which he has. A religion which promises the justice of heaven is declared to be defeatism, and a belief in an overruling Providence, a sublimated Oedipus complex. There is no more hope for the poor than for the prosperous. All is futility.

The earlier forms of the evolutionary philosophy replaced the older theological doctrine of prevenient and irresistible grace. That philosophy has been found to be equally mechanistic and incapable of solving the problems of our human life. It is as foreign to our present intellectual mood to say that mankind will inevitably progress as it was for the seventeenth century to say that the elect could not go to hell if they chose. But this is far from saying that there are not discoverable laws of human progress, or that human persons cannot live normally when in adjustment with those personality-producing activities of the cosmos which environ them. Deprive humanity of either one of these optimisms and life becomes unintelligible. But what man of us who has ever attempted to co-ordinate the findings of the various investigators would believe that calling ourselves comrades in doom is the only way to face reality? There is within us the inexpugnable conviction that while the extension of the circumference of human knowledge gives us an ever expanding contact with the unknown, it just as truly gives us data by which can be organized and administered a more intelligent appreciation of our worth as persons.

III

It is not strange that in such a moment of defeatism persons who are really responsible for the situation should extol religion. Failing to act intelligently and with social-mindedness they call upon religion to do what they ought to have done themselves. God is made responsible for human mistakes and called upon to rectify them.

But a religion is not something external to humanity. It is as concrete as a state. It is no more divorced from social processes than are political parties. Religious people both individually and collectively implement an ideology. If that be one of passive resistance in which men await divine acts it might well be that it will be replaced by the direct action of those who do not camouflage inertia by pietism. But such direct action does not need to be antireligious or even indifferent to religion. There is an international Christianity as truly as there is international communism and if it is to be efficient in developing social hopefulness it must share in the processes of change and reconstruction. The security which it promises must be something more than a perpetuation of the *status quo* whose injustices are to be compensated by the joys of post-mortem heaven. True security lies in an adjustment to and a direction of change.

We may not see the heavenly city or the better social order of the future, but we can feel secure in a knowledge that we are on the way. To go from Chicago to Boston one chooses an eastward bound train. Once upon it, one can securely expect to arrive. It is a function of a Christian church and of Christian people to point out a way which can be trusted to lead toward the desired end. He who believes that co-operation and the recognition of personal rights lead toward a better human society will no more choose the way of violence and expect God to work miracles in his behalf than the man who wants to go east would expect God to work a miracle if he got on a train that was going west.

But if defeatism is not to lead to sanctified inertia, what way to hope does Christianity offer?

First of all it can offer the hopefulness which comes from a belief that human beings are more than chemical laboratories driven by the sex instinct. True, Christian thought has never suffered from myopic optimism when considering human nature. We may have outgrown the sublimated imperialism that believed in a humanity every member of which was born damned because of its ancestors' rebellion. But we have not outgrown the backward pull which such pessimism pictured. Christianity, however, facing a very real humanity holds that human life can move onward to more personal and intelligent living. In theological terms the belief is in salvation. This hopefulness is conditioned by the recognition of the fact that progress towards personal value is not mechanical but the outcome of life in accordance with the cosmic laws and activities from which humanity has emerged. It has never regarded human beings as living in a cosmic vacuum. Whatever form this conviction has taken — whether it has been in the analogies of Hebraism, the idealism of Plato, the dialectic of Aristotle or the recognition of the scientific formulas of today — it has believed in God. This God is not a remote sovereign but a conditioning activity. Humanity must cooperate with this environing activity.

Stripped of such a terminology, Christianity holds that love is a practicable basis upon which to build human relations because God is love. A course of conduct which makes personal values subordinate to economic or political ends, therefore, is sure to bring suffering. The creative activities of the universe are against it. Temporary success of such violation is as certain to be overcome as a stone forced into the air is destined to succumb to gravitation.

It is the primary function of the church to persuade men and women to accept the truth of this belief. That takes more than abstract idealism. It cannot promise progress without insisting upon its cost. To recognize personal values in the economic and political world is to socialize privilege at the cost of the privileged. That is an expensive process which demands the basic conviction of the Christian religion. Quixotic enthusiasm will not do. Love must involve an intelligent recognition of social process. An ideal must be something more than a program superimposed upon people morally unprepared.

Christian people live in a world of change subject to social forces. It does not seem the function of religion to supply scientific recognition of the laws of change or of the institutions which conserve and further change, but it can give men and women a sense of direction which they can follow as their intelligence demands. For religion, as the Christian church conceives it, is not a passive submission to forces that would go in opposite directions but an extension of its own sense of personal values to the world in which it actually lives.

Such a view of Christian faith is neither a camouflaged defeatism nor a withdrawal from human affairs in the interest of individual salvation nor yet a limitation of its influence to a preparation for heaven. It is a religion for social guidance rather than for introvert pietism. Its basis seems as scientifically sound as the effort to live intelligently with the impersonal forces of nature. If men choose to live in a way which cooperates with the personality-producing activities of the universe, hopefulness becomes a sane optimism. It is at the same time a warning that hopefulness which rests on any other than a personal basis and seeks to make force or selfishness supreme is doomed to produce sorrow and misery. We may not see the destination of our journey, but we do not look for that destination to come to us or distrust the direction in which we are going. We may not be as intelligent as we should like in dealing with economic and international problems, but we can feel and courageously follow the conviction that humanity in undertaking to live in accordance with the conditions which are set by the universe itself can hope to produce a better social order in which justice shall be given rather than demanded and the welfare of human beings as personalities be superior to the institutions and the economic mechanisms which may be its servants. To carry such convictions into the actual world in which we live demands freedom for different programs, but the pursuit of a single, ultimate end.

THE CHURCH, THE TRUTH, AND SOCIETY

EDGAR SHEFFIELD BRIGHTMAN
Boston University

THE CHRISTIAN church in recent years has been challenged by historical forces led by men whose aim is the extermination of all religion except the deification of their own will. The long period of public indifference to Christianity is thus drawing to its close; and a time has come when society must choose definitely for or against Christianity.

Yet precisely at this time there is perhaps greater confusion than ever about what Christianity is and about the nature and function of the church. The last thing that a group of moderns interested in religion can hope to accomplish is to define religion in a way acceptable to all members of the group. A definition which suits some seems to others intolerably narrow, and to still others vaguely and aimlessly broad. Indeed, some Christians object to the very word "religion" on the ground that it implies that possibly there is some religion outside of Christianity; and some religious persons trained in the Christian tradition disclaim the name of Christian because they deem it to be partisan, exclusive, and intolerant. Yet others, from sincere loyalty to Christian ideals, maintain their Christian life out of all relation to the Christian church, which they take to be disloyal to spiritual Christianity.

The church has begun to respond to this situation. The response is slow, far too slow for the needs of the times. But leaders of the church have a historical perspective and a faith in the future which render them immune to panic and to wild schemes. They are unwilling to embark on hasty action. What they are willing and eager to undertake is a new self-appraisal, looking to a reconstruction of the present order. This self-appraisal has been in process for some years now in concrete form. The names of such places as Stockholm, Geneva, Jerusalem, Oxford, Edinburgh, Utrecht, and Madras suggest the organized and purposeful character of this new self-appraisal. The word " ecumenicity " — world-wideness — sums up the new outlook. Movements toward church union in Canada (the United Church) and the United States (Congregationalists and Christians, Methodists, Presbyterians and Episcopalians) and on the mission field (notably in India) are further aspects of the new spirit.

Valuable as it might be to explore this new evolution of ecumenical Christianity, such is not the purpose of the present investigation. Recent movements have been mentioned only as a background for a more venturesome and probably less profitable undertaking, namely, an attempt by an individual who avows a Christian faith to make clear to himself and others what he thinks of the church. We are to ask what the church is and should be, and what its relation is, on the one hand, to the ideal of the truth as it has been developed in secular thought, and, on the other hand, to the larger human society of which the church is a part. The church, the truth, and society are topics which lead to inexhaustible questions. It is with no hope of answering these questions that the present inquiry is undertaken. If any ideas are suggested which make any of the important problems clearer, the goal will have been achieved.

Borden Parker Bowne once wrote an essay on "The Church and the Truth," which appeared in his book, *Studies in Christianity*. When a contemporary American philosopher was asked to read and criticize the chapter, his comment was: "The church and the truth — what have these two to do with each other?" If this comment be taken at its face value, our problem has begun to disintegrate. The process of disintegration would be carried further if we accepted the opinion of those who believe that society has no need for the church and no use for the truth. There is enough substance in these cynical comments, not to disintegrate our problem, but to show its radical implications. Does the church welcome truth? Has it usually welcomed truth bravely, or has truth survived in spite of the inquisitions and oppositions of the church? Has the church served its God with half the zeal wherewith it served its king? What would become of the church if it welcomed all truth as God's truth, and were faithful to its function as the conscience of society? Again, what would happen to truth and society if the church were utterly to fail? What will happen to both church and society unless both recognize frankly that all of the principles and behavior of both are subject to the judgment of truth? We have seen parts of the church indifferent to any truth except the truth of which it supposes itself already to be in possession, and to any society except the household of faith. We have also seen parts of the church lay claim to a monopoly on truth and society, in the sense that all search for truth not in harmony with church doctrines has been censored and all Christendom has been viewed as subject to the spiritual overlordship of the church. What is the value of these policies? Problems swarm about us as we enter our field of inquiry.

I. CHURCH, TRUTH, AND SOCIETY AS EMPIRICAL FACTS

Before we can do anything fruitful with the delicate and complicated problems on which we have touched, it is essential for us to see what the facts are that give rise to our problems. All thinking is an interpretation of some actual experience.[1] We need, then, to ask exactly what we experience as church and truth and society. In dealing with terms surrounded by theory and dogma, it is not easy or natural to set those theories aside even temporarily in order to inspect their empirical bases. This must, however, be done if the problem is to be seen clearly. The method we thus adopt is akin to what Husserl, Scheler, and others call phenomenology. What, we ask, are church, truth, and society experienced as being? What are they *de facto,* regardless of their claims *de jure?*

First of all, what is truth empirically? In the broadest sense, it is whatever is accepted or believed as truth, that is, as a correct description of what is or ought to be. Since this leaves us with an utter chaos of conflicting truth-claims, we may narrow the concept and still remain empirical by declaring truth to be whatever is accepted as truth by those who are socially recognized as seekers for truth. This social definition may be supplemented by a historical one reading: " Truth consists of those beliefs which have survived the testing of many generations or which result from the use of historically tested methods." Yet at each stage of history, the social test is resorted to; and therefore the empirical definition of truth, useful as it is in pointing out the area in which some real truth may be found, affords and can afford no standard for determining which are the best methods. For, on a strictly factual basis, scientific methods of observation and experiment, Roman Catholic methods of logical deduction from biblical revelation, Mohammedan methods of logical deduction from the Koran, and economic methods of competitive profit-seeking, all alike conform to the historical definition of truth. All of these methods have survived the testing of many generations. So too have the institutions of war and prostitution. A purely descriptive definition of truth leaves us with a conflict of truth-claims on many levels, with no measure of the height or depth of the levels.

What, we next ask, is society as an empirical fact? The social mind — if it is not a mere verbal fiction — is neither writing nor reading this chapter. Empirically, then, so far as you and I are concerned, society is not the social mind. Neither is it all the human beings in the world; no one (leaving God or the Absolute out, as we must empirically) has ever come anywhere near to experiencing all the human beings in the world, even if we may all be conscious of them generically by use of the concept of humanity.

However, a critic might ask, if experience means consciousness, and you can be conscious in any sense of all human beings, why do you not admit that you experience them? This raises a fundamental question, which must be faced squarely. It is the question of what Ralph Barton Perry has called "the egocentric predicament" (a useful name-calling which points out a real problem). Every experience I have is my experience. No matter how social or objective my interests may be, no matter what I am referring to, the interests and the references are my interests, my references. In one sense, then, the answer to the critic is that strictly and literally all my experience is individual; all experience is experience of myself. Hence, when I am conscious of "all humanity," I do not literally include all humanity in my consciousness; I simply experience myself as believing in all humanity. Empirically, the case is just the same as a belief in "all angels" or "all ghosts" or "all fairies." I experience myself as believing in all men, angels, ghosts, or fairies. I do not experience "all men" any more than I experience "all fairies."

Empirically, then, society is no more than certain experiences of individuals. Social psychology is a branch of the psychology of individuals; indeed, the same "social situations" (if we may be allowed a highly metaphysical concept for a moment!) may lead to very different social experiences on the part of the various individuals in the group, although political mass meetings, whether in Nuremberg, Moscow, or Chicago, probably achieve far more uniformity than do sermons, symphony concerts, or lectures on philosophy. If all social and historical experience is empirically the experience of individuals, then the problem of truth is far less simple than our statement made it, for both the social and the historical definitions must root in present experiences of present individual persons.

Exactly what is our empirical base of supplies when we talk about society? Empirically, society is that series of experiences which individuals ascribe to the influence of other individuals (or groups of individuals) on their experience. This cannot be construed as meaning that actually society is nothing but our social experiences. It means, rather, that when we talk about society the only evidence that we have empirically for the existence of that society is found in our own experiences, including, of course, our experiences of reasoning and believing. No one can believe that society consists of his own consciousness; but no one ought to pretend to believe that he has any empirical evidence for society other than what he finds in his own consciousness. We all, however, make distinctions within our own consciousness between experiences that are more obviously social and others that are far less so. The qualities which we discern in sense perception no one would seriously believe to be social products. The individual's choice from among competing social stimuli is not always itself socially determined. But when we experience perceptions, the stimuli for which we spontaneously ascribe to the bodies of other persons, we are having social experience as empirically as we can ever have it — especially when those perceptions are of gestures or words which we interpret as language. Even if there is E. S. P. — the extra-sensory perception of the investigators at Duke University — social experience is still the same in principle. It consists always of the interpretation of signs in my own experience as being either communications from others or effects of their activity. The whole world experiences no more about "society" than the individual persons in the world experience. Knowledge of this fact should tend to keep abstractions and dogmatic assertions about society within bounds.

In addition to this "social" conception of society, there is also, as there was with truth, a historical conception. The empirical basis of a historical view of society is to be found in those experiences which we interpret as signs of the activity of men who lived long ago — such experiences as our perceptions of documents, books, monuments, inscriptions, or artifacts. The validity of historical knowledge rests on the validity of our present beliefs in the proper explanation of these experiences.

This somewhat prolonged discussion of empirical definitions of truth and society was a necessary preliminary to an empirical definition of the church. The church is a social institution, and our experiences of the church are part of our social experiences. From this empirical-social point of view the church consists of all experiences of individuals which arise in connection with what they acknowledge as a church, that is, as a body of Christian believers organized for purposes of Christian worship and other appropriate activity. Empirically, Quakers, Baptists, Christian Scientists, Witnesses of Jehovah, Latter-day Saints, angels of Father Divine, Anglo-Catholics, Methodists, Roman Catholics, Lutherans, and Presbyterians are all on an equality. They are all experienced as church groups. By some, they are all experienced as being members of the church universal. It must be added that in many of these groups, especially since the war of 1914, experience of the local church quite overbalances experience of the church universal. That is to say, the church is experienced in terms of the welfare of a local group without much regard to wider interests. The brute fact of provincialism looms large among the rank and file, and ecumenicity is the experience of a select few.

As in the definitions of truth and society, so here, the historical must supplement the social. The historical definition is of prime importance for the Christian church, for it would be a contradiction in terms to call a church Christian if it did not experience some sort of historical consciousness of Christ. Historically, therefore, the church consists of those persons who relate themselves and their social organization to Jesus Christ. Since the source of our experience of Jesus is in the Bible, a church is empirically impossible without some knowledge of the Scriptures. Many members of most churches lay great stress on sacraments and orders and their perpetuation in traditional forms, although others, notably the Friends, minimize these matters. The empirical fact of insistence on a specific form of baptism or of ordination of the clergy or of the sacrament of the Lord's Supper is well-known as the most divisive force within the ecumenical church, far more divisive than doctrine or race. So scandalous is this division that it seems to many to be more truly an exhibition of a competitive struggle for power than of anything related to the spirit of Christ. Yet in talking about the church empirically we must face these empirical facts objectively, regardless of the value-judgment that we or anyone else may pass upon them.

II. TRUTH, SOCIETY, AND CHURCH AS IDEALS

As we have seen, truth, society, and the church are experienced by individuals as facts of which they are conscious. But experience is more than the awareness of actual present facts, or memory of past facts. Every person finds in his experience also the conception of kinds of possible facts that might be and ought to be actual. Such experiences we call ideals. Every normal human being frequently compares the actual with the ideal. Life consists partly of the effort to make ideals conform more closely to one another. It is hard to say whether the conflict of the ideal with the actual or the conflict of ideals with one another is the more serious and tragic aspect of life. At the present time, certainly, the world conflict of incompatible ideals seems to be even more acute and destructive than the conflict of ideal aspiration with actual fact. It is far easier to write a poem, to carry on scientific research, or to achieve personal character than it is to arrive at a solution of the conflicting ideals of capital and labor, or of democracy and totalitarianism. It is in the realm of ideals that the battles of man are fought and his destiny decided.

To say that I believe a proposition to be true is a mere description of a psychological situation. It is purely *de facto*. But when I give reasons for my belief I appeal to an ideal of truth which I acknowledge and which I believe you and all reasonable beings ought to acknowledge. Such an appeal changes the situation from a *de facto* experience to one that claims a status *de jure*. To use the language of Plato, the former is simply an opinion about truth, while the latter is knowledge. The ideal by which we criticize our empirical opinions and achieve knowledge contains at least three factors: the love of truth (the purpose to know — the Platonic ἔρως, Spinoza's *amor intellectualis dei*), respect for reason (for consistency and coherence of all our thought and experience — the Platonic σύνοψις, Leibniz's *vérités de raison* and Hegel's " the true is the whole "), and respect for fact (scientific verification — which Plato treated lightly in the *Republic*[2] and the *Timaeus;*[3] but it appears in Leibniz's *vérités de fait* and Hegel's phenomenology). A proposition approaches truth insofar as it expresses a love of truth unmixed with personal, economic, or political interests, conforms to the demands of reason, and is consistent with observed fact. At times one element in this ideal is emphasized more than another, but the great minds of the race have almost always acknowledged all three as equally essential to a well-rounded view of the ideal of truth. Those who are unaware of the ideal of truth, or reject it, may entertain some true opinions, but they have no trustworthy means of testing their opinions or of learning new truths.

The ideal of truth underlies and grounds all other ideals: for if any pretended ideal is not true — that is, not a true ideal — how can it pretend to be anything more than a false opinion about an ideal? If we apply this principle to social ideals, it is most searching and embarrassing in its implications.

Every society is more than the empirical facts which were described in the previous section. Every society is an ideal in at least two senses. Our concept of any society to which we belong or to which we are related is an ideal — an intellectual construct — which goes far beyond anything any or all members of the society have experienced, and sets up what we believe to be the truth about that society. This is the objective ideal of truth about a society. Then there is also the ideal of the purpose, the goal (the policy, the aim) of the society. This is the normative ideal of a society's function. It is obvious that neither ideal is perfectly attained, and that each ideal is approximated only by the most rigorous loyalty to truth. No research can completely determine what the United States, for example, really is, if only for the reason that conditions change while the research is going on, and the research (e.g., the Gallup polls) may itself tend to change the facts. Neither can any philosophy — political, economic, or religious — finally determine what the purposes of the

United States are or ought to be. Social ideals — like Kantian principles — are infinite tasks (*unendliche Aufgaben*),
but — like Kant's also — they are rational tasks which give
a society its meaning.

Truth is empirically believed in; and it is also an ideal.
Society is many empirical facts; it is also an experience of
judging those facts by an ideal. The church is a complex
series of empirical facts within society; it, too, is an idealizing
experience, which presupposes the validity of ideals of truth
and society.

Let us remember that we are thinking now as Christians
about the Christian church. If our loyalty to the ideal of
truth had led us to find an explanation of our experience and
purpose other than God, or had compelled us to conclude
that someone or something else was more worthy of our allegiance than Jesus Christ, then we could have no ideal of
the church except, at best, that of a collection of misguided
individuals who had better be about some useful business.
We might even accept Voltaire's ideal, " *Écrasez l'infâme,*"
and seek to crush the wretch. But as believers in God and
in Jesus Christ we must have some ideal of a church. To
believe in God and in Christ is to believe, among other
things, in man's cooperation with man and with God for
living as Jesus taught. Such cooperation, when consciously
organized, becomes a church (a κυριακόν).

It is one thing to acknowledge the ideal that Christians
ought, *de jure,* to be organized as a church. It is quite another to interpret the empirically existing churches with reference to the ideal. The practical importance of ideals is
nowhere more vividly (and sadly) illustrated than in the
Christian church. On matters ordinarily called practical,

that is, on most questions of morals and daily living, Christians of all churches are agreed. The law of love in the Golden Rule and in the thirteenth chapter of 1 Corinthians is universally acknowledged, but conflicting ecclesiastical ideals make the law of love " of none effect " in many of the relations of Christians to non-Christians, of Catholics and Protestants to each other, and of sect to sect among Protestants. It is necessary for Christians to become more conscious of this conflict among ideals if it is ever to be overcome intelligently.

One way of coping with the conflict of ideals is the way of what is known as tolerance, which really means good manners toward those whom we believe to be in error. Tolerance is important, especially from a governmental standpoint. Civil liberties are to be preserved at all costs, especially in days when regard for such liberties is sometimes stigmatized as Communist propaganda. But tolerance is more than a democratic civic duty; it is also a demand of reason. The only procedure for dealing with deviations from the ideal of truth is not hatred or intolerance, but simply renewed appeal to the ideal of truth. Christian truth demands love even to our enemies; " love suffereth long and is kind." No reader of Paul's psalm to love could possibly justify an attitude of intolerance.

Nevertheless, the way of tolerance is no solution of the problem of the ideal of the church. In a letter to the magazine *Newsweek,* Dean Hiram R. Bennett of the Cathedral Church of St. John in Wilmington, Delaware, wrote about the magazine's discussion of nomenclature in the church. He went on to say that " it will only be fair to the great Anglican Communion, of which the Episcopal Church is a part, to take it on its own valuation, which is that it is the ancient Catholic Church of English-speaking races." [4] As a journalistic principle, Dean Bennett's maxim is sound. But as an ideal of social and religious truth, it is hopeless. According to it, each church, or at least each " great " church, is to be taken at its own valuation. Then the Roman Catholic, the Greek Catholic, the Anglican, the Baptist, the Methodist, and the Congregational churches, for example, are all to be accepted on their own valuation of themselves. The result of such an extension of tolerance is a relativism that has no regard for truth or for the hope of rational agreement. Unless tolerance is accompanied by freedom of rational discussion and rational criticism — a freedom used both toward others and toward oneself — tolerance is a name either for indifference or for arrogance. If I tolerate indifferently, I do so like Gibbon, because it makes no difference what anyone believes; if I tolerate arrogantly, I do so like Rome, because I am certain that I am right and hence I can afford to be merciful. In either case, tolerance, taken by itself, suffers from an insufficient reverence for the ideal of truth as a universal goal and as an instrument of self-criticism.

If, therefore, we are to grasp the problem of the ideal of the church not merely as participants in a present situation, but as believers in the God who has placed eternity in our hearts, we have to face an ultimate decision, which American Christianity, for the sake of peace and harmony, has long sought to evade. Is the church to be defined as the body of those who accept the biblical revelation as final or as the body of those who believe in an ever-present and progressive revelation of God? Unpopular as the terminology may be, the conflict between ideals of fundamentalism and of liberalism, of Catholic dogma and Protestant conscience, of religions of authority and religions of the spirit, lies at the bottom of all thought about the church. As we have said, any Christian church must revere and use the Scriptures. But it is one thing to view the Scripture as absolute and literal authority; it is another to view it as a historical laboratory manual of Christian experiments which can be tested over and over by later generations and which lead to new experiments and new insights as the centuries advance. On the one hand is the letter, on the other the spirit. On the one hand is deuteronomic centralization of worship in Jerusalem; on the other is Jeremiah with his " Trust ye not in lying words, saying, the temple of Jehovah, the temple of Jehovah, the temple of Jehovah, are these."

One might almost say that one ideal of the church puts Scripture above God, while the other puts God above Scripture. The former may be called the dogmatic, the latter the metaphysical ideal of the church. It is to the dogmatic ideal, sincerely held, sincerely limiting God's plans to the explicit declarations of Scripture, that the divisive theories about sacraments and orders may be traced. The dogmatic ideal has great practical value; it is definite, it gives the church concrete powers in this world, and its valuation of Scripture has kept religious life vital. But its authoritarian basis in the end makes discussion impossible. When dogma faces dogma, each posing as absolute revelation, only abject surrender or bitter conflict can ensue. When dogma rests on Scripture, the interpretation of Scripture becomes the foundation stone of the church. The only way satisfactorily to insure unity in scriptural interpretation is the Roman Catholic way, which makes the church the authoritative interpreter. But this way seems to the Protestant to violate the ideal of free loyalty to truth. Yet Protestants who reject Rome and still hold to the dogmatic ideal of the church are in a precarious position, as Rome well knows. They either accept the interpretation of Calvin or of Barth as ultimate, or allow each individual to interpret as he will. Whichever they do, their views are subject to the results of historical criticism, which are devastating to literalism.

If we turn to the metaphysical ideal of the church, are we any better off? Metaphysics is fully as unpopular today as is Christian dogma. Is metaphysics any improvement on dogmatism? A dogmatic metaphysics surely would not be. But any conception of the Christian church must be metaphysical in some sense, because any idea of God (even the humanistic) is metaphysical. The Christian faith is a faith about God, his relations to Christ, and his place in reality. To define this faith in any way is to be metaphysical. Even the dogmatic ideal is metaphysical in its content. But we have to distinguish between metaphysical conceptions (which are any conceptions about what is truly real) and metaphysical method (which is rationally coherent interpretation of our entire experience). Dogmatism thus uses metaphysical conceptions but, at the vital point, rejects metaphysical method. The metaphysical ideal of the church is the ideal of the church as the body of those who use metaphysical method in their relations to a metaphysical Christian God. Otherwise stated, the church is the body of those who follow Christ and who test their Christian living and their thinking by their experience, reasonably interpreted. In the church, thus conceived, the principle of Christ, " By their fruits ye shall know them," is taken quite literally.

Fruits are what grow out of the inner nature of a tree in harmonious relations with its environment. The metaphysical ideal of the Christian church is that of a life that is in harmony with God and that is tested by its fruits.

The value of the church, then, is tested by the quality of its living cooperation with God; the ideal of the church is that of an eternally growing experience. The biblical revelation is taken by those who hold this ideal to be the revelation of a method of growth rather than the revelation of a fixed body of doctrine. This conception of the church [5] gives it an adventurous and experimental task, and at the same time recognizes the divine initiative and the divine leadership as immanent in the whole history of the church. Divine revelation is not concentrated in the first century, but is a continuous process of growth in the experience of divine values. If the dogmatic ideal locates ecclesiastical authority on earth in the infallible Word and the infallible Church, the metaphysical ideal locates ultimate authority in God alone, a God who not merely tolerates differences of opinion, but also uses those differences as a means of bringing his followers nearer to him, and nearer to one another. Tolerance, hopeless of fruitage on the dogmatic view, on the metaphysical view is accompanied by self-criticism, open-mindedness, and growth. The metaphysical ideal may not offer any greater prospect of immediate agreement among churches than does the dogmatic, but it proposes a method of growth toward harmony and a more generous view of divine purpose.

III. THE CONCEPT OF SOCIAL FUNCTION

With the definition of the empirical and ideal conceptions of truth, society, and the church, the foundations of this essay have been laid and its goal in principle attained. It remains to make explicit certain important implications.

The only actual truth we have is truth that is socially found and that functions socially. No individual ever discovered any truth unless he built on his social heritage. Truth, then, is a social function, whatever else it may be. And the church, as a part of society, obviously functions socially.

Let us now inquire exactly what is meant by the concept of social function. In the broadest sense, the social function of anything consists of the actual social consequences which follow from its existence, regardless of whether those consequences are hurtful or helpful. But usually when we speak of social function we mean, more specifically, a relation to the purposes of society. Whatever fulfills a social purpose of any kind has a social function relative to that purpose. Social purposes may aim at the realization of brute empirical desires, as when a state seeks territorial aggrandizement regardless of questions of right; or social purposes may aim at the realization of ideals, as when a group of scientists conduct an experiment or when a group of worshipers seek to learn the will of God.

Thus we have both empirical social purpose and ideal social purpose, and hence both empirical and ideal social functions.

IV. THE SOCIAL FUNCTION OF TRUTH

In speaking of the social function of truth we must keep in mind the distinction between the empirical and the ideal. Empirical truths, truth-claims, are, of course, far more abundant than is love for ideal truth. Their abundance is an important social fact. The more empirical " truths " are believed in without regard for empirical truth, the more difficult it is for truth to exercise its ideal social function. Sincere belief that error is truth is a means of perpetuating error and social malfunction.

The social function of ideal truth may be summarized with a brevity in inverse ratio to its importance. The following items are the chief factors in the ideal social function of truth:

First: To define the best available ends for social action to pursue (intrinsic social values). (It lies quite beyond our present purpose to develop the details of such a theory of value.)

Secondly: To criticize ends empirically striven for in the light of the ideal definition.

Thirdly: To discover or create new ends — new works of music or of literature, or new philosophical or religious truths.

Fourthly: To discover and apply the appropriate means for achieving the ideal ends of social life. (Mr. John Dewey regards it as the sole function of intelligence to find and use instruments for the control of experience; but his instrumentalism must be supplemented, or rather preceded, by an intrinsicalism; if we do not know truth about the ends of life, no truth about means will serve any ideal social function. Mr. Dewey's thought is pungent and wholesome precisely because he acknowledges ideal social ends in spite of his theory.)

Fifthly: To point society to supersocial truth. Truth obviously functions in society. But the ideal of truth is an ideal about what is reasonable and actual regardless of whether society approves it or not. Social approval may be essential to the functioning of truth; it is not essential to its trueness.

Sixthly: To admonish society of the tentativeness of present insight into truth, and to warn against the confusion of probability with certainty. Empirical truth is never wholly ideal.

If one considers these six social functions of truth with the Christian church in mind, it will become clear that there is a very close relation between the functions of truth and the functions of the church, which we shall next consider.

V. THE SOCIAL FUNCTION OF THE CHURCH

It is not our aim to appraise in detail the empirical social functions of the church. Those functions have been mixed. They have combined intolerance, conflict with science and philosophy, hatred, persecutions and wars, with love of God and humanity, improvement in the status of woman, support of education, art, and hospitals, and countless social reforms. At almost any stage of history in almost any church, the wheat and the tares will be found growing together, and evidence for both could be piled up indefinitely.

Our interest at present is in the ideal social functions of the church. In enumerating them it is necessary to adopt some order, but it is not to be supposed that the order chosen is intended to express the relative importance of the functions mentioned. In fact, it would be truer to regard these functions as co-ordinate in value. Certainly no church could be viewed as fulfilling its proper obligations to society if it omits any one of these functions.

The first function of the church is that of allegiance to the ideal of truth. This function, it is true, is not peculiar to the church. It is one which every social institution — the school, the stage, commerce, and the state — owes to society as a logical and a moral obligation. Continued nonpayment of the debt does not cancel the obligation. All institutions have made token-payments in recognition of that obligation. All institutions have fallen short. There are two institutions especially obligated, by their very nature, to be loyal to truth. They are the school and the church. The school emphasizes man's search for truth; the church emphasizes the truth itself as searching for man. When the school fails in its allegiance to truth man is disloyal to himself; when the church fears or opposes truth it is guilty of disloyalty to God himself. It has committed a treasonable blasphemy which vitiates all of its social functioning. More deeply even than the school the church is obligated to be truth-loving, truth-seeking, open-minded, critical, and constructive. Where it fails in this, truth-lovers are alienated, and cynical truth-scorners in forum and mart are delighted to welcome the church into their ranks; worst of all, the church then betrays its God.

The church's second function is also one which it shares with all other social institutions, yet with a special degree of obligation. It is that of acknowledging its membership in and its responsibility to human society as a whole. Every social group or institution is necessarily a part of humanity, and every group is in duty bound to respect the rights of all. Some institutions, however, by their very nature have broader social obligations than others. Organized baseball in America has the function of furnishing clean and sportsmanlike amusement. It has no obligation to politics or religion or art, except to keep out of them; it makes no direct contribution to science or philosophy, and is interested in their truth-seeking only insofar as it directly affects baseball. But the church, as an interpreter of God to the world, must be universal. Any God worthy of worship must be a universal God of all races, nations, and civilizations. The church, therefore, must be universal in spirit. A provincial or parochial church is a contradiction in terms. The concept of a national church, an established church, or of a local community church, threatens this universally human function of the church. National churches and community churches may, it is true, achieve a truly ecumenical standpoint, but they do so in spite of their mode of organization, not on account of it.

The third function (like all of those yet to be mentioned) is peculiar to the church. A Christian church cannot be at all unless it is an institution committed to the task of preserving and reinterpreting the lessons of the Christian Scriptures and of Christian history. An institution which has forgotten its own past has become another institution, just as a person suffering from total amnesia has become another person. Without the Bible there is no historical basis for knowledge of the teachings or of the religious value of Jesus Christ; and a Christianity without Christ is a self-contradiction. Likewise it would be folly for the church to forget Christian history. If the principles of Christ have been tested and confirmed through the ages, the church owes to society the spread of this knowledge. If the church has failed in its loyalty or, on the other hand, has learned new truths, it is obligated here, too, to share its experiences. The alternative to this historical task is to forget history and to begin in each generation with barbarism — a method that is being far too successfully approximated by many in our times.

The fourth social function of the church, perhaps its most important function, is that of holding up before society the ideal of the will of God. This ideal is a dangerous one, for it lures men into identifying the will of God with their own pet schemes and programs. Leaders of the church easily find the will of God in the same place where greater power and larger salaries for themselves are located. But the potency of the ideal of the will of God lies in its paradoxical character. It must indeed be the will of a good and just God that each person shall "follow the gleam" by being true to the results of what he deems to be his own best thinking and insight; but it is utterly incompatible with the ideal of the will of God to regard any present insight as the best that God has in store for us or can reveal to us. Thus the will of God is immanent in the best insight of the present; but it is transcendent in leading beyond it. The church errs when it regards all human endeavor as essentially sinful; it errs equally when it regards men as good enough when they are doing the best they can. If the European church often commits the former error, the American tends easily to fall into the latter. The ideal of the will of God should keep the church from both errors and should cause the church to function more vitally in the social order.

The fifth social function of the church is to teach worship and reverence, that is, devotion to the supreme source of all goodness, beauty, truth, and holiness. The prayers, rituals, and sacraments of the church, from a social standpoint, have this one function. If they increase devotion to the highest values by leading men to the source of all value, then they are giving society what it most needs. Unfortunately, the very forms of worship have often exhibited a conflict of ideals and dogmatic arrogance instead of setting society an example which makes the values harmonious and attractive. Worship is the supreme experience of value. In fostering worship, the church is not only the conscience, but the very soul of society.

The church's sixth social function is that of continuing as the one lasting international and supernational force in the world. Feeble as the church's power has been in preserving world peace, no one should forget that the church is the only permanent historical institution making for friendly co-operation among nations, and also the only institution which by right is in a position to rebuke the state or to point at a king with the words, " Thou art the man." This function is of supreme importance in a time like the present, when the experiences back of the Book of Revelation, re-enacted in Germany and Russia, are in danger of being repeated on a world-wide scale. When the church is true to herself, she never renders unto Caesar that which is God's.

Closely related to the sixth (as well as to the second) function is the seventh social function of the church, which in a sense summarizes all the others. It is that of exemplifying its faith in divine values by striving by all the means in its power for the conditions which make spiritual values attainable. This means work for the rights of every oppressed individual and group, for a just and free social order, for economic and international relations which do not blaspheme every principle of truth and value.

In a word, then, the social function of the church is to cooperate with God in the salvation of society. Its task is to make the ideal real in the actual experience of humanity. This goal, rather than an otherworldly or an individualistic conception, will alone justify the church as a social institution.

NOTES

[1] The word "experience" is used here to mean any actual conscious process or processes of any kind, whether sensory or affective or conative or intellectual, whether spontaneous or critical, whether passive or active. Thus the term has, on the one hand, a far wider range than does the "experience" of traditional empiricism with its restriction to sense experience as the only type worthy of the eulogistic word; on the other hand, it is far narrower than the "experience" of John Dewey, which is coextensive with all objects which ever affect conscious experience, and so is really synonymous with nature. For reasons which cannot be developed here it seems more sensible to look upon nature as an inference from, or an interpretation of, our experience than to identify the one with the other. Our experience is our evidence for nature; it is not identical with nature. Nature is there whether we experience it or not.

[2] 529 B.

[3] 68 D.

[4] July 17, 1939.

[5] For a somewhat related discussion, see Dr. Harris Franklin Rall's essay on "Given or Gathered," in *Christendom*, Spring 1939.

LET THE CHURCH BE THE CHURCH!

ERNEST FREMONT TITTLE
First Methodist Church, Evanston, Illinois

MEETING at Madras, in December 1938, the International Missionary Council said: " In the presence of . . . disasters and forebodings, we see the judgment of God's righteousness upon our society; but we see also His judgment upon our churches — so enmeshed in the world that they dare not speak God's full word of truth unafraid, so divided that they cannot speak that word with full power, so sullied by pettiness and worldliness that the face of Christ cannot be clearly discerned in them, or His power go forth through them for redemption." It also said: " Yet, in all humility and penitence, we are constrained to declare to a baffled and needy world that the Christian Church, under God, is its greatest hope." [1] Can these statements be reconciled, one with the other? For my own part, I believe they can be.

True, we who constitute the churches are so much under the influence of a secular culture that our outlook often is not God's but man's. Corrupted by pride and self-centeredness, we are prone to listen to the voice of self-interest rather than to the voice of God. In many cases our standard of success is the selfsame standard which the world recognizes, not the standard of Christ; so that, as individuals, we measure success in terms of money and power and, as churches, we measure it in terms of financial support and institutional prestige. Nor have our churches as yet completely withdrawn from their unholy alliance with Moloch and Mars. Even so, we can hardly doubt that Jesus Christ is the Way, the Truth, and the Life and that there is no other way out of the world's misery. Insofar as the world accepts him as its Lord and Master, there is notable increase of security and of freedom, opportunity, happiness, and hope. Insofar as it denies, betrays, and crucifies him, there is terrible increase of insecurity and of fear and hatred and violence and cruelty, until, as now, all the lights of a humane and civilized culture threaten to go out. Hence, confessing our own selfishness and worldliness, we nonetheless may feel bound to suppose that the Christian church, under God, is the world's greatest hope. To be sure, the church cannot save the world. Only God can save the world. But God in history employs human agents to carry out his redemptive purpose; and if it be true that Jesus Christ is "the real and living way," it would seem to be entirely credible that the Christian church, although not the only agency, is the chief agency on which God must now depend. There is no other institution that is profoundly concerned to mediate Christ to the world.

This must be said, however. The church as we now know it is not, in every case, "the greatest hope of the world." Looking at the church in his own community, many a man, ethically sensitive and socially minded, has found himself asking, Can anything truly redemptive come out of that? As a matter of fact, the church, as we now know it, is not always in very deed the church. In some cases, it occupies a churchly building and it recites the creed, it reads the Scriptures, it uses the prayers of the church; yet it is not in very deed the church, for its supreme allegiance is not given to

God, its " gospel " is but a travesty of the gospel of Christ, the pattern of its life bears but scant resemblance to the pattern that is laid down in the New Testament.

" Let the church be the church." That challenge, which came from the world conference assembled at Oxford in the summer of 1937, requires now to be met. The purpose of this paper is to explore its meaning.

I

To the church in Ephesus, St. Paul writes:

You belong to God's own household, you are a building that rests on the apostles and prophets as its foundation, with Christ Jesus as the cornerstone; in him the whole structure is welded together and rises into a sacred temple in the Lord, and in him you are yourselves built into this to form a habitation for God in the spirit.[2]

In the light of this passage, " Let the church be the church " might be understood to mean, Let the church be a habitation for God — a community of Christians in which God may dwell and make manifest his kingdom and power and glory.

Let the church be a habitation for God, *not merely another socially minded organization.* Unless it has a vital faith in God born of its own experience of his presence and power, the church has little to say to the world that is not being said by other institutions. Has it anything worth saying to a world that, having lost sight of God, has lost confidence in itself and is today, without hope, moving rapidly to disaster? The church must be a religious fellowship based on a living faith in God if it is to be used of God to save the world from madness and despair.

Let the church be a habitation for God, *not merely an agency of propaganda for the national state*. A church whose supreme allegiance, under stress, is given to the state cannot be a habitation for God. A church which takes its orders, not from God, but from the state, whether it be a fascist or a democratic state, is in reality not a church but simply an agency of government whose function is to maintain the morale of the people, especially when they are being sold down the river.

In almost every part of the world, there is now a growing tension between the church and the state. In Russia, the church is barely able to exist. In Germany, many of the bravest and best of its leaders are in prison. In Italy, it is tolerated — on conditions that are humiliating, to say the least. In Japan, native Christians, like all other citizens, are required to bow before the shrine of the emperor — an act which does not necessarily call for the ascription of divinity to the emperor's person but which, undoubtedly, is intended to symbolize a primary allegiance to the state. In Japanese dependencies, such as Korea and Manchukuo, an attempt is now being made to bring the church, as well as the school, under the complete control of military authority. In one case, a church which had caused the Ten Commandments to be inscribed on the front of its house of worship was peremptorily told, " You must have the first four of these commands erased, inasmuch as they have political implications." In the United States, the church has been accorded no little freedom. So far as the national government is concerned, the church, in peacetime, may say anything it has a mind to. But what if the Congress should declare war? The decision of the United States Supreme Court in the Macintosh case leaves little room for doubt that, in that event, Christians, like all other citizens, would be expected to consider that their supreme allegiance was due to the will of the Congress, *not* to the will of God. In more than one part of the world, the command, " Thou shalt have no other gods before me," is now supposed to have " political implications " and may be expected, if consistently obeyed, to produce political repercussions.

Jesus, when he was confronted with the question, " Is it lawful for us to give tribute unto Caesar, or not? " answered, " Render unto Caesar the things that are Caesar's, and unto God the things that are God's." And his enemies " marveled at his answer, and held their peace." [3] But this unexpected answer, which closed the mouths of ancient Pharisees, has opened the mouths of modern Pharisees, who, although they may remember nothing else that Jesus ever said, never weary of quoting, "Render unto Caesar the things that are Caesar's," being careful, however, not to finish the quotation. There are now many persons inside as well as outside the church who take the position that Christians should leave in the hands of Caesar all questions of major importance. To be sure, Caesar may be advised by the secular press, by " patriotic " societies, by chambers of commerce, by makers of munitions, by the shipbuilding industry, and, indeed, by any industry that has a private ax to grind; but not by the church. The church, according to some of its own members, does not know enough to give advice to Caesar. People who have an eye to their own interests know enough to whisper in the ear of Caesar; it is only Christians who, having the welfare of the world at heart, are too dumb to talk!

Let the church repudiate the assertion of its own incompetence to pass judgment upon matters which for millions of human beings are matters of life and death. Let the church stand fast in the position that was taken at Oxford:

> Since we believe in the holy God as the source of justice, we do not consider the state as the ultimate source of law but rather as its guarantor. It is not the lord but the servant of justice. There can be for the Christian no ultimate authority but very God. . . . It is true that our Lord told his disciples to render to Caesar the things that are Caesar's and to God the things that are God's. But it is God who declares what is Caesar's. Therefore, whatever the choice may be, the Christian must always, whether as a member of the church or as a citizen, obey the will of God. . . . The primary duty of the church to the state is to be the church, namely, to witness for God, to preach his word, to confess the faith before men, to teach both young and old to observe the divine commandments, and to serve the nation and the state by proclaiming the will of God as the supreme standard to which all human wills must be subject and all human conduct must conform.[4]

Let the church be a habitation for God — " the God and Father of our Lord Jesus Christ." [5] The God in whom our generation has put its trust is not the God and Father of our Lord Jesus Christ. In a modern play entitled *Wings Over Europe,* the minister of the navy undertakes to say what a demand for naval reduction means to him. As he sees them, battleships represent the security, the power, and the glory of empire. " And now," he exclaims, " I am bidden to scrap them in the name of a Christ in whom I do not believe and in disregard of Jehovah, God of Battles, in whom I do believe." In a " Christian " country, that, of course, is not the sort of thing that one is expected to say. And, in fact, people ordinarily do not come right out and say that they have no faith in Christ. They merely act as if they had none. Having said that Christ is very God of very God, they quietly ignore him and put their trust in battleships, bombing planes, mines, tanks, guns, flame throwers, hand grenades, and a devil's brew of lethal gases. Today, unbelief in the might of spiritual forces is widespread. Even among Christians there is a not uncommon suspicion that a God whose power is only the power of truth and right and love is unable to cope with imperial gangsters on the march. Hence, in some quarters, the revival of an apocalypticism that pins its hopes on a violent invasion of history by a God who has at his command something more formidable than truth and right and love. And hence, in many quarters, a growing belief that there must be at least one more war to end war and to make the world safe for democracy.

Let the church be a habitation for God, *even the Father of our Lord Jesus Christ*. Let the church believe that truth and right and love, far from being impotent, are the mightiest forces in history. Let it maintain that evil cannot be overcome with more evil but only with good and that God, working through men who do good even at great cost to themselves, is able to overcome lies, injustice, and tyranny. Let the church declare that Christ crucified, unto imperialists a stumbling block and unto militarists foolishness, is the power and the wisdom of God.

II

To the church in Corinth, St. Paul writes, " Now ye are the body of Christ, and severally members thereof." [6] This, undoubtedly, is Paul's great and favorite conception of the

Christian society. In letter after letter [7] he puts forth and
develops the idea that the church is the body of Christ.

Now, Protestantism has thought of the church as being a
pulpit for the proclamation of the word of God. It has not
commonly thought of the church as being a fellowship
which embodies the spirit of Christ and is thus enabled to
minister to every need of the world. In the main, evangelical Protestantism has not been very much concerned about
the world. Profoundly concerned for the salvation of human individuals, it has assumed, however, that the salvation
of individuals is in no way related to the political, economic,
and social conditions of the world. But in view of what child
labor does to the soul of a child, of what crime- and vice-
breeding slums do to the souls of those who dwell in them,
of what enforced unemployment does to the soul of the unemployed, and of what the fascist state does to the soul of
its people, this purely individualistic conception of salvation
can hardly be maintained.

Also, it is now quite clear that the church, unless it undertakes to improve the conditions of the world, will itself by
the world be either corrupted or destroyed. The spirit of
Antichrist *has found embodiment* in social institutions
which, day after day, are shaping the souls of men, including
churchmen. It has found embodiment in totalitarian systems which are determined either to transform the church
into their own likeness or to put an end to its existence. A
purely individualistic Christianity which is unconcerned for
the world is proving itself to be impotent alongside of anti-
Christian collectivisms which are changing the conditions
of the world by molding and directing the total life of the
individual. It is now all-important that the church should

be thought of as a fellowship which embodies the spirit of Christ and is thus enabled to minister to every need of the world. Let the church be to Christ what his own body was in the days of his flesh. Let it confront anti-Christian collectivisms with a world-wide fellowship that embodies the faith and purpose of Christ.

The church is itself an employer of labor. It employs administrators and preachers and teachers and secretaries and sextons. It employs editors and typesetters and bankboys and packers and salesmen. As an employer, let the church make ample provision, even unto old age, for the needs of its employees, including not only bishops but bankboys, not only those who write but those who set type. As an employer, let the church practice its own pronouncements on the rights of labor, including labor's right to organize for its own protection. Let it act in accordance with the most advanced standards of employer-employee relationship. Let it take the initiative in the raising of such standards. As an employer, let the church be the body of Christ, expressing *his* concern for the last and least of its employees.

The church is itself an investor. No small part of its income for world service is derived from investments. Let the church give attention to the character of its investments! It cannot afford to invest in antisocial enterprises, such as armament industries, breweries, and slum properties. Nor can it afford to invest in enterprises in which labor is being notoriously exploited. It could well afford, by its investments, to promote and encourage cooperative enterprises which embody a principle — cooperation — which is, indubitably, a Christian principle and one that, as is now becoming ever more apparent, is essential to the solution of some of the most desperate problems of national and international life. As an investor, let the church be the body of Christ, expressing *his* concern for righteousness and justice.

Today, the church is set in a world in which nation is arrayed against nation, race against race, and class against class. In such a world, let the church, in its own fellowship, demonstrate the possibility of a human community that transcends all barriers of race and nation and class. There is now far too much truth in the statement:

> Wherever racial inequality exists it is reflected just as much in our churches as in our economic, political, or cultural associations: the church is as exclusive of the black man or the yellow man, as the golf club. Blacks and whites can belong together and work together in the Communist Party. But they cannot worship together in the Church of Jesus Christ.[8]

Let the church be the body of Christ, in whom there can be neither Jew nor Greek, bond nor free.

Thanks to widespread unemployment, to the awful persecution of Jews and other minorities, and to the obscene operations of war, the church, today, is set in a world in which there is appalling suffering. In the United States, the present number of the unemployed is greater than the total membership of the Methodist Church, and rickets and pellagra are now appearing. In such a world, let the church be the hands of Christ, ministering to human need wherever it exists. The Society of Friends has set an example that might well be followed by every other church on earth. In time of war, it has ministered on both sides of the conflict to the tortured bodies and souls of men. At all times, it has fed the hungry, clothed the naked, sheltered the homeless, befriended the victims of "civilization." And, so doing, it has proclaimed the gospel of the love of God in a language that all men understand.

In the world of today, the cross looms as a dread possibility not only for the Christian but also for the Christian church. In some places, the church is now being ordered to render unto Caesar the things that are God's, on penalty of persecution if it refuses to do so. In other places, almost any day, it may be called upon both to say and to do things that are in utter contradiction of its own nature and mission. In such a world, let the church be the body of Christ, consenting if necessary to suffer but never to surrender that which makes it the *church*. Let the church not attempt to save its property, its financial support, or its social prestige on conditions that would involve the corruption of its spiritual life. Let the church not shrink from the fellowship of the sufferings of Christ, that it may know the power of his resurrection; that in days to come, having been the church and not merely the tool of nationalism and imperialism, it may be used of God to heal the hurt of the world.

III

"The Christian church, under God, is the greatest hope of the world." Therefore, "let the church *be* the church." By being the church it can, without inconsistency, call upon the world to repent of tempers and practices that are driving it mad and leading it to destruction.

Of calls for repentance there is now, to be sure, a plenty. They are, indeed, as grasshoppers for multitude, and they come from every corner of the earth. The only trouble with them is that they are addressed by sinners, not to themselves, but only to other sinners. Undoubtedly, the governments of Germany, Italy, and Japan are guilty in the eyes of God. But what other government on earth is now in a morally comfortable position to cast the first stone at them? Has British imperialism no present sins to repent of? Has French imperialism now nothing, even in Africa, to be ashamed of? Has the United States no racial doctrine or practice of which it now needs to repent? To be sure, there are varying degrees of guilt. Americans who exclude Jews from golf clubs are not as guilty as are Germans who physically mistreat them. Americans, Englishmen, and Frenchmen who, in the mills of Shanghai, indecently underpay Chinese labor, coining wealth for themselves out of the sweat and hunger of their fellows of another race — they, no doubt, are not as guilty as are Japanese violators and killers. But the fact remains that there is now no nation on earth whose hands are clean. The pot has been calling the kettle black, the kettle has been returning the compliment, and the world has been going to perdition. It is now quite clear that there is nothing to be gained by earnest attempts on the part of unrepentant sinners to persuade not themselves but other sinners to go to the mourners' bench.

The world now desperately wants to be saved. It cannot be saved unless and until it repents of its sins. It is, however, the Christian faith that men can repent and that the human heart can, by the grace of God, be radically transformed. Let the church, repenting of its own sins and seeking the forgiveness of God, call upon the people, not of other nations, but of its own nation, to repent of that cruel love of money and of power which is the deadly sin of the world. Let the church, putting its own house in order, call for the building of an economic order which, embodying the justice and the solicitude of God, will provide for all men the material conditions of intellectual and spiritual development. And let it call for the building of an international order in which no nation will insist upon being judge in its own cause, no nation will claim individual ownership of undeveloped territories, no nation will seek its own gain at the expense of its neighbors, but all nations will be placed in the way of security, opportunity, and hope.

Let the church be the church, that, calling for repentance and for " works worthy of repentance," it may proclaim the gospel of the saving grace of God. To a world that is bedeviled, confused, threatened with disaster, and now terribly afraid, the church, if only it be the church, may bring hope of redemption. For the God of Christian faith is a living God who, in history, is working for the salvation of individuals and, *therefore,* for the salvation of the world itself — those political institutions, social customs, and economic practices which so largely condition the spiritual development of men. By the action of political and economic forces, God is now bringing home the fact that men are members one of another, so that no nation can prosper unless all are enabled to prosper, no nation can have security unless all are made secure. In Jesus Christ, God is reconciling the world unto himself, creating in it a new mind, a new outlook on life, a new desire and ambition, so that growing numbers of men, beholding the glory of his kingdom and the imperative need of his righteousness, are now turning away from false gods and false hopes and gladly devoting themselves to God, even the Father of our Lord Jesus Christ.

Let the church be the church, that, calling upon the world

to repent and to do works worthy of repentance, it may also say: " Be of good cheer. We are not alone in a terrible time, with nothing to depend upon save our own resources. We are in the hands of God, who by the action of his power within us is able to do exceeding abundantly above all that we ask or think; unto whom be the glory in the church and in Christ Jesus throughout all generations forever and ever. Amen."

NOTES

[1] *Madras Series* (International Missionary Council, 1939), I, 173, 177.

[2] Eph. 3:20–21 (Moffatt).

[3] Luke 20:22–26.

[4] *The Oxford Conference — Official Report* (Chicago: Willett, Clark & Co., 1937), pp. 67–70.

[5] Eph. 1:3; II Cor. 1:3.

[6] I Cor. 12:27.

[7] Rom. 12:4 f.; Eph. 4:1–16; Col. 1:18.

[8] Gregory Vlastos, *Christian Faith and Democracy* (Association Press, 1939), p. 49.

BIBLIOGRAPHY OF THE WRITINGS OF HARRIS FRANKLIN RALL

To March, 1940 *

I. BOOKS

DER LEIBNIZSCHE SUBSTANZBEGRIFF. Halle: Erhardt Karras, 1899.

THE SOCIAL MINISTRY OF JESUS. In *The Social Ministry,* edited by Harry F. Ward (New York: Eaton & Mains; Cincinnati: Jennings & Graham, 1910), pp. 27–55.

A NEW TESTAMENT HISTORY. New York: Abingdon Press, 1914.
Second half translated into Burmese.

A WORKING FAITH. New York: Abingdon Press, 1914.

SANCTIFICATION. In *The International Standard Bible Encyclopedia* (Chicago: Howard-Severance Co., 1915), pp. 2681–85.

THE LIFE OF JESUS. New York: Abingdon Press, 1917.
Translated into Korean.

TEACHER'S MANUAL FOR THE LIFE OF JESUS. New York: Abingdon Press, 1918.

THE TEACHINGS OF JESUS. New York: Abingdon Press, 1918.
Also published in Spanish, Korean and Hindustani translations.

* Editor's Note. The editor is happy to express his sincere gratitude and deep appreciation to Miss Mabel Frances Gardiner, librarian of Garrett Biblical Institute, and to her assistants in the Garrett Library, who are largely responsible for compiling the data for this bibliography.

It has seemed best to publish this bibliography in four parts, as follows: I. Books. II. Pamphlets. III. Articles. IV. Book Reviews. Within each of the four parts the order of arrangement is chronological.

TEACHER'S MANUAL FOR THE TEACHINGS OF JESUS. New York: Abingdon Press, 1918.

MODERN PREMILLENNIALISM AND THE CHRISTIAN HOPE. New York: Abingdon Press, 1920.
Reprinted as pamphlet from the above: WAS JOHN WESLEY A PREMILLENNIALIST? Toronto: Methodist Book and Publishing House, 1921.

THE COMING KINGDOM. New York: Abingdon Press, 1924.

THE NATURE OF REVELATION. Fourth Biennial Meeting of the Conference of Theological Seminaries and Colleges in the United States and Canada (Evanston, Ill., 1924), pp. 24–30.

THE MEANING OF GOD. Nashville, Tenn.: Cokesbury Press, 1925.
Emory University, Quillian Lectures.
Reprinted in part as a chapter in *God in Christian Thought,* compiled by H. J. Harwood. Rangoon, Burma, 1939.

THE PATH TO GOD. In *Week-Day Sermons in King's Chapel,* edited by Harold E. B. Speight (New York: Macmillan Co., 1925).

THE STORY OF THE FAMILY OF OTTO AND ANNA STEINER RALL. Privately printed. Chicago, 1925.

MODERN PHILOSOPHY: ORIGINS OF ITS METHOD; THE SERVICE OF FOUR FAMOUS THINKERS TO THE CHRISTIAN FAITH. In *An Outline of Christianity; The Story of Our Civilization,* Vol. 4, edited by Francis J. McConnell (New York: Bethlehem Publishers, Inc., 1926), pp. 131–50.

CHRISTIANITY AND JUDAISM COMPARE NOTES. By Harris Franklin Rall and Samuel S. Cohon. New York: Macmillan Co., 1927.

CHRISTIANITY TODAY (editor and joint author). Nashville, Tenn.: Cokesbury Press, 1928.

THE TEACHING OF JESUS. In *The Abingdon Bible Commentary,* edited by Frederick Carl Eiselen, Edwin Lewis, David G. Downey (New York: Abingdon Press, 1929), pp. 904–13.

RELIGION AS SALVATION. Mimeographed lectures on theology. Evanston, Ill., 1929, 1932, 1936, 1939.

WHAT DOES BEHAVIORISM MEAN FOR RELIGION? In *Behaviorism: A Battle Line,* edited by William P. King (Nashville, Tenn.: Cokesbury Press, 1930), pp. 288–304.

THE JESUS OF THE NEW TESTAMENT AND THE JESUS OF TO-DAY. In *The Minister and His Bible,* Annual College of Preachers (New York: General Conference Commission on Courses of Study of the Methodist Episcopal Church, 1930–31), pp. 23–29.

THE SIGNIFICANCE OF THE DOCTRINE OF THE SPIRIT FOR PRESENT-DAY LIFE. Seventh Biennial Meeting of the Conference of Theological Seminaries and Colleges in the United States and Canada (Chicago, 1931), pp. 71–80.

THE PREACHER MUST BRING GOD. In *" They Went Forth, and Preached Everywhere, the Lord Working With Them,"* Annual College of Preachers (New York: General Conference Commission on Courses of Study of the Methodist Episcopal Church, 1931–32), pp. 47–50.

THEOLOGY, EMPIRICAL AND CHRISTIAN. In *Contemporary American Theology,* edited by Vergilius Ferm (New York: Round Table Press, Inc., 1933), pp. 243–73.

THE QUEST FOR GOD THROUGH JOY; THE QUEST FOR GOD THROUGH SUFFERING; THE QUEST FOR GOD THROUGH SERVICE. In *The Quest for God through Worship,* edited by Philip Henry Lotz (St. Louis: Bethany Press, 1934), pp. 58–59, 134–35, 226–27.

THE EXPERIENCE OF GOD IN THE SOCIAL ORDER. In *Experience,* Annual College of Preachers (New York: General Conference Commission on Courses of Study of the Methodist Episcopal Church, 1935), pp. 57–61.

A FAITH FOR TODAY. New York: Abingdon Press, 1936.

WHAT FAITH MEANS. In *Faith,* Annual College of Preachers (New York: General Conference Commission on Courses of Study of the Methodist Episcopal Church, 1936), pp. 18–23.

THE MEANING OF GOD FOR OUR PREACHING. In *Preaching,* Annual College of Preachers (New York: General Conference Commission on Courses of Study of the Methodist Episcopal Church, 1937), pp. 24–28.

THE CERTAINTY OF GOD. In *God,* Annual College of Preachers (New York: General Conference Commission on Courses of Study of the Methodist Episcopal Church, 1937), pp. 16–19.

RELIGION AND PUBLIC AFFAIRS (editor and joint author). In Honor of Bishop Francis John McConnell. New York: Macmillan Co., 1937.

SOME CURRENT CONCEPTIONS OF MAN. In *Man,* Annual College of Preachers (New York: General Conference Commission on Courses of Study of the Methodist Episcopal Church, 1938), pp. 47–52.

JESUS AND THE FAMILY OF GOD. In *The Family of God,* Annual College of Preachers (New York: General Conference Commission on Courses of Study of the Methodist Church, 1939).

TOWARDS A CHRISTIAN PHILOSOPHY. Probable title of a volume to appear in autumn 1940.

II. PAMPHLETS

THE OBLIGATION OF METHODISM TO TOMORROW. Baltimore, 1910.

WHAT TO READ. Privately printed. Baltimore, 1910.
Also in many printings by the American Bible Society under the title, HOW TO USE THE BIBLE.

STUDIES IN PAUL. Outline of addresses at Epworth League Institutes. Chicago, 1911.

A Christian's Financial Creed. First published in 1914 by the Colorado Conference of the Methodist Episcopal Church, then in successive editions and printings by the Commission on Finance, and by other churches.

The Master Teacher. Denver: Iliff School of Theology, 1914.

The Conference Course of Study. New York: General Conference Commission on Courses of Study, 1918.

A Teaching Mission. Philadelphia: Board of Home Missions and Church Extension of the Methodist Episcopal Church [1918?].

The Brotherhood and Social Service. New York: Methodist Brotherhood [1920?].

Doctrinal Preaching and the New Day. Philadelphia: Board of Home Missions and Church Extension of the Methodist Episcopal Church, 1921.

A Statement of the Methodist Faith. Prepared for the Board of Home Missions and Church Extension and contained in the pamphlet, *Facts Concerning the Methodist Episcopal Church*. New York: Methodist Book Concern, 1921, 1922.
Printed in Czech, Lithuanian, Polish, Russian, Slovak, Italian, Portuguese, Spanish, Arabic, Finnish, Hungarian.

What Can I Believe? Minneapolis, 1922. Last edition, Chicago: Board of Education of the Methodist Episcopal Church, 1933.

What Can We Believe? Seattle, Wash.: Plymouth Congregational Church, 1922.

I Believe. Chicago: American Institute of Sacred Literature, 1924, and in later reprintings.

The Religion of the Bible in the World Today. Chicago: American Institute of Sacred Literature, 1925.

WHAT IS SPIRITUALITY? Chicago: Board of Sunday Schools of the Methodist Episcopal Church [1930?].

THE CHRISTIAN CONCEPTION OF GOD. One of fourteen pamphlets on *The Significance of Christ in the Modern World.* New York: Board of Foreign Missions of the Methodist Episcopal Church, 1931.

THE GARRETT OF TOMORROW. Evanston, Ill.: Garrett Biblical Institute, 1937.

PLANNING THE COLLEGE COURSE FOR MINISTERIAL STUDENTS. Nashville, Tenn.: General Board of Christian Education, 1937.

WHAT HAVE CHRISTIANS TO SHARE WITH NON-CHRISTIANS? Chicago: Movement for World Christianity, 1937.

WHICH WAY THEOLOGY? Evanston, Ill.: Garrett Biblical Institute [1937?].

III. ARTICLES

DO WE NEED A METHODIST CREED? *Methodist Review,* March–April 1907, LXXXIX, 221-30.

THEOLOGY AND THE HISTORICAL METHOD. *Methodist Review,* March–April 1910, XCII, 194-210.

THE LIFE AND TEACHINGS OF JESUS, a special course of lessons for adult classes prepared under the auspices of the Committee on Curriculum of the Board of Sunday Schools of the Methodist Episcopal Church. *Adult Bible Class Monthly,* Jan. to Dec., 1916, IX.

PREMILLENNIALISM AND THE SCRIPTURES. *Sunday School Journal,* Feb. 1916, XLVIII, 96-98.

PREMILLENNIALISM AND JUDAISM. *Sunday School Journal,* March 1916, XLVIII, 177-79.

PREMILLENNIALISM AND THE WORK OF THE KINGDOM. *Sunday School Journal,* April 1916, XLVIII, 271–73.

THE CHRISTIAN HOPE. *Sunday School Journal,* May 1916, XLVIII, 365–67.

WHY I DO NOT ACCEPT PREMILLENNIALISM, in a symposium on premillennialism. *Sunday School Journal,* March 1917, XLIX, 149–51.

PREMILLENNIALISM. I. THE ISSUE. *Biblical World,* July 1919, LIII, 339–47.

PREMILLENNIALISM. II. PREMILLENNIALISM AND THE BIBLE. *Biblical World,* Sept. 1919, LIII, 459–69.

PREMILLENNIALISM. III. WHERE PREMILLENNIALISM LEADS. *Biblical World,* Nov. 1919, LIII, 617–27.

A STEWARDSHIP CREED. *Christian Advocate,* Jan. 22, 1920, XCV, 119.

METHODISM AND PREMILLENNIALISM. *Methodist Review,* March–April 1920, CIII, 209–19.

METHODISM TODAY. *American Journal of Theology,* Oct. 1920, XXIV, 481–501.

WILL YOU? *Epworth Herald,* April 23, 1921, XXXII, 410–11.

THE NATION TO-MORROW — A STORY IN DEMOCRACY. *Epworth Herald,* Oct. 29, 1921, XXXII, 1062–63.

THE NATIONS TO-MORROW — A WORLD SURVEY. *Epworth Herald,* Nov. 5, 1921, XXXII, 1084–85.

INDUSTRY TO-MORROW; A TEST FOR CHRISTIANITY. *Epworth Herald,* Nov. 26, 1921, XXXII, 1167–69.

WHAT WILL BE THE RELIGION OF TO-MORROW? *Epworth Herald*, Dec. 10, 1921, XXXII, 1220–21.

ARE LAYMEN INTERESTED IN THEOLOGY? *Zion's Herald*, Sept. 27, 1922, C, 1226.

A CHRISTIAN'S FINANCIAL CREED. *Christian Advocate*, March 13, 1924, XCIX, 313.

NOT INTELLECTUAL CREDENCE BUT PERSONAL TRUST, in a symposium on "The Faith Once Delivered to the Saints." *Methodist Review*, March–April 1924, CVII, 253–57.

WHAT ABOUT OUR MINISTRY? *Methodist Review*, May–June 1924, CVII, 401–12.

MAKING A METHODIST THEOLOGY. *Methodist Quarterly Review*, Oct. 1925, LXXIV, 579–96.

THE HISTORIC MEANINGS OF RELIGIOUS EXPERIENCE. *Religious Education*, Oct. 1925, XX, 330–36.

EXPLANATORY NOTES AND LESSON EXPOSITION, on the Improved Uniform Lessons. *Church School Journal*, Jan. to April, 1926, LVIII.

THE GOSPEL OF JOHN; ITS DISTINCTIVE PURPOSE, CONTENT, AND AUTHORSHIP. *Church School Journal*, Feb. 1926, LVIII, 86–87.

EXPLANATORY NOTES AND LESSON EXPOSITION, on the International Uniform Lessons. *Church School Journal*, Jan. to June, 1927, LIX.

MAKING YOUR OWN BIBLE. *Senior Quarterly*, Jan.–March 1927, XLV, 2–4.

THE CREED OF JESUS. *Christian Advocate*, Jan. 13, 1927, CII, 40–41.

JESUS IN THE THOUGHT OF TO-DAY; A Glimpse of Some Recent Books on Jesus. *Christian Advocate*, May 12, 1927, CII, 584–86.

THE POPE AND THE PROFESSOR. *Religious Education,* March 1928, XXIII, 178–79.

LECTURE FOUNDATIONS AND RELIGIOUS BOOKS. *Christian Advocate* (Nashville, Tenn.), May 18, 1928, LXXXIX, 617–19.

WHAT IS THE MATTER WITH RELIGION AND WHAT IS TO BE DONE ABOUT IT? In a symposium. *Religious Education,* June 1928, XXIII, 509–11.

LUTHER B. WILSON; THE CHURCH OF A LIVING FAITH; BEHIND THE EDITOR'S BACK; THE DUTY OF HATRED; GREAT DEEDS AT KANSAS CITY; ABOUT WAR AND PEACE; UNFINISHED BUSINESS. Editorials in the *Northwestern Christian Advocate,* June 1928, LXXVI.

BELIEF AND FAITH AND EDUCATION; GOD AND MR. BARNES; THE MEN THAT STOOD BY; " A PREFACE TO MORALS; " ADVENTURES IN FRIENDSHIP; WHO IS THE EDUCATED MAN? WHO WAS THE MURDERER? WE THANK GOD AND TAKE COURAGE. Editorials in the *Northwestern Christian Advocate,* May and June, 1929, LXXVII.

JESUS AS TEACHER TO-DAY. *Adult Bible Class Monthly,* Jan. 1930, XXIII, 29–30.

HOW MEN ARE THINKING ABOUT GOD. *Methodist Review,* May–June 1931, CXIV, 309–17.

A DISCUSSION GROUP AND WHAT IT ACCOMPLISHED. *Church School Journal,* July 1931, LXIII, 374–75.

WHICH WAY RELIGION? *Christian Advocate, Northwestern Edition,* Aug. 13, 1931, LXXIX, 806.

PUTTING OVER THE CHRISTIAN MESSAGE. *Christian Advocate, Central Edition* (and other editions), Sept. 17 and 24, 1931, LXXIX, 923–24, 949.

THE IDEA OF GOD IN RECENT LITERATURE. *Religion in Life,* Winter 1932, I, 55–69.

THE CLIMATE OF RELIGION. *Religion in Life,* Spring 1934, III, 245–56.

A FAITH FOR TO-DAY. A series of articles appearing in the *Church School Journal,* Jan. to Dec., 1935, LXVII, under the following titles: A FAITH FOR TO-DAY; WHAT IS CHRISTIANITY? WHAT IS THE BIBLE AND HOW SHALL WE USE IT? HOW SHALL WE THINK ABOUT GOD? KNOWING GOD; GOD AND THE WORLD; GOD AND THE WORLD OF EVIL; CONCERNING PRAYER; WHAT DOES IT MEAN TO BE SAVED? CONCERNING SOCIAL SALVATION; I BELIEVE IN THE CHURCH; THE LIFE TO COME.

EDINBURGH 1937; THE SECOND WORLD CONFERENCE ON FAITH AND ORDER. *Church School Journal,* Dec. 1937, LXIX, 620–21.

AFTER EDINBURGH. *Religion in Life,* Winter 1938, VII, 22–35.

THOU SHALT LOVE THYSELF. *Epworth Herald,* Aug. 20, 1938, XLIX, 484–85.

THE STORY OF CREATION. *Christian Advocate, Northwestern Edition* (and other editions), Sept. 8, 1938, LXXXVI, 926.

THE CHURCH GIVEN OR GATHERED? *Christendom,* Spring 1939, IV, 164–73.

HOW FAR SHOULD OUR CHRISTIANITY BE EXPERIMENTAL, EXPLANATIONAL, SOCIAL? *World Christianity,* Fourth Quarter, 1939, III, 29–33.

THE AUTHORITY OF OUR FAITH. *International Review of Missions,* Jan. 1940, XXIX, 130–39.

IV. BOOK REVIEWS *

A New Dictionary of Religion and Ethics. *Journal of Religion*, March 1922, II, 210–12.
Review of Shailer Mathews and G. B. Smith: *A Dictionary of Religion and Ethics.*

Some Modern Interpretations of Christianity. *JR*, March 1925, V, 196–202.
Review of Harry Emerson Fosdick: *The Modern Use of the Bible;*
E. G. A. Holmes: *Dying Lights and Dawning;*
Albert C. Knudson: *Present Tendencies in Religious Thought;*
Shailer Mathews: *The Faith of Modernism;*
Carl S. Patton: *Religion in the Thought of Today;*
Gerald Birney Smith: *Principles of Christian Living;*
Herbert A. Youtz: *The Supremacy of the Spiritual.*

Interpreting Modern Christianity. *JR*, July 1926, VI, 432–35.
Review of Benjamin W. Bacon: *The Apostolic Message;*
William P. Merrill: *Liberal Christianity.*

The Heresy of the Orthodox. *Christian Century*, Nov. 6, 1929, XLVI, 1376.
Review of William Peter King: *Faith in the Divine Fatherhood.*

---

* Editor's Note. Since Professor Rall has, unfortunately, never kept track of the book reviews he has written, and since he has written many hundreds of them and in innumerable magazines and journals, it has been found impracticable to make the listing of his reviews anywhere near complete. We list here merely those which have appeared in two magazines, the *Journal of Religion* and the *Christian Century*. These magazines will be abbreviated (after the first citation of each) *JR* and *CC* respectively.

THE ENDLESS QUEST. *CC*, March 4, 1931, XLVIII, 308–9.
Review of W. R. Matthews: *God in Christian Experience.*

REALISTS OF MANY KINDS. *CC*, Feb. 3, 1932, XLIX, 156–57.
Review of D. C. Macintosh: *Religious Realism.*

THE GROUNDS OF HOPE. *CC*, Jan. 3, 1934, LI, 20.
Review of John Baillie: *And the Life Everlasting.*

A GERMAN RELIGIOUS PSYCHOLOGIST. *CC*, March 7, 1934, LI, 330.
Review of Georg Wobbermin: *The Nature of Religion.*

PARADISE REGAINED. *CC*, July 4, 1934, LI, 900.
Review of Shailer Mathews: *Immortality and the Cosmic Process;*
William Pepperell Montague: *The Chances of Surviving Death.*

A RECALL TO ORTHODOXY. *CC*, Nov. 7, 1934, LI, 1415–16.
Review of Edwin Lewis: *A Christian Manifesto.*

SELF-CRITICAL LIBERALISM. *CC*, Jan. 2, 1935, LII, 21–22.
Review of Walter M. Horton: *Realistic Theology.*

WHAT DOES CHRISTIANITY OFFER? *CC*, Jan. 16, 1935, LII, 82.
Review of Oscar Macmillan Buck: *Christianity Tested.*

RELIGION FOR UNDERGRADUATES. *CC*, Oct. 2, 1935, LII, 1248.
Review of Horace T. Houf: *What Religion Is and Does.*

WHAT THE THINKERS THINK. *CC*, May 13, 1936, LIII, 706–7.
Review of Henry Nelson Wieman and Bernard Eugene Meland: *American Philosophies of Religion.*

"CATHOLICISM OF THE WORD." *CC*, July 7, 1937, LIV, 871–72.
Review of Nathaniel Micklem: *What Is the Faith?*

GOD'S OTHERNESS. *CC*, Sept. 8, 1937, LIV, 1104.
Review of Emil Brunner: *God and Man: Four Essays on the Nature of Personality.*

THE MYSTERY OF MAN. *CC*, Dec. 8, 1937, LIV, 1528–29.
Review of Nicolas Berdyaev: *The Destiny of Man.*

REVIEW of *The Validity of Religious Experience,* by Albert C.
Knudson.
"Critical Reviews," *JR*, July 1938, XVIII, 323–25.

GOD'S PART AND MAN'S. *CC*, Nov. 2, 1938, LV, 1332–33.
Review of Edgar P. Dickie: *Revelation and Response.*

AN ANGLICAN THEOLOGY. *CC*, Jan. 4, 1939, LVI, 19–20.
Review of Oliver Chase Quick: *Doctrines of the Creed.*

WAYS TO A KNOWLEDGE OF GOD. *CC*, Oct. 4, 1939, LVI, 1203.
Review of Norman MacLeish: *The Nature of Religious Knowledge.*

BRUNNER IN REVOLT. *CC*, Jan. 3, 1940, LVII, 17–19.
Review of Emil Brunner: *Man in Revolt.*

The *Garrett Tower,* a quarterly publication which has appeared
since 1925 and which was initiated by Dr. Rall, has contained
reviews of current theological literature from his pen in each
issue since its founding. Totaling some hundreds, the list is
too long for printing here. Occasional reviews in other peri-
odicals are likewise omitted.